Englische Grammatik

ELLEN HENRICHS-KLEINEN

ENGLISCHE GRAMMATIK

Die Zeiten

Aktiv und Passiv

Hilfsverben

Indirekte Rede

Infinitiv und Gerundium

If-Sätze

Nomen (Plural, Genitiv)

Artikel

Adjektiv und Adverb

Pronomen

Präpositionen

Konjunktionen

Die Wortstellung

Bassermann

Der Text dieses Buches entspricht den Regeln der neuen
deutschen Rechtschreibung.

ISBN 3 8094 1674 6

© 2004 by Bassermann Verlag,
einem Unternehmen der Verlagsgruppe Random House GmbH, 81673 München

© der Originalausgabe by FALKEN Verlag, einem Unternehmen der
Verlagsgruppe Random House GmbH, 81673 München

Umschlaggestaltung: Büro Norbert Pautner, München
Satz: Grunewald GmbH, Kassel
Druck: Ludwig Auer GmbH, Donauwörth
Printed in Germany

817 2635 4453 6271

Contents

Inhalt

Contents
Inhalt

Contents
Inhalt

Contents
Inhalt

Introduction

Einleitung

Dieses Buch ist ein Lern- und Arbeitsbuch zur englischen Grammatik für Schüler aller Lern- und Altersstufen. Es wurde aus der Praxis heraus konzipiert, d. h. es basiert auf Erfahrungswerten gewonnen aus der Korrektur von Klassenarbeiten, Tests, Hausaufgaben etc. Im Schulalltag wird immer wieder deutlich, dass Schwierigkeiten von Schülern im Fach Englisch besonders auf Problemen mit der englischen Grammatik beruhen. Nicht nur jüngere Schüler sind betroffen, sondern auch viele Oberstufenschüler, wie Kursarbeiten oft sehr deutlich erkennen lassen. Anliegen dieses Buches ist es Schülern fundiertes Grundwissen im Grammatikbereich zu vermitteln sowie Sicherheit und Übung in der Anwendung der Grammatikstrukturen zu geben. Daraus resultiert die Zweischichtigkeit des vorliegenden Buches, das zum einen Lernbuch, zum anderen Übungsbuch ist.

Es handelt sich um eine Schulgrammatik, die alle schulrelevanten Themen abdeckt. Leicht verständliche Erklärungen in deutscher Sprache mit den entsprechenden, im Unterricht gebräuchlichen englischen Fachausdrücken, einprägsame Regeln, anschauliche Beispiele und übersichtliche Tabellen vermitteln dem Schüler eine solide Wissensgrundlage. Die Untergliederung des Buches in Kapitel zu den einzelnen Wortarten oder Strukturen ermöglicht ein systematisches Durcharbeiten ebenso wie eine Beschränkung auf ausgewählte Kapitel oder eine Verwendung des Buches als Nachschlagewerk um sich zu bestimmten Themenkreisen zu informieren.

Zu jedem Kapitel werden dann eine Vielzahl von Übungen unterschiedlichster Form gegeben, die den Aufgabenstellungen in Klassenarbeiten entsprechen. Der Schwierigkeitsgrad der Übungen eines Kapitels ist steigend. Am Ende des Buches befindet sich ein Lösungsanhang, mit dessen Hilfe sich der Schüler selbst korrigieren kann.

Um bestmögliche Resultate zu erzielen empfiehlt sich beim Lernen folgende Vorgehensweise:

1. Auswahl des Kapitels, das dem Schüler Schwierigkeiten macht oder das Thema der nächsten Arbeit darstellt;
2. Durcharbeiten der Erklärungen, Regeln, Beispiele etc. um das nötige Basiswissen zu erlangen;
3. Lösung der Übungen (bei Oberstufenschülern vorwiegend der letzten Übungen eines Kapitels) um das theoretisch Erlernte anzuwenden;
4. Korrektur mit Hilfe des Lösungsanhangs;
5. Nacharbeiten der noch fehlerhaften Aufgaben und erneute Überprüfung.

Die Übungen, gezielt und regelmäßig eingesetzt, helfen Lücken im Bereich der englischen Grammatik zu schließen und Sicherheit im Umgang mit grammatikalischen Strukturen zu erlangen. Eine erfolgversprechende Vorbereitung auf den Unterricht, auf Klassen- oder Kursarbeiten ist dank des Lösungsanhangs auch ohne Hilfe möglich, sodass die vorliegende englische Grammatik für all diejenigen eine wertvolle Stütze darstellt, die ihre Kenntnisse und Fähigkeiten im Fach Englisch verbessern oder vertiefen wollen.

The Verb

Das Verb/das Tätigkeits-wort

Dem Verb wird in dieser englischen Grammatik ein sehr breiter Raum gewidmet, da ohne Verb kein vollständiger Satz gebildet werden kann und die meisten Schüler mit dieser Wortart Probleme haben.

Verben werden unterteilt in **Vollverben (Verbs)** und **Hilfsverben (Auxiliaries)**. Vollverben sind alle Verben, die den vollen Begriff einer Tätigkeit ausdrücken, zum Beispiel to go, to write, to come, to see etc.

Hilfsverben dienen dazu die Zeit- und Aussageverhältnisse der Vollverben auszudrücken. Hilfsverben im Englischen sind: to have*, to be*, to do*, may, can, shall, will, must, ought to, used to, need*.

Ein Verb hat drei **Stammformen,** die man zur Bildung der verschiedenen Tenses (Tempora/Zeiten) benötigt:

1. Verbform: Infinitive (Infinitiv/Grundform)
Beispiel: to go – gehen
Der Infinitiv wird im Englischen mit "to" gekennzeichnet, im Deutschen endet er auf „-en".
2. Verbform: Past Tense (Imperfekt oder Präteritum/Vergangenheit)
Beispiel: went – ging
3. Verbform: Past Participle (Partizip Perfekt/Mittelwort der Vergangenheit)
Beispiel: gone – gegangen

Im Englischen unterscheidet man **regelmäßige Verben** (sie bilden die 2. und 3. Verb-/Stammform auf "-ed") und **unregelmäßige Verben.**
Beispiel: *regelmäßig:* to look – looked – looked
        unregelmäßig: to go – went – gone
Eine Liste der am häufigsten gebrauchten unregelmäßigen Verben befindet sich im Anhang (siehe S. 249). Man muss sie lernen.

Bei den Verbformen unterscheidet man zwischen **Finite Forms (finiten oder konjugierten/gebeugten Formen)** und **Infinite Forms (infiniten oder nicht konjugierten/nicht gebeugten Formen).**

Diese Hilfsverben können auch Vollverben sein.

▶ Finite Formen des Verbs sind von einer Person und vom Numerus (Einzahl, Mehrzahl) abhängig.

Beispiel: I go, he goes, they go, Paul went

▶ Infinite Formen des Verbs sind:

1. **Infinitive** (Infinitiv/Grundform)

    Beispiel: to go – gehen

2. **Gerund** (Gerundium/Tätigkeitswort, das zum Hauptwort geworden ist)

    Beispiel: going – das Gehen

3. **Participle** (Partizip/Mittelwort)

    Beispiel: going – gehend   (Present Participle; Partizip Präsens/Mittelwort der Gegenwart)

    gone – gegangen   (Past Participle; Partizip Perfekt/Mittelwort der Vergangenheit)

The Tenses – Active Voice
Tempora – Aktiv/die Zeiten – Tatform

Im Englischen gibt es acht Zeiten:

1. Present Tense (Präsens/Gegenwart)
2. Past Tense (Imperfekt oder Präteritum/Vergangenheit)
3. Present Perfect (Perfekt/vollendete Gegenwart)
4. Past Perfect (Plusquamperfekt/Vorvergangenheit)
5. Future I (Futur I/Zukunft I)
6. Future II (Futur II/Zukunft II)
7. Conditional I (Konditional I)
8. Conditional II (Konditional II)

Diese Zeiten erhalten oft die Zusatzbezeichnung **"Simple"**, womit die **einfache Form** der Zeit gemeint ist. Zu allen Zeiten gibt es **Verlaufsformen**, die entweder **"Progressive Form"** oder **"Continuous Form"** oder **"ing-Form"** genannt werden. Die Zeiten werden unterteilt in **Active Voice (Aktiv/Tatform)** und **Passive Voice (Passiv/Leideform)**.

▶ Bei Aktiv tut das Subjekt des Satzes selbst etwas.

   Beispiel: I drive home. – Ich fahre nach Hause.

▶ Bei Passiv wird etwas mit dem Subjekt gemacht.

   Beispiel: I am driven home. – Ich werde nach Hause gefahren.

Present Tense Simple
Präsens/Gegenwart

Bejahter Satz	Verneinter Satz	Fragesatz
I work	I don't* work	Do I work?
you work	you dont't work	Do you work?
he works	he doesn't** work	Does he work?
she works	she doesn't work	Does she work?
it works	it doesn't work	Does it work?
we work	we don't work	Do we work?
you work	you don't work	Do you work?
they work	they don't work	Do they work?

Die Bildung des Present Tense Simple:

▶ 1. Verbform – bei he, she, it (3. Person Singular) + Endung "-(e)s" –.
    Beispiel: I work
            aber: he works

▶ Die Verneinung und die Frage werden mit "do" oder – bei he, she, it – mit "does" und der 1. Verbform gebildet.
    Beispiel: I don't like hamburgers.   – Ich mag keine Hamburger.
              He doesn't work.   – Er arbeitet nicht.
              Beachte: kein "-s" am Vollverb!
    Beispiel: Do you watch TV?   – Schaust du fern?
              Does he go to school? – Geht er zur Schule?

Zu beachten ist:

▶ Bei Verben, die auf Zischlaut oder "-o" enden, wird in der 3. Person Singular "-es" angehängt.
    Beispiel: to watch   – he watches
              to go   – he goes
▶ Ein "-y" am Verbende wird in der 3. Person Singular zu "-ie", wenn kein Vokal (a, e, i, o, u) vorausgeht.
    Beispiel: to hurry   – he hurries
▶ "Have" wird in der 3. Person Singular zu "has".
    Beispiel: to have   – he has

---

* don't = do not ** doesn't = does not

► "To be" hat im Present Tense drei Formen (am, are, is):

I am	– ich bin
you are	– du bist
he, she, it is	– er, sie, es ist
we are	– wir sind
you are	– ihr seid
they are	– sie sind

► "Can", "must" und "may" haben in der 3. Person Singular kein "-s". Das nachfolgende Verb steht im Infinitive (Infinitiv/Grundform).

Beispiel: He can come.   – Er kann kommen.

She must go.   – Sie muss gehen.

Present Tense Simple wird verwendet

Anwendung

► bei *regelmäßig* wiederholten oder *gewohnheitsmäßigen Handlungen.*

Beispiel: He often goes to the cinema. – Er geht oft ins Kino.

Signalwörter:		
	usually	– gewöhnlich
	always	– immer
	sometimes	– manchmal
	occasionally	– gelegentlich
	normally	– normalerweise
	every . . .	– jeden/s . . .
	never	– nie
	seldom	– selten
	often	– oft

► bei *allgemein gültigen Feststellungen.*

Beispiel: The sun rises in the east. – Die Sonne geht im Osten auf.

► wenn *mehrere Handlungen* nacheinander geschehen.

Beispiel: He sits down, drinks a cup of tea, and then begins to read. – Er setzt
sich, trinkt eine Tasse Tee und beginnt dann zu lesen.

► bei zukünftigem *Geschehen,* das durch Fahrplan, Programm etc. bereits *festgelegt* ist.

Beispiel: The train leaves at 7 o'clock. – Der Zug fährt um 7 Uhr ab.

► bei Verben mit *statischer Bedeutung* und Verben des *Denkens* und *Erkennens*
und der *Sinneswahrnehmung,* die keine Verlaufsform (ing-Form) bilden.
Dazu gehören:

to be	– sein		to have	– besitzen
to believe	– glauben		to hear	– hören
to belong	– gehören		to know	– wissen
to contain	– enthalten		to like	– mögen
to doubt	– zweifeln		to love	– lieben
to forget	– vergessen		to mean	– bedeuten
to hate	– hassen		to notice	– bemerken

Das Verb
Tempora – Aktiv

to prefer	– vorziehen	to smell	– riechen nach
to remain	– bleiben	to taste	– schmecken
to realize	– erkennen	to think	– denken
to remember	– sich erinnern	to understand	– verstehen
to see	– sehen	to want	– wollen
to seem	– scheinen	to wish	– wünschen etc.

Exercises
Übungen

Übungen

I. *Decide whether to put an "-s" behind the verb.*
 Entscheide, ob ein "-s" ans Verb gehört!

1. I (read).
2. Paul (see).
3. The Bakers (live).
4. Mr and Mrs Palmer (read).
5. The boys (like).
6. You (see).
7. They (come).
8. Maud (play).
9. The children (write).
10. The teacher (explain).
11. Mother (cook).
12. We (visit).
13. The neighbour (work).
14. The secretary (telephone).
15. The workers (put).
16. The three girls (walk).
17. The girl (think).
18. The dog (bark).
19. It (rain).
20. The flowers (grow).
21. Paul and his brother (play).
22. The telephone (ring).
23. My father (drive).
24. The pictures (hang).

II. *Decide whether an "-e-" is missing.*
 Entscheide, ob ein "-e-" fehlt!

1. He read-s.
2. She watch-s.
3. Mary teach-s.
4. Peter do-s.
5. The student look-s.
6. The lady say-s.
7. The bus park-s.
8. She push-s.
9. Susan rush-s.
10. The postman bring-s.

III. *Decide whether the "-y" turns into "-ie-" when the "-s" is added.*
 Entscheide, ob das "-y" zu "-ie-" wird, wenn "-s" angehängt wird!

1. Michael (hurry).
2. The teacher (annoy).
3. He (say).
4. The boss (stay).
5. Mrs Mayer (worry).
6. The cat (play).
7. The butcher (carry).
8. The pupil (try).
9. It (vary).
10. The child (cry).

***Setze in die richtige Präsensform! Bilde entweder Aussagesätze, verneinte
Aussagesätze oder Fragen!***

1. ... you (to live) in Brighton?
2. I (not/to live) in England.
3. The Parkers (to live) there.
4. Mr Parker (to work) at the harbour.
5. He (not/to like) his work.
6. Mrs Parker (to like) her job as a secretary.
7. She (not/to want) to stay at home all day.
8. The children, Cindy and Bert, (to go) to school.
9. Cindy (to go) to a comprehensive school, Bert (to attend) a grammar school.
10. They (to come) home at 5 p. m.
11. They (to wear) school uniforms.
12. After school Cindy (to take) the bus home.
13. Bert (to have) a bike, so he (to cycle) home.
14. In the evening the Parkers (to watch) TV or (to play) games.
15. They (not/to go) to bed late, because they (to get up) very early every day.

Present Tense Continuous
Präsens/Gegenwart Verlaufsform

Beispiel-formen

Bejahter Satz*	Verneinter Satz*	Fragesatz
I am working.	I am not working.	Am I working?
You are working.	You are not working.	Are you working?
He is working.	He is not working.	Is he working?
She is working.	She is not working.	Is she working?
It is working.	It is not working.	Is it working?
We are working.	We are not working.	Are we working?
You are working.	You are not working.	Are you working?
They are working.	They are not working.	Are they working?

Die Bildung des Present Tense Continuous:
Eine Präsensform von "to be" (am/are/is) + 1. Verbform + Endung "-ing"

---

*Es können auch Kurzformen verwendet werden: I'm = I am; you're = you are; he's = he is; isn't = is not etc.

Das Verb
Tempora – Aktiv

Beispiel: He   **is**   **sing**   **ing.**

Form	1. Verb-	Endung
von "to be"	form	"-ing"

Bildung

Rechtschreibbesonderheiten:

*Recht-
schreibung*

▶ Bei Verben, die mit stummem "-e" enden, fällt das "-e" bei der ing-Form weg.
Beispiel: to give – giving

▶ Bei Verben, die mit betontem "-er", "-ir", "-ur" enden, verdoppelt sich das "r"
in der ing-Form
Beispiel: to occur – occurring

▶ Bei Verben mit kurzem, betontem Vokal (a, e, i, o, u) wird der darauf folgende Konsonant (Mitlaut) in der ing-Form verdoppelt.
Beispiel: to put – putting

▶ Bei Verben, die mit "-ie" enden, wird das "ie" in der ing-Form zu "y".
Beispiel: to lie – lying

Present Tense Continuous wird verwendet

Anwendung

▶ hauptsächlich bei Handlungen, die *im Moment des Sprechens* geschehen.
Beispiel: He is just watching a film. – Er sieht sich gerade einen Film an.

Signalwörter:	at the moment	– im Moment
	just (now)	– gerade (jetzt)
	right now	– gerade jetzt
	Look!	– Schau!
	Listen!	– Hör mal!
	now	– nun

▶ bei Handlungen, die *gegenwärtig ausgeübt* werden, wobei der Augenblick
des Sprechens jedoch nicht einbegriffen sein muss.
Beispiel: Mary is writing a book. – M. schreibt (zur Zeit) an einem Buch.

▶ bei *zukünftigen,* durch Vereinbarungen bereits *festgelegten* Handlungen; die
zukünftige Bedeutung wird dann meist durch eine entsprechende Zeitangabe verdeutlicht.
Beispiel: We are having a party next weekend. – Wir geben nächstes Wochenende eine Party.

▶ bei Handlungen, die *wiederholt,* aber nur innerhalb eines genau *begrenzten
Zeitraums* geschehen.
Beispiel: I am helping him just for this week. – Ich helfe ihm nur diese
Woche.

Beachte: Verben mit statischer Bedeutung und Verben des Denkens und
Erkennens (siehe S. 18) bilden keine ing-Form.

Exercises

Übungen

I. *Form the ing-Form. Mind the spelling.*
   Bilde die ing-Form! Achte auf die Rechtschreibung!
   Beispiel: *to make – making*

1. to leave
2. to ride
3. to refer
4. to sit
5. to hide
6. to read
7. to cook

8. to type
9. to meet
10. to have
11. to bring
12. to get
13. to repair
14. to come

II. *Put the verbs in brackets in the correct Present Tense Continuous form.*
   Setze die Verben in Klammern in die richtige Form des Präsens Verlaufs-form!

1. We (to discuss) the problem at the moment.
2. Look! Carmen (to play) with Susan now.
3. The children (to open) their presents right now.
4. Listen! The Coopers (to make) a lot of noise again.
5. The students (to write) a test now.
6. Oliver (to leave) the house at the moment.
7. Look! The workers (to clean) the street.
8. Susan can't come. She (to telephone) at the moment.
9. The sun (to shine) now.
10. Look! The cat (to play) with the little ball.
11. Officer, I (to watch) the man now.
12. The girls (to cut) the film now.
13. The teacher (to correct) the tests at the moment.
14. She (to go) by bus today.
15. My mother (to bake) a cake now.
16. At the moment the children (to sleep).
17. Listen! Our neighbours (to have) a party.
18. Sally can't answer the phone now. She (to wash) her hair.
19. Look! Robin (to climb) on the tree.
20. We (to have) dinner at the moment.

III. *Translate the following sentences.*
   Übersetze folgende Sätze!

1. Kommenden Samstag haben wir ein Fußballspiel.
2. Im Augenblick übe ich für unsere Klassenarbeit.
3. Herr Steiger repariert gerade sein Auto.
4. Wir essen gerade zu Abend.
5. Hör mal! Der Hund des Nachbarn bellt schon wieder.
6. Er liest gerade ein interessantes Buch.
7. Mein Vater arbeitet im Moment im Garten.
8. Susan besucht gerade ihre Freundin.
9. Die Sekretärin telefoniert gerade.
10. Komm, wir (Let's) gehen schwimmen. Die Sonne scheint.
11. Herr Meyer schreibt gerade einen Brief und Frau Meyer strickt.
12. Schau! Die Feuerwehr kommt.
13. Frau Cooper liegt gerade auf dem Balkon und sonnt sich.
14. Die Arbeiter bauen gerade ein neues Haus.
15. Er fotografiert gerade die Sehenswürdigkeiten.
16. Die Schüler machen gerade einen Lesewettbewerb.
17. Im Moment nehmen wir an einem Französischkurs teil.
18. Sie sitzt gerade in ihrem Zimmer und liest.
19. Die Mutter schimpft gerade ihren Sohn, weil er nicht ordentlich schreibt.
20. Er geht gerade mit dem Hund spazieren.

Present Tense Simple and Present Tense Continuous in Contrast

Präsens/Gegenwart und Präsens/Gegenwart Verlaufsform im Vergleich

Vergleich

	Present Tense Simple	Present Tense Continuous
Bildungs-weise	Infinitiv, bei he, she, it + "-(e)s"	am / are / is + Infinitiv + "-ing"
Beispiel-formen	I look he looks they look	I am looking he is looking they are looking
Anwendung	▶ bei Dauerzuständen ▶ bei regelmäßig wieder-holten Vorgängen ▶ bei allgemein gültigen Feststellungen ▶ bei zukünftigem Ge-schehen, das durch Fahr-plan, Programm etc. bereits festgelegt ist ▶ bei nacheinander geschehenden Handlungen ▶ bei Verben mit statischer Bedeutung, bei Verben des Denkens und Erkennens (to be, to belong, to doubt etc.; siehe S. 18)	▶ bei momentanen Handlungen ▶ bei wiederholt geschehenden Handlungen eines begrenzten Zeit-raumes ▶ bei zukünftigen, bereits vereinbarten Handlungen

Signalwörter	often – oft
	usually – gewöhnlich
	sometimes – manchmal
	always – immer
	never – nie
	seldom – selten
	normally – normalerweise
	every – jeden/s
	occasionally – gelegentlich
	           etc.
		just – gerade
		just now – gerade jetzt
		now – nun
		at the
		moment – im Augenblick
		Look! – Schau!
		Listen! – Hör mal!
		right now – gerade jetzt
		         etc.
		next ...
		the
		following – kommenden
		         ... etc.

Exercises
Übungen

I. *Decide whether to use Present Tense Simple or Present Tense Continuous.*
Entscheide, ob du Präsens oder Präsens Verlaufsform benutzen musst

1. Sometimes Susan (to watch) science fiction films, but she normally (to prefer) love stories.
2. Look! Mr Cooper (to work). He usually (to start) work at about 8 o'clock.
3. We (to go) to a football match next Saturday.
4. Can you (to answer) the phone, please, I (to have) a bath right now.
5. I never (to eat) spinach, but we (to have) some this evening.
6. When I (to see) him, we always (to go) to a pub.
7. We usually (to meet) when we (to go) to work.
8. Listen! Mrs Jones (to play) the piano. You can (to hear) her very clearly.
9. When John (to sleep), he sometimes (to talk).
10. Sorry, Mr Smith, I cannot (to speak) to you right now, because I (to be) very busy.
11. Paul and Tim (to go) to London three times a year, but next summer they (to stay) at home.
12. Occasionally he (to go) to the cinema, but he (to go) to the theatre at least once a week.
13. John (not/to be) here, he (to work) late this evening.
14. At the moment I (not/to like) fish.
15. Peter always (to sing) while he (to have) a bath.
16. Look! It (to rain) outside, so we can't (to go) to the beach.
17. Susan (to hate) potatoes, because she (to think) they (to be) bad for her.
18. I must (to go) home now, because my parents (to wait) for me.
19. Sam can't (to go) to Mexico next summer, so he (to visit) his grandmother.
20. Mary (to love) chocolate, and she (to eat) some every day.

II. *Translate the following sentences.*
Übersetze die folgenden Sätze!

1. Hör mal! Frau Simon spielt schon wieder Klavier, obwohl sie weiß, dass ihre Nachbarin krank ist und im Bett liegt.
2. Manchmal verlässt die alte Dame den ganzen Tag ihre Wohnung nicht, doch heute verbringt sie den ganzen Tag im Garten.
3. Er besucht gelegentlich seinen Bruder in Hampstead, aber ansonsten verreist er nicht sehr oft.
4. Lady Mary nimmt ihren Tee täglich um 17 Uhr ein, doch Butler Charles ist krank. Deshalb serviert heute Sue den Tee.
5. Bill lernt gerade seine Französischvokabeln, obwohl er normalerweise um diese Zeit draußen spielt, aber er schreibt morgen eine Klassenarbeit.

6. Siehst du! Hier auf dem Foto liegen Susan und Mary gerade am Strand.
7. Im Moment arbeiten meine Brüder im Park, aber es ist nur ein Ferienjob. Sie besuchen das College, haben aber im Augenblick Sommerferien.
8. Frau Cooper liebt italienisches Essen, aber momentan isst sie nur Gemüse und Obst, da sie abnehmen möchte.
9. „Was machst du hier im Krankenhaus?" „Ich bin mit Sam hier. Er wird gerade geröntgt." (to have an X-ray)
10. Ich berichte gerade vom Autorennen in Indianapolis. Wagen Nr. 5 überholt gerade Wagen Nr. 3. Es ist eine Überraschung, denn Wagen Nr. 3 gewinnt gewöhnlich.

Past Tense Simple
Imperfekt oder Präteritum/Vergangenheit

regelmäßge Verben

Beispiel-formen

Bejahter Satz	Verneiner Satz	Fragesatz
I looked.	I didn't* look.	Did I look?
You looked.	You didn't look.	Did you look?
He looked.	He didn't look.	Did he look?
She looked.	She didn't look.	Did she look?
It looked.	It didn't look.	Did it look?
We looked.	We didn't look.	Did we look?
You looked.	You didn't look.	Did you look?
They looked.	They didn't look.	Did they look?

unregelmäßiges Verb

Bejahter Satz	Verneiner Satz	Fragesatz
I went.	I didn't* go.	Did I go?
You went.	You didn't go.	Did you go?
He went.	He didn't go.	Did he go?
She went.	She didn't go.	Did she go?
It went.	It didn't go.	Did it go?
We went.	We didn't go.	Did we go?
You went.	You didn't go.	Did you go?
They went.	They didn't go.	Did they go?

* *didn't = did not*

Das Verb
Tempora – Aktiv

Die Bildung des Past Tense Simple:

regelmäßige Verben: 1. Verbform + "-ed"

Beispiel: I looked.

Bildung

Rechtschreibbesonderheiten beim Anhängen von "-ed":

▶ Endet die 1. Verbform auf "-e", wird nur "-d" angehängt.
   Beispiel: like – liked
▶ "y" nach Konsonant (Mitlaut) wird zu "i".
   Beispiel: tidy – tidied
▶ Endet die 1. Verbform auf betontem "-er", "-ir" oder "-ur", verdoppelt sich das "-r".
   Beispiel: prefer – preferred
▶ Ein einfacher Endkonsonant wird nach kurzem, einfachem, betontem Vokal (a, e, i, o, u) verdoppelt.
   Beispiel: stop – stopped

unregelmäßige Verben: 2. Verbform

Beispiel: I went.

Zu beachten ist:

▶ "To be" hat zwei Vergangenheitsformen (was/were):

Besonder-heiten

I was	– ich war
you were	– du warst
he, she, it was	– er, sie, es war
we were	– wir waren
you were	– ihr wart
they were	– sie waren

▶ "May" bildet die Vergangenheit mit "was/were allowed to".
   Beispiel: I was allowed to go the cinema. – Ich durfte ins Kino gehen.
▶ "Must" bildet die Vergangenheit mit "had to" (siehe auch S. 101).
   Beispiel: I had to work till 7 p.m. – Ich musste bis 19 Uhr arbeiten.
▶ Frage und Verneinung werden mit "did" + 1. Verbform gebildet.
   Beispiel: Did he come yesterday? – Kam er gestern?
   No, he didn't come. – Nein, er kam nicht.

Past Tense Simple wird verwendet

▶ für *einmalige (a)* oder *aufeinanderfolgende (b)* oder *wiederholte (c)* Vorgänge, die in der Vergangenheit angefangen haben und abgeschlossen sind.

Anwendung

   Beispiel: (a) They moved in last week. – Sie zogen letzte Woche ein.
   (b) The teacher opened his book and began to read. – Der Lehrer öffnete sein Buch und begann zu lesen.
   (c) She wrote to him every week. – Sie schrieb ihm jede Woche.

Signalwörter:	yesterday	– gestern
	(2 months) ago	– vor (2 Monaten)
	... ago	– vor ...
	in 1960	– 1960
	the other day	– neulich
	the day before yesterday	– vorgestern
	last (week)	– letzte (Woche)
	last ...	– letzte ...

Beachte: Im Deutschen steht statt Imperfekt (Vergangenheit) oft
Perfekt (vollendete Gegenwart)
Beispiel: Ich habe gestern gearbeitet. (Perfekt)
statt: Ich arbeitete gestern. (Imperfekt)
Die englische Übersetzung für beide Sätze muss aber
lauten:
I worked yesterday. Also: Vorsicht beim Übersetzen!

Exercises

Übungen

I. *Write down the Past Tense form.*
Schreibe die Vergangenheitsform auf!

1. to occur (geschehen)
2. to come (kommen)
3. to plan (planen)
4. to give (geben)
5. to see (sehen)
6. to destroy (zerstören)
7. to change (wechseln)
8. to apply (sich bewerben)
9. to paint (malen)
10. to work (arbeiten)
11. to enjoy (genießen)
12. to hear (hören)
13. to listen to (zuhören)
14. to arrive (ankommen)
15. to drink (trinken)
16. to put (stellen, legen etc.)
17. to write (schreiben)
18. to drive (fahren)
19. to read (lesen)
20. to understand (verstehen)

II. *Put the verbs in brackets in the Past Tense. Mind the negative sentences and
the questions.*
*Setze die Verben in Klammern in die Vergangenheit! Achte auf verneinte
Sätze und Fragesätze!*

1. Last year we (not/to go) on holiday.
2. The Mayers (to go) to Italy last year.
3. She slowly (to get up), (to go) to the door, and (to open) it.
4. Dunlop (to invent) the tyre.

5. When (you/to buy) your new T-shirt?
6. (you/to see) Mary yesterday?
7. How (you/to like) the match last week?
8. Sam (to open) the door and the dog (to begin) to bark.
9. He (to write) his first book when he (to be) 25.
10. Yesterday the alarm clock (to ring) an hour too early, so I (to get) to the office at 8 o'clock.
11. In 1996 Martin (to pass) his exam and (to start) to work as a lawyer.
12. Malcolm X (to be) a famous Civil Rights leader.
13. In 1995 they (to have) a terrible accident. Martha (not/may/to leave) hospital till summer.
14. Some years ago we (to sell) our house in Kingston and (to move) to a better area.
15. When he (to be) 6 years old, he (already/can/to play) the piano.

III. Write a short biography of George Washington.
Schreibe eine Kurzbiographie von George Washington!
- 1732 / Bridges Creek / to be born
- the 1750s / to become / commander-in-chief of Virginia
- 1759 / to marry / wealthy young widow
- 1759 / people / to elect him / to the Virginia Parliament
- 1774–1775 / to be / delegate / to the 1st and 2nd Continental Congress, which / to choose him / commander-in-chief of the Continental Army in the Revolutionary War
- at the battle of Yorktown / he / to defeat / British Army / 1781
- 1789 he / to become / 1st President of the United States
- he / to keep / America / neutral / during the French Revolution
- the Americans / to elect / him / for a second term of office / 1793
- 1799 / he / to die / Mount Vernon, Virginia

Past Tense Continuous

Imperfekt oder Präteritum/Vergangenheit Verlaufsform

Bejahter Satz	Verneinter Satz	Fragesatz
I was going.	I wasn't* going.	Was I going?
You were going.	You weren't** going.	Were you going?
He was going.	He wasn't going.	Was he going?
She was going.	She wasn't going.	Was she going?
It was going.	It wasn't going.	Was it going?
We were going.	We weren't going.	Were we going?
You were going.	You weren't going.	Were you going?
They were going.	They weren't going.	Were they going?

Die Bildung des Past Tense Continuous:

▶ Eine Vergangenheitsform von "to be" (was/were) + 1. Verbform + Endung "-ing"

Beispiel: He <u>   **was**   </u>   <u>   **read**   </u>   <u>   **ing.**   </u>

           Form von to be   1. Verbform   Endung "-ing"

▶ Rechtschreibbesonderheiten der ing-Form siehe S. 21.

Past Tense Continuous wird verwendet

▶ um den Ablauf einer Handlung zu einem *bestimmten Zeitpunkt (a)* oder während eines *bestimmten Zeitraumes (b)* der Vergangenheit zu bezeichnen.

Beispiel: (a)   Yesterday at 8 o'clock I was working. – Gestern habe ich um 8 Uhr gearbeitet.

          (b)   Between 10 o'clock and 11 o'clock we were having a meeting. – Zwischen 10 und 11 Uhr hatten wir eine Sitzung.

Wahl der Zeit bei mehreren Vorgängen:

▶ Fanden mehrere Vorgänge *gleichzeitig* in der Vergangenheit statt, benutzt man bei allen *Past Tense Continuous.*

Beispiel: I was watching TV while Susan was playing cards. – Ich sah fern, während Susan Karten spielte.

---

* wasn't = was not   ** weren't = were not

▶ Fanden mehrere Vorgänge *nacheinander* in der Vergangenheit statt, benutzt man bei allen *Past Tense Simple*.

Beispiel: The doctor looked at Paul, took his temperature and sent him home immediately. – Der Arzt schaute Paul an, maß seine Temperatur und schickte ihn sofort nach Hause.

▶ Wenn eine Handlung bereits „im Gange war", als ein neues Ereignis eintrat, steht die ältere Handlung im Past Tense Continuous, das neue Ereignis jedoch im Past Tense Simple.

Beispiel: We were lying on the beach,   when the accident happened. –
    Wir lagen am Strand,   **als der Unfall passierte.**
        ältere Handlung   neues Ereignis

Beachte: Verben mit statischer Bedeutung und Verben des Denkens und Erkennens (siehe S. 18) bilden keine ing-Form.

Exercises
Übungen

Übungen

I. *Bob's parents were away on holiday, but they came home earlier than expected. Write down what they saw when they came home.*
    Bobs Eltern waren in Urlaub, aber sie kamen früher als erwartet nach Hause zurück. Schreibe auf, was sie sahen, als sie nach Hause kamen!

1. Bob – to dance with Mary
2. Peter – to drink father's whisky
3. Susan and Mary – to use mother's make-up
4. some children – to have a bath in the swimming pool
5. the dog – to lie on the most expensive armchair
6. Paula – to wear mother's nicest evening dress
7. the children – to play father's favourite jazz record
8. some hamburgers – to lie on the floor
9. three children – to dance on the table
10. empty bottles – to lie around everywhere
11. Bob – to smoke cigars
12. four girls – to play cards on the bed
13. the cat – to try to escape from the chaos
14. the neighbours – to come to complain
15. the telephone – to ring

II. *Write down what the people were doing at the same time.*
   Schreibe auf, was die Leute zur gleichen Zeit taten!
   Beispiel: *Bob – to do his homework / Sam – to listen to his records upstairs*
             While Bob was doing his homework, Sam was listening to his
             records upstairs.

 1. father – to type a few letters in his study / I – to tidy up the attic
 2. the stewardesses – to serve dinner / Mr Scott – to sleep in his chair
 3. Mrs Martin – to try to sleep / the children – to make a terrible noise
 4. the boys – to play tennis / their mothers – to enjoy a quiet afternoon
    at home
 5. the band – to play on the football field / all the spectators – to wait for
    the match to start
 6. the actors – to practise for the performance / the workers – to decorate
    the stage
 7. my aunt – to talk on the telephone / I – to do all her housework
 8. the children – to sleep / their parents – to watch TV
 9. Lord and Lady Southerby – to have tea / their servants – to prepare dinner
10. the patient – to tell his story / the doctor – to look out of the window
11. the reporter – to interview the famous film star Sandy / she – to polish
    her nails
12. the students – to write their final tests / the teacher – to watch them
    carefully
13. Mrs Burrell – to do her shopping / Mr Burrell – to collect money for
    the pools
14. the children – to have lunch at school / Mrs Cooper – to visit a friend
    of hers
15. the new neighbours – to move in / we – to work in the garden

III. *Write down what people were doing when . . .*
    Schreibe auf, was die Leute taten, als . . .!
 1. We – to sleep – when the window suddenly broke.
 2. When the two cars crashed, the old lady – to wait – at the traffic lights.
 3. The Bakers – to have – tea when the telephone rang.
 4. I – to write – a letter to my pen-friend when I suddenly heard a noise.
 5. The band – to play – when suddenly the lights went out.
 6. We – to drive – along a small country road when suddenly a deer
    jumped in front of our car.
 7. Mrs Cooper – to do – her shopping when she noticed that she had
    forgotten her purse.
 8. Mr Sutton – play – tennis when it started to rain.
 9. When Jane arrived home, her friend – to wait – for her in the living-room.
10. When I discovered him, he – to breathe – still.

11. When the police found him, he – to try – to hide in a garage.
12. We – to sit – in the garden when suddenly the door opened.
13. When I came home, my parents – to sleep – already.
14. When the teacher – to explain – the new words, he was suddenly hit on the head by a piece of paper.
15. We – to stand – on the bridge when we suddenly saw a man trying to climb on the railing.

Past Tense Simple and Past Tense Continuous in Contrast

Imperfekt oder Präteritum/Vergangenheit und Imperfekt oder Präteritum/Vergangenheit Verlaufsform im Vergleich

	Past Tense Simple	Past Tense Continuous
Bildungs-weise	regelmäßige Verben: 1. Verbform + "-ed" unregelmäßige Verben: 2. Verbform	"was/were" + 1. Verbform + "-ing"
Beispiel-formen	I looked he went they went	I was looking he was going they were going
Anwendung	Vorgänge, die in der Vergangenheit angefangen haben und abgeschlossen sind	
	► für einmalige oder wiederholte Vorgänge in der Vergangenheit	► um den Ablauf einer Handlung zu einem bestimmten Zeitpunkt/Zeitraum der Vergangenheit zu bezeichnen
	► bei nacheinander stattfindenden Vorgängen in der Vergangenheit Signalwörter: then – dann after that – danach	► bei mehreren gleichzeitigen Vorgängen in der Vergangenheit Signalwort oft: while – während
	► bei einem neuen Ereignis, das eine bereits laufende Handlung (ing-Form) unterbricht Signalwort oft: suddenly – plötzlich	► wenn eine Handlung bereits „im Gange war", als ein neues Ereignis eintrat Signalwort oft: when – als

Exercises

Übungen

I. *Put into the correct Past Tense form.*

Setze in die richtige Vergangenheitsform!

1. While Peter and Mary (to lie) beside the swimming-pool, we (to have) a drink at the hotel bar.

2. When I (to walk) down Station Road yesterday, I (to meet) Mr Meyer, an old friend of my father's.

3. While Sue (to get off) the bus, a few rude youngsters (to try) to get in at the same time.

4. I (to want) to visit you yesterday, but you (not/to be) at home. It (to be) at 3 o'clock. What (you/to do) at that time?

5. He (to recognize) me at once, although I (to wear) a scarf around my face.

6. When the old lady (to try) to cross the street, suddenly a car (to come) round the corner and nearly (to hit) her.

7. He (to eat) some sandwiches and then (to help) himself to some biscuits.

8. When my friend (to come) to see me yesterday I (not/can/come) down-stairs, because I (to have) a shower.

9. When it (to start) to rain, the children (to try) to put up their tent.

10. He (to climb) through the window, (to switch on) the lights and (to go) into the kitchen.

11. When she (to hear) the terrible news, she (to burst) into tears.

12. While the doctor (to examine) Mr. Samson, his wife (to wait) in the wai-ting-room.

13. Some weeks ago he (to break) his arm, but nevertheless he (to go) to work some days later.

14. What (you/to do) when the robbery (to take place)?

15. While the mechanic (to check) the engine, Sam (to wait) in the little office.

16. We (to watch) TV when it (to start) to rain. So mother (to switch) off the TV, because she (to be) afraid of the lightning.

17. The organizer (to announce) the very famous singer. Some minutes later she (to appear) on the stage.

18. When he (to work) for this company, he (not/to like) his job.

19. Paul (to be) very eager when he was a schoolboy. When his friends (to play), he (to sit) in his room and (to study).

20. Last weekend we (to visit) friends of ours in the afternoon, then we (to go) to the cinema.

II. *Translate the following sentences.*
Übersetze die folgenden Sätze!

1. Der Kommissar betrat mit dem Fremden die Bar und fragte: „Was haben Sie gestern zwischen 9 und 10 Uhr gemacht?"

2. Der Fremde antwortete: „Als der Mord geschah, saß ich in der Bar und spielte mit Mr. Doodle Karten."

3. „Hat irgend jemand anders Sie gesehen?" wollte Kommissar Montag wissen.

4. „Während wir Karten spielten, beobachtete uns ein junger Mann, der die ganze Zeit an der Theke stand."

5. Der Kommissar wurde langsam nervös.

6. Schließlich dachte er einen Moment nach und fragte dann den Fremden: „Was machte der Mann in dem Moment, als Sie die Bar betraten?"

7. „Als ich ihn das erste Mal sah, stand er in der Ecke und sprach leise mit dem Kellner."

8. Montag schien sehr erstaunt zu sein, als er dies hörte.

9. Während er sich mit dem Fremden unterhielt, hörte er, dass Mr. Doodle mit dem Kellner sprach.

10. Montag verstand nicht, worüber sie sprachen.

11. Während er immer noch versuchte die beiden zu verstehen, kam Inspektor Datson herein.

12. Als er sah, was sich in der Bar abspielte, eilte er zu Kommissar Montag.

13. Er gab ihm ein Stück Papier, das der Fremde sofort erkannte.

14. Während Montag den Zettel anstarrte, überlegte der Fremde, wie er aus der Bar fliehen könnte.

15. Als er plötzlich zur Tür rannte, wurde er von den beiden Polizisten, die draußen warteten, verhaftet.

Present Perfect Simple
Perfekt/vollendete Gegenwart

regelmäßiges Verb

Bejahter Satz	Verneinter Satz	Fragesatz
I have looked.	I haven't* looked.	Have I looked?
You have looked.	You haven't looked.	Have you looked?
He has looked.	He hasn't** looked.	Has he looked?
She has looked.	She hasn't looked.	Has she looked?
It has looked.	It hasn't looked.	Has it looked?
We have looked.	We haven't looked.	Have we looked?
You have looked.	You haven't looked.	Have you looked?
They have looked.	They haven't looked.	Have they looked?

unregelmäßiges Verb

Bejahter Satz	Verneinter Satz	Fragesatz
I have gone.	I haven't gone.	Have I gone?
You have gone.	You haven't gone.	Have you gone?
He has gone.	He hasn't gone.	Has he gone?
She has gone.	She hasn't gone.	Has she gone?
It has gone.	It hasn't gone.	Has it gone?
We have gone.	We haven't gone.	Have we gone?
You have gone.	You haven't gone.	Have you gone?
They have gone.	They haven't gone.	Have they gone?

Die Bildung des Present Perfect Simple:

regelmäßige Verben: "have" – bei he, she, it "has" – + 1. Verbform + "-ed"

  Beispiel: I have looked.

    He has looked.

Rechtschreibbesonderheiten beim Anhängen von "-ed" siehe S. 27.

unregelmäßige Verben: "have" – bei he, she, it "has" – + 3. Verbform

  Beispiel: I have gone.

    He has gone.

---

* *haven't = have not*
** *hasn't = has not*

Beachte: *Im Deutschen wird das Perfekt bei einigen Verben mit „sein", bei einigen mit „haben" gebildet.*

Beispiel: Er ist gerannt. Er hat gemacht.

Im Englischen jedoch wird das Present Perfect immer mit einer Form von "have" gebildet.

Beispiel: He has run. He has made.

Present Perfect wird verwendet

▶ für Vorgänge, die in der Vergangenheit angefangen haben und *bis in die Gegenwart* reichen.

Anwendung

Beispiel: I have known him for 2 years now. – Ich kenne ihn nun schon seit 2 Jahren.

Beachte: Im Deutschen steht in diesem Fall Präsens (Gegenwart)!

▶ für Vorgänge, die *gerade erst abgeschlossen* sind.

Beispiel: I have just opened the window. – Ich habe gerade das Fenster geöffnet.

▶ für Vorgänge, die in der Vergangenheit angefangen haben und abgeschlossen sind, deren *Auswirkungen* jedoch bis in die Gegenwart reichen; der Zeitpunkt der Handlung interessiert dabei nicht.

Beispiel: Prices have gone up. – Die Preise sind gestiegen.

▶ um auszudrücken, dass etwas *einmal, mehrmals oder nie vor dem Zeitpunkt des Sprechens* geschehen ist. Es darf jedoch keine Zeitangabe der Vergangenheit stehen.

Beispiel: I have never been to Wales. – Ich bin noch nie in Wales gewesen.

Signalwörter:	
just*	– gerade (erst vorbei)
already*	– schon
since	– seit (Zeitpunkt)
for	– seit (Zeitspanne)
till now	– bis jetzt
up to now	– bis jetzt
so far	– bisher
not … yet	– noch nicht
ever*	– jemals
never*	– noch nie
this morning, year etc.	– heute Morgen, dieses Jahr etc. (aber nur, wenn die entsprechende Tageszeit/Jahreszeit zum Zeitpunkt des Sprechens bereits angefangen hat, aber noch nicht vorüber ist)

Beachte: Die Signalwörter mit * stehen vor dem Vollverb.

Beispiel: I have never seen Big Ben.

Exercises

Übungen

I. *David is a very good boy. His mother, Mrs Cary, praises him when she talks to her neighbour, Mrs Samuel, whose son Paul seems to be a nuisance. Make up sentences.*

David ist ein sehr lieber Junge. Seine Mutter, Frau Cary, lobt ihn, als sie mit ihrer Nachbarin, Frau Samuel, spricht, deren Sohn Paul eine Plage zu sein scheint. Bilde Sätze!

Beispiel: *Mrs C.: David / never / to smoke a single cigarette*
David has never smoked a single cigarette.

1. Mrs S.: Paul / to smoke / for 4 years
2. Mrs C.: David / never / to go to a disco
3. Mrs S.: Paul / not to be at home / for 3 nights
4. Mrs C.: David / never / to write a bad test
5. Mrs S.: Paul / already / to write five bad tests / this year
6. Mrs C.: David / never / to go out with girls / so far
7. Mrs S.: Paul / to take out two different girls / this week
8. Mrs C.: David / to do the shopping for me three times / this week
9. Mrs S.: Paul / not to help me with the housework / since my last birthday
10. Mrs C.: Yes, David / always / to be a good boy and Paul / always / to cause trouble

II. *Mary is applying for a holiday job. The boss is interviewing her. You ask the questions!*

Mary bewirbt sich für einen Ferienjob. Der Chef befragt sie. Du stellst die Fragen!

1. you / ever / to work / in your holidays / before?
2. you / ever / to organize / anything special / in school?
3. you / already / to pass / your O-level?
4. since when / you / to be / in Stroud?
5. you / already / to learn / how to type?
6. you / to apply / for another holiday job?
7. you / ever / to have / an interview before?
8. you / already / to ask / your parents?
9. you / ever / to be / abroad?
10. you / ever / to have / any opportunity to practise your German?

III. Translate the following sentences.

Übersetze die folgenden Sätze!

1. Wie lange kennst du ihn?
2. Er hat gerade das Fenster geschlossen.

3. Wir haben schon fünf Übungen gelöst.
4. Sie sind schon 10 Meilen gewandert.
5. Er hat den ganzen Abend noch mit niemandem gesprochen.
6. Ich bin noch nie in Australien gewesen.
7. Seit er Hundebesitzer ist, geht er jeden Tag zweimal spazieren.
8. Fred hat noch nie Shakespeare gelesen.
9. Ich habe ihn seit langem nicht mehr gesehen.
10. Er hat gerade das Büro verlassen.
11. Seid ihr schon mal zu Fuß bis Greenwich gegangen?
12. Er hat diese Krankheit seit 2 Jahren.
13. Seit 4 Wochen hat sie nichts für die Schule getan.
14. Sie ist (bis jetzt) immer eine gute Schülerin gewesen.
15. Ich habe bis jetzt noch nicht mit dem Direktor gesprochen.
16. Seit 2 Jahren spricht sie nicht mehr mit ihm.
17. Hast du schon die neue Platte von David Bowie gehört?
18. Unsere Nachbarin ist bis jetzt immer sehr freundlich gewesen.
19. Ich war schon 2 Jahre lang nicht in Urlaub.
20. Seit er in der Firma arbeitet, verdient er viel mehr.

Present Perfect Continuous
Perfekt/vollendete Gegenwart Verlaufsform

Bejahter Satz	Verneinter Satz	Fragesatz
I have been working.	I haven't* been working.	Have I been working?
You have been working.	You haven't been working.	Have you been working?
He has been working.	He hasn't** been working.	Has be been working?
She has been working.	She hasn't been working.	Has she been working?
It has been working.	It hasn't been working.	Has it been working?
We have been working.	We haven't been working.	Have we been working?
You have been working.	You haven't been working.	Have you been working?
They have been working.	They haven't been working.	Have they been working?

Beispiel-formen

*haven't = have not **hasn't = has not

Die Bildung des Present Perfect Continuous:

▶ "have" – bei he, she, it (3. Person Singular) "has" – + "been" + 1. Verbform + "-ing"

Beispiel: They have been waiting.

▶ Rechtschreibbesonderheiten beim Anhängen von "-ing" siehe S. 21.

▶ Verben, die keine ing-Form bilden, siehe S. 18.

Present Perfect Continuous wird verwendet

▶ für Handlungen, die in der Vergangenheit begannen und *noch andauern*. Im Gegensatz zum Present Perfect Simple, das das *Ergebnis* einer Handlung betont, betont Present Perfect Continuous die *Dauer* einer Handlung.

Beispiel: I have been working for 2 hours now. – Ich arbeite nun schon seit 2 Stunden. (Die passende Frage ist: Wie lange ...?)

Aber Present Perfect Simple:

I have already typed five letters. – Ich habe schon fünf Briefe getippt. (Das Ergebnis ist wichtig.)

Signalwörter: all day / month, etc.　　　– den ganzen Tag / Monat etc.
　　　　　　　the whole morning, etc.　– den ganzen Morgen etc.
　　　　　　　how long　　　　　　　– wie lange
　　　　　　　since　　　　　　　　– seit (einem Zeitpunkt)
　　　　　　　for　　　　　　　　　– seit (einer Zeitspanne)

▶ um auszudrücken, dass eine noch nicht weit zurückliegende Handlung der Vergangenheit zu unbeabsichtigten *Folgen in der Gegenwart* geführt hat.

Beispiel: I can't dance tonight. My legs are aching. I've been playing football all afternoon. – Ich kann heute Abend nicht tanzen. Meine Beine schmerzen. Ich habe den ganzen Nachmittag Fußball gespielt.

Exercises

Übungen

I.　Form sentences about what the persons have been doing all day.
　　Bilde Sätze! Was haben die Personen den ganzen Tag gemacht?

1. Simon / to do / crossword puzzles / all day

2. Peter and Paul / to play football

3. Mother / to work in the house

4. I / to be to the swimming pool

5. The young children / to play in kindergarten

6. The neighbours / to lie in the sun

7. Susan / to knit her new pullover

8. David / to try to repair his bike
9. Grandfather / to sit in his armchair and / to read
10. The cat / to chase mice and / to play in the sun

II. *Put the verbs in brackets in the correct Present Perfect Form. Use either Present Perfect Simple or Present Perfect Continuous.*
   Setze die Verben in Klammern in die richtige Perfektform! Benutze entweder Perfekt oder Perfekt Verlaufsform!

1. I (to learn) English for 6 years now.
2. We (to live) in that area since 1970.
3. He (already / to solve) two crossword puzzles this morning.
4. It (to rain) all day.
5. I hope you (not / to wait) for him for a long time.
6. Charles really looks pale. He (not / to eat) anything today.
7. My father (to work) in this company for 2 years now.
8. He (to know) Jim for a long time.
9. ... you ever (to see) any fish in this river?
10. Since when ... you (to sit) here?
11. The children can't go out. They (not / to finish) their homework yet.
12. My uncle (already / to find) a good new job in the city.
13. Mr Cooper (to drive) this car for six months now. He (already / to drive) 40 000 miles.
14. You (to tell) me this story twice now, but I (never / to believe) it.
15. Michael (to drink) all evening. He (already / to drink) several bottles of beer.
16. Mrs Smith (to talk) to Susan all afternoon now. She (not / to talk) to anybody else.
17. Sam (just / to clean) his car. It looks like new.
18. Michael, you (not / to listen) to me for the last five minutes.
19. What a mess! What ... you (to do)?
20. The Millers (to take) photos of London all day. They (already / to take) nearly fifty photos.

III. *Translate the sentences. Use the correct Present Perfect form.*
   Übersetze die Sätze! Benutze die richtige Perfektform!

1. Susan macht seit 3 Wochen eine Diät und hat schon 5 Pfund abgenommen.
2. Mr Seller hat schon den ganzen Morgen Kunden. Er hat bereits zwei Autos verkauft.
3. Paul spielt seit 2 Stunden Schach. Er hat noch nie gegen Tom gespielt.
4. Ich lebe jetzt seit 2 Jahren in den USA und habe mein Heimatland noch nicht vermisst.

5. Mrs Chatter telefoniert schon seit einer halben Stunde mit ihrer Freundin. Sie hat schon über £ 5 für das Gespräch ausgegeben.
6. Was hast du den ganzen Nachmittag gemacht? Hast du auf mich gewartet?
7. Harry spart schon seit Monaten für ein Motorrad. Er hat bereits £ 100 gespart.
8. Ich suche meine Brille schon seit 10 Uhr, aber ich habe sie noch immer nicht gefunden.
9. Ich bin noch nie in Amerika gewesen, aber ich habe schon viel über dieses Land gelesen.
10. Er arbeitet schon 5 Jahre in dieser Firma und bis jetzt hat es noch nie Probleme gegeben.
11. Maud sitzt schon 2 Stunden an ihrem Schreibtisch und hat immer noch nicht alle Fragen beantwortet.
12. Er spielt seit 2 Jahren Golf im Club und hat bereits einige Preise gewonnen.
13. Hast du schon gefrühstückt oder hast du bis jetzt geschlafen?
14. „War der Briefträger schon da?“ – „Ja, ich habe die Post schon auf deinen Schreibtisch gelegt.“
15. Er wohnt schon seit 2 Monaten hier, aber er hat noch keinen neuen Job gefunden.

Past Tense Simple and Present Perfect Simple in Contrast

Imperfekt oder Präteritum/Vergangenheit und Perfekt/vollendete Gegenwart im Vergleich

Vergleich

	Past Tense Simple	Present Perfect Simple
Bildungs-weise	regelmäßige Verben: 1. Verbform + "-ed" unregelmäßige Verben: 2. Verbform	regelmäßige Verben: "have/has" + 1. Verbform + "-ed" unregelmäßige Verben: "have/has" + 3. Verbform
Beispiel-formen	I looked/went he worked/saw they rushed/came	I have looked/have gone he has worked/has seen they have rushed/have come
Anwendung	▶ für einmalige, aufeinander folgende oder wiederholte Vorgänge, die in der Vergangenheit angefangen haben und <u>abgeschlossen</u> sind	▶ für Vorgänge, die in der Vergangenheit anfingen und <u>bis in die Gegenwart</u> reichen ▶ für Vorgänge, die in der Vergangenheit anfingen und <u>gerade erst abgeschlossen</u> sind ▶ für in der Vergangenheit abgeschlossene Vorgänge, deren <u>Auswirkungen bis in die Gegenwart</u> reichen ▶ für Vorgänge, die einmal, mehrmals, nie vor dem Zeitpunkt des Sprechens passierten, jedoch ohne Zeitangabe
Signal-wörter	yesterday – gestern ... ago – vor ... in 1960 – 1960 the other day – neulich last ... – letzte ... etc.	just – gerade already – schon since – seit (Zeitpunkt) for – seit (Zeitspanne) till now – bis jetzt up to now – bis jetzt so far – bisher never – noch nie ever – jemals not yet – noch nicht this morning – heute Morgen

Zum Gebrauch der entsprechenden Continuous-Formen siehe S. 30ff. und 39ff.

Exercises

Übungen

I. *Put the verbs in brackets into Past Tense or Present Perfect.*
   Setze die Verben in Klammern ins Imperfekt oder ins Perfekt!

1. Pauline (not/to see) her mother since she (to arrive) last week.
2. Mr Martins (to look at) the new plans yesterday, but he (not/to decide) yet if he will accept them.
3. I never (to like) horror films, so I (not/to watch) the one on TV last night.
4. My grandfather always (to enjoy) a glass of red wine with his meal, but since he (to have) his heart attack, he (not even/to look at) alcohol any more.
5. When the new immigrants (to arrive) in the United States, they often (not/can/to speak) English.
6. Soon after their arrival they (to find out) that they (must/to learn) English immediately.
7. Since the days of the American colonies, immigrants (to make) this experience over and over again.
8. The same (to be) true of the immigrants of the 1970s, but they (continuously/to try) to learn English ever since they (to land) in America.
9. Every group of immigrants (to consider) America as a country of nearly unlimited opportunities.
10. Mr Bart (to come) to America 10 years ago and (to live) there ever since.
11. Last year he (to get) married and he (already/to teach) his wife some Italian.
12. His parents (to visit) him three times, although they (never/to want) to travel across the Atlantic.
13. When they first (to see) the Statue of Liberty they (to be) very disappointed.
14. Since 1993 they (to visit) their son every year.
15. When they (to come) to the party last night, all the other guests (to be) already there.
16. We never (to like) wine, but since beer prices (to go up) we also (to stop) drinking beer.
17. I (always/to hate) sports and I never (to play) tennis in my life.
18. Mrs O'Donovan (to work) in Frankfurt for more than 5 years, but she (not/to visit) the Opera house yet.
19. We (to be) very happy when my grandmother (to come) to visit us, but she (to stay) 6 weeks with us now and (to make) trouble since the day she (to arrive).
20. (you/really/to enjoy) this show? I never (to see) anything more stupid than that in my whole life.

II. *Translate the following sentences.*
   Übersetze die folgenden Sätze!

1. Stephen ist noch nicht lange hier, aber er hat schon drei Steaks gegessen.
2. Als John das erste Mal nach Deutschland kam, konnte er kein Wort Deutsch sprechen.
3. Wir wohnen nun schon 3 Wochen in unserem neuen Haus und haben unsere Nachbarn immer noch nicht kennen gelernt.
4. Seit Mr Sellers nach Hamburg gezogen ist, haben wir nichts mehr von ihm gehört.
5. Erwin war noch nie im Wilden Westen.
6. Als er letztes Jahr nach New Mexico kam, war er erstaunt, dass es immer noch Indianer dort gab.
7. Jetzt lebt er schon seit 8 Monaten in New Mexico und hat schon viele indianische Wörter gelernt.
8. Als ich ihn vor einigen Wochen besuchte, versuchte er gerade sich mit einem alten Häuptling zu unterhalten.
9. Einige Tage später erzählte mir der Häupting in Englisch:
10. „Erwin hat in den 8 Monaten, seit er herkam, mehr Wörter gelernt, als ich jemals gekannt habe."
11. Obwohl er schon hunderte von Indianern gesehen hat, hat er noch keinen Cowboy getroffen.
12. Als er in den Westen kam, glaubte er, dass dort nur Cowboys lebten.
13. Bald fand er heraus, dass es mehr Indianer als richtige Cowboys in New Mexico gab.
14. Seit Beginn dieses Jahrhunderts hat sich die Anzahl der Indianer in den USA vervierfacht (to quadruple).
15. Als Columbus Amerika entdeckte, lebten 1 Million Indianer in den heutigen USA.
16. In den folgenden 4 Jahrhunderten wurde ihre Zahl immer kleiner.
17. In der zweiten Hälfte des 19. Jahrhunderts erreichte sie ihren niedrigsten Stand.
18. Seitdem steigt die Zahl der Indianer wieder kontinuierlich.
19. Im Gegensatz dazu sind die echten Cowboys heute fast ausgestorben.
20. In den vergangenen Jahrzehnten haben immer mehr weiße Amerikaner ihr Interesse an der indianischen Kultur gezeigt.

Past Perfect Simple

Plusquamperfekt/vollendete Vergangenheit

regelmäßiges Verb

*Beispiel-
formen*

Bejahter Satz	Verneinter Satz	Fragesatz
I had worked.	I hadn't* worked.	Had I worked?
You had worked.	You hadn't worked.	Had you worked?
He had worked.	He hadn't worked.	Had he worked?
She had worked.	She hadn't worked.	Had she worked?
It had worked.	It hadn't worked.	Had it worked?
We had worked.	We hadn't worked.	Had we worked?
You had worked.	You hadn't worked.	Had you worked?
They had worked.	They hadn't worked.	Had they worked?

unregelmäßiges Verb

Bejahter Satz	Verneinter Satz	Fragesatz
I had gone.	I hadn't* gone.	Had I gone?
You had gone.	You hadn't gone.	Had you gone?
He had gone.	He hadn't gone.	Had he gone?
She had gone.	She hadn't gone.	Had she gone?
It had gone.	It hadn't gone.	Had it gone?
We had gone.	We hadn't gone.	Had we gone?
You had gone.	You hadn't gone.	Had you gone?
They had gone.	They hadn't gone.	Had they gone?

Die Bildung des Past Perfect Simple:

Bildung

regelmäßige Verben: "had" + 1. Verbform + "-ed"
Beispiel: I had worked.
Rechtschreibbesonderheiten beim Anhängen von "-ed" siehe S. 27.

unregelmäßige Verben: "had" + 3. Verbform
Beispiel: I had gone.

Beachte: Im Deutschen wird Plusquamperfekt bei einigen Verben mit der Vergangenheitsform von „sein", bei einigen mit der Vergangenheitsform von „haben" gebildet.

---

* hadn't = had not

Beispiel: Ich hatte gearbeitet.

Ich war gegangen.

Im Englischen wird Past Perfect jedoch immer mit "had" gebildet.

Beispiel: I had worked.

I had gone.

Anwendung

Past Perfect wird verwendet

▶ für Handlungen, die zu einem bestimmten *Zeitpunkt der Vergangenheit bereits abgeschlossen* waren. Dies wird entweder durch eine zweite, nachfolgende Handlung im Past Tense, Vergangenheit (a) oder durch eine entsprechende Zeitangabe (b) gekennzeichnet.

Beispiel zu (a): After I had done my homework,   I played tennis. –
Nachdem ich meine Hausaufgaben
gemacht hatte,   spielte ich Tennis.

(1. Handlung: (2. Handlung:
Past Perfect)   Past Tense)

Beispiel zu (b): By that time he had already left. – Inzwischen war er schon
gegangen.

▶ für Handlungen, die vor einem bestimmten *Zeitpunkt der Vergangenheit* begannen und bis zu diesem oder über diesen hinaus *andauerten.*

Beispiel: They had known each other for a long time when they got married.
– Sie kannten sich schon lange, als sie heirateten.

Beachte: Im Deutschen steht gewöhnlich Imperfekt (Vergangenheit).
Beispiel: „kannten" für "had known"

Past Perfect Continuous
Plusquamperfekt/vollendete Vergangenheit Verlaufsform

Beispielformen

Bejahter Satz	Verneinter Satz	Fragesatz
I had been going.	I hadn't* been going.	Had I been going?
You had been going.	You hadn't been going.	Had you been going?
He had been going.	He hadn't been going.	Had he been going?
She had been going.	She hadn't been going	Had she been going?
It had been going.	It hadn't been going.	Had it been going?
We had been going.	We hadn't been going.	Had we been going?
You had been going.	You hadn't been going.	Had you been going?
They had been going.	They hadn't been going.	Had they been going?

hadn't = had not

Die Bildung des Past Perfect Continuous:

▶ "had" + "been" + 1. Verbform + "-ing"

Beispiel: I had been going.

I had been smiling.

▶ Rechtschreibbesonderheiten beim Anhängen von "-ing" siehe S. 21.

Past Perfect Continuous wird verwendet

▶ für Handlungen, die vor einem bestimmten *Zeitpunkt der Vergangenheit* begonnen hatten und bis zu diesem Zeitpunkt *andauerten*.

Beispiel: He had been waiting for 10 minutes before she arrived. – Er wartete schon 10 Minuen, als sie ankam.

Beachte: Im Deutschen steht Imperfekt (Vergangenheit)!

Beispiel: „wartete" für "had been waiting"

In der Anwendung entspricht das Past Perfect Continuous einem in die Vergangenheit gerückten Present Perfect Continuous.

Signalwörter: for – seit (einer Zeitspanne)

since – seit (einem Zeitpunkt)

how long – wie lange ...

▶ für Handlungen, die vor einem bestimmten *Zeitpunkt der Vergangenheit* begonnen hatten und kurz vor diesem *beendet* waren.

Beispiel: I had just been watching TV at that time. – Ich hatte gerade um diese Zeit ferngeschaut.

Exercises

Übungen

I. *Form sentences. Mind the tenses! The first action gets Past Perfect, the second (later) action Past Tense.*

Bilde Sätze! Achte auf die Zeiten! Die erste Handlung steht im Plusquamperfekt, die zweite (spätere) Handlung im Imperfekt!

Beispiel: *a) they – to buy a new house*

b) to move in

After they had bought a new house, they moved in.

1. **a)** the children – to tidy up their room
   b) to play in the garden
2. **a)** the tourists – to visit the British Museum
   b) to have tea at the Ritz
3. **a)** the Millers – to have their traditional Christmas dinner
   b) to open the parcels

4. **a)** I – to mix my colours
   b) to start to paint
5. **a)** Mrs Simons – to make the breakfast
   b) to call the children
6. **a)** he – to pass the final exam
   b) to go to university
7. **a)** the vicar – to make his speech
   b) they all – to sing a song
8. **a)** Sally – to take a few lessons in tennis
   b) to buy a tennis racket
9. **a)** he – to be on holiday for 4 weeks
   b) to find it difficult to get used to work again
10. **a)** the employee – to learn English at night school
    b) to get a higher position in his firm.

II. *Put the verbs in brackets into the correct Past Perfect form.*
Setze die Verben in Klammern in die richtige Plusquamperfektform!

1. The boy scout (to walk) for half an hour when it began to rain.
2. When he came home, his mother (already/to lay) the table.
3. When I met you first in 1992, how long ... you (to work) in our firm then?
4. Then we came to the house Mary (to live) in when she was a little girl.
5. How long ... you (to learn) English when you got the job as an interpreter?
6. After the children (to be) in England they were more interested in the English language.
7. Before we decided to spend our holiday in Greece we (to study) all the brochures from the travel agency.
8. After the cleaning lady (to break) the expensive vase she wasn't allowed in Lady Margaret's room any more.
9. Mrs Scott (to have) the letter for some days before she showed it to me.
10. Before Alan started work with that company, he (already/to apply) for many other jobs.
11. After the students (to hear) so much about England they wanted to visit England themselves.
12. She (to take) a sleeping tablet before she went to bed.
13. When we (to finish) our work, we saw that we (to forget) an important part.
14. After the students (to get) their certificates they had a big party.
15. Before she moved to the seaside she (to have) a terrible flat.
16. My father was late yesterday because he (to miss) the bus.
17. When the show was nearly over, Mrs Late ... still (not to arrive).
18. After they (to discover) the burglary they called the police at once.
19. She was sent to hospital immediately after the doctor (to give) her a check-up.
20. Before she had the accident she (to be) a good swimmer.

Past Tense, Present Perfect and Past Perfect – Mixed Exercises

Gemischte Übungen zu Imperfekt, Perfekt und Plusquamperfekt

Übungen

I. *Put the verbs in brackets into the correct tense.*
   Setze die Verben in Klammern in die richtige Zeit!

1. When Roger (to come) home from school, his mother (to wait) for him for almost 2 hours.
2. She asked him: "Why (you/not/to come) earlier? Dinner (to be) ready for over an hour now."
3. Roger replied: "I (to want) to be punctual, but we (must/to stay) in school longer."
4. "What (you/to do) that you (must/to stay) so long?" his mother asked.
5. "When the teacher (to come) in, we (to jump) over the tables in our classroom."
6. "I (not/to hear) such a stupid thing for years", exclaimed his mother.
7. When Inspector Blockhead (to arrive) at the hotel, he (to find) that a terrible crime (to be committed).
8. He (not/to stand) there long when suddenly one of the guests (to want) to speak to him.
9. He (to say) that he (to watch) TV when suddenly he (to hear) a shot.
10. He (to run) to the window at once and (to see) a woman leaving the hotel in a hurry.
11. She (to wear) a grey fur coat.
12. When the guest (to mention) the grey fur coat, the inspector immediately (to know) who the woman (to be).
13. He (to write) down the address and (to tell) one of the officers to go there directly.
14. The officer (to do) as he (to be told).
15. The inspector (to smile) and (to say): "I'm very happy to say that we (already/to solve) the case."
16. He added: "I (to have) a feeling that this woman (to be) the murderer from the moment we (to come) here."
17. This (to be) the first case in over 2 years which Inspector Blockhead (to finish) in such a short time.
18. 2 hours later the officer (to return) with the woman in the grey fur coat.
19. He (to arrest) her while she (to try) to drive to the airport.
20. Inspector Blockhead (to be promoted) and (to be) happy ever since.

II. *Translate the following sentences.*
Übersetze die folgenden Sätze!

1. Als Columbus Amerika entdeckte, glaubte er, dass er einen kürzeren Weg nach Indien gefunden hätte.
2. Seit damals haben wir herausgefunden, dass Columbus sich geirrt hatte.
3. Nachdem die ersten Siedler nach Amerika gekommen waren, begannen sie bald überall Dörfer und Städte zu bauen.
4. Vom Ende des 17. Jahrhunderts bis zum Ende des 19. Jahrhunderts fand eine ständige Westwärtsbewegung statt.
5. Gegen 1890 waren die letzten großen, freien Gebiete besiedelt.
6. Seitdem hat sich die Situation für die Einwanderer grundlegend geändert.
7. Während sie in den ersten Jahrzehnten dieses Jahrhunderts in den Industriezentren Arbeit fanden, sind die Einwanderer in den letzten Jahren zu einem Problem geworden.
8. Vor dem 2. Weltkrieg kamen die Einwanderer hauptsächlich aus Europa, aber seit den 50er Jahren hat die Zahl der Einwanderer aus der Dritten Welt kontinuierlich zugenommen.
9. Außerdem hat die Zahl der illegalen Einwanderer in jüngster Zeit zugenommen.
10. 1987 begann die Regierung damit vielen illegalen Einwanderern die Chance zu geben amerikanische Staatsbürger (citizens) zu werden.
11. Niemals zuvor hatten so viele Menschen auf einmal die Möglichkeit gehabt Bürger der Vereinigten Staaten zu werden.
12. Als wir das letzte Mal in den USA waren, erfuhren wir, dass viele Mexikaner schon jahrelang auf das neue Gesetz gewartet hatten.
13. Auch in England nahm die Zahl der Einwanderer in den 70er und in den frühen 80er Jahren stark zu.
14. 1986 versuchte die britische Regierung die Flut der Einwanderer durch ein neues Gesetz zu stoppen.
15. Seitdem sind weniger Einwanderer nach Großbritannien gekommen.
16. Als er hereinkam, stellte er fest, dass die anderen Gäste bereits alle Sandwiches gegessen hatten.
17. Obwohl er sich schon den ganzen Nachmittag auf ein Steak gefreut hatte, konnte er jetzt nichts essen.
18. Der Gastgeber (host) sagte zu ihm: „Wir haben 2 Stunden auf Sie gewartet, aber als Sie um 8 Uhr immer noch nicht hier waren, haben wir mit dem Essen angefangen."
19. „Wir sprachen gerade von Ihnen, als Sie zur Tür hereinkamen."
20. Der Gast erwiderte: „Ich konnte leider nicht früher kommen, da ich noch im Büro arbeiten musste."

Future I ("Will"-Future) Simple
Futur I/Zukunft I

Bejahter Satz	Verneinter Satz	Fragesatz
I will* work.	I won't** work.	Will I work?
You will work.	You won't work.	Will you work?
He will work.	He won't work.	Will he work?
She will work.	She won't work.	Will she work?
It will work.	It won't work.	Will it work?
We will work.	We won't work.	Will we work?
You will work.	You won't work.	Will you work?
They will work.	They won't work.	Will they work?

Die Bildung des Future I:

"will" + 1. Verbform

Beispiel: I will work:

Beachte: will – werden (nicht „wollen")

I will. – Ich werde.

I want. – Ich will.

Future I ("Will"-Future) wird verwendet

▶ um *zukünftiges Geschehen* auszudrücken, das der Sprecher nicht beeinflussen kann.

Beispiel: It will rain tomorrow. – Morgen wird es regnen./... regnet es.

▶ um einen *Entschluss* auszudrücken, der spontan im Moment des Sprechens gefasst wird.

Beispiel: Wait a minute, I'll help you. – Warte einen Moment, ich werde dir helfen/ich helfe dir.

▶ im *Hauptsatz eines If-Satzes* (Bedingungssatzes) vom Typ I (siehe S. 129 ff.).

Beispiel: It it rains, we'll stay at home. – Wenn es regnet, werden wir zu Hause bleiben/bleiben wir zu Hause.

▶ bei *Vermutungen* von zukünftigem Geschehen.

Beispiel: I think Mary will arrive late. – Ich glaube, M. wird spät ankommen.

Signalwörter:
next ... – nächste ...
the following ... – folgenden
in 2010 – im Jahre 2010
in 2 weeks, etc. – in 2 Wochen etc.
tomorrow – morgen

*will = 'll **won't = will not

Beachte: In der Verwendung des Futurs ist das Englische wesentlich konsequenter als das Deutsche. Im Deutschen kann oft Präsens stehen, wenn im Englischen Futur benutzt werden muss.

Future I ("Will"-Future) Continuous
Futur I/Zukunft I Verlaufsform

Bejahter Satz	Verneinter Satz	Fragesatz
I will* be working.	I won't** be working.	Will I be working?
You will be working.	You won't be working.	Will you be working?
He will be working.	He won't be working.	Will he be working?
She will be working.	She won't be working.	Will she be working?
It will be working.	It won't be working.	Will it be working?
We will be working.	We won't be working.	Will we be working?
You will be working.	You won't be working.	Will you be working?
They will be working.	They won't be working.	Will they be working?

Beispiel-formen

Die Bildung des Future I Continuous:
"will" + "be" + 1. Verbform + "-ing"
Beispiel: I will be working.
Rechtschreibbesonderheiten der ing-Form siehe S. 21.

Bildung

Future I Continuous wird verwendet
▶ um auszudrücken, dass ein Vorgang zu einem *bestimmten Zeitpunkt* oder in einem bestimmten *Zeitraum der Zukunft gerade ablaufen* wird.
  Beispiel: When you are asleep, I'll be sitting in the train. – Wenn du schläfst, werde ich im Zug sitzen.
▶ um auszudrücken, dass ein *zukünftiger Vorgang* für ganz *sicher* oder *selbstverständlich* gehalten wird.
  Beispiel: I'll be seeing Mary tomorrow at the office. – Ich werde Mary (sicherlich) morgen im Büro sehen.

Anwendung

Beachte: Verben mit statischer Bedeutung und Verben des Denkens und Erkennens (siehe S. 18) bilden keine ing-Form.

---

*will = 'll **won't = will not*

Exercises

Übungen

I. *Answer the questions in complete sentences.*
   Beantworte die Fragen in ganzen Sätzen!
   Beispiel: *When will you leave? (3rd of June)*
   We will leave on the 3rd of June.

1. When will you arrive in New York?
   (4th of June, in the evening)
2. How many days will you spend there?
   (3 days)
3. Will you visit the Empire State Building?
   (no/not to visit the Empire State Building/but to see the Statue of Liberty)
4. Will you stay at the Hilton?
   (no/not to stay at the Hilton/but to stay at a cheaper hotel)
5. What will you do on the fourth day?
   (to fly to Chicago)
6. What will you do in Chicago?
   (to visit an uncle of mine)
7. How many days will you stay in Chicago?
   (only 2 days)
8. Will you do a lot of sightseeing in Chicago?
   (no/not to have time for that)
9. Where will you go next?
   (to go to L. A. by Greyhound bus)
10. Will that be the last part of your journey?
    (yes/after that/to return to England)

II. *Write down what they will do in complete sentences.*
    Schreibe in ganzen Sätzen, was sie tun werden.
    Beispiel: *to fly from Frankfurt to London*
    We will fly from Frankfurt to London.

1. to arrive at Heathrow at 10 p.m.
2. to take the tube to the city
3. to arrive at the George Hotel at about 11 o'clock
4. not to go out on the first evening/because/to be tired
5. only to have a drink at the hotel bar
6. to go to bed at about 12 o'clock
7. next morning/to visit Portobello Road Market
8. Perhaps/to buy presents for the family

9. to have lunch at a pub
10. in the afternoon/to go shopping in Oxford Street
11. on Sunday morning/to go to Hyde Park and/to listen to the people at Speakers' Corner
12. not to stay there very long/because/to meet some friends at the Park Lane Hotel for tea.
13. In the evening/to go to the theatre to see the famous musical "Cats".
14. On Monday morning/to take a boat to Greenwich
15. There/to see the "Cutty Sark" and the Royal Observatory
16. In the afternoon/to go back to London by train
17. to visit the Tower of London and/to admire the famous Crown Jewels
18. Later/to have dinner at Dickens Inn
19. not to have time to stay there very long/because/to return to Germany early the next morning
20. at 8 o'clock/to have to be at the airport.

III. The Grays are going to move house next month. They are dreaming of what they'll be doing then. Form sentences.

Die Grays ziehen nächsten Monat um. Sie träumen davon, was sie dann tun werden. Bilde Sätze!

Beispiel: *Next month/to sit in our new living-room*
Next month we will be sitting in our new living-room.

1. we/to watch the fire in the new fireplace
2. mother/to prepare dinner in her new kitchen
3. the cat/to lie in front of the fireplace
4. later/we/to play cards
5. our parents/to talk to the new next-door neighbours
6. Paul/to help Grandma with the washing-up in the kitchen
7. the baby/already/to sleep/upstairs
8. on the first Sunday in our new house/we/to have breakfast on the balcony
9. Grandma/to sit in her favourite armchair
10. we hope/the sun/to shine

IV. Tomorrow at 7 p.m. the famous "Black Cats" band will be on stage. Write down what other people will be doing then.

Morgen um 19 Uhr wird die berühmte Band "The Black Cats" auf der Bühne sein. Schreibe auf, was andere Leute zu dieser Zeit tun werden!

1. Simon and his friends, who are fans of this group, (to sit) on the ground in front of the stage and (to clap).
2. The girls (to cry) enthusiastically, because they think the boys of the band are great.

3. Reporters (to try) to get the best photos of the members of the band.
4. The roadies (to work) hard behind the stage.
5. The television broadcasting team (to check) all cameras.
6. The parents (to sit) in front of the TV and (to hope) to see their children in the audience.
7. The hot dog vendors (to prepare) snacks for the interval.
8. Hairdressers (to wait) behind the stage in case they are needed.
9. Technicians (to control) the different connections for the radio stations.
10. Reporters (already/to scribble) down notes for the following day's articles.

"Going to"-Future
"Going-to"-Futur/"Going-to"-Zukunft

Beispiel-
formen

Bejahter Satz	Verneinter Satz	Fragesatz
I am* going to arrive.	I am not going to arrive.	Am I going to arrive?
You are* going to arrive.	You are not going to arrive.	Are you going to arrive?
He is* going to arrive.	He is not going to arrive.	Is he going to arrive?
She is going to arrive.	She is not going to arrive.	Is she going to arrive?
It is going to arrive.	It is not going to arrive.	Is it going to arrive?
We are going to arrive.	We are not going to arrive.	Are we going to arrive?
You are going to arrive.	You are not going to arrive.	Are you going to arrive?
They are going to arrive.	They are not going to arrive.	Are they going to arrive?

Bildung

Die Bildung des "Going to"-Future:
Gegenwartsform von "to be" (am/are/is) + "going to" + 1. Verbform
Beispiel: I am going to arrive. – Ich **werde** ankommen.
Beachte: "To be going to" + 1. Verbform hat nichts mit *gehen* zu tun, sondern bedeutet *werden*.

---

*Statt "am", "are", "is" können auch die Kurzformen "'m", "'re" und "'s" verwendet werden.

56

Das "Going to"-Future wird verwendet

▶ um eine *logische Schlussfolgerung* auszudrücken.

Beispiel: Billy is coughing. He is going to be ill tomorrow. – Billy hustet. Er wird morgen krank sein.

▶ um eine *Absicht* auszudrücken, die zum Zeitpunkt des Sprechens bereits besteht (also keinen spontanen Entschluss wie beim "Will"-Future).

Beispiel: I am going to bring you the book tonight. – Ich werde dir das Buch heute Abend bringen.

Present Tense Simple Referring to Future
Präsens/Gegenwart in futurischer Bedeutung

Die Formen des Present Tense Simple:

I arrive

he arrives

(Ausführliche Beispielformen siehe S. 17).

Die Bildung des Present Tense Simple:

1. Verbform – bei he, she, it (3. Person Singular) + "-(e)s" –

Beispiel: I come

he comes

Present Tense Simple wird in futurischer Bedeutung verwendet

▶ um auszudrücken, dass *Vorgänge oder Zustände* von außenstehenden Personen oder Institutionen *festgelegt* sind (z. B. Fahrplan, Programm).

Beispiel: The new film starts next Friday. – Der neue Film beginnt nächsten Freitag.

Present Tense Continuous Referring to Future
Präsens/Gegenwart Verlaufsform in futurischer Bedeutung

Die Formen des Present Tense Continuous:

I am arriving.

He is arriving.

(Ausführliche Beispielformen sowie Rechtschreibbesonderheiten beim Anhängen von "-ing" siehe S. 20 f).

Die Bildung des Present Tense Continuous:

Gegenwartsform von "to be" (am/are/is) + 1. Verbform + "-ing"

Beispiel: He is working.

Present Tense Continuous wird in futurischer Bedeutung verwendet

▶ bei Tätigkeits- und Vorgangsverben (z. B. to arrive, to come, to go, to leave etc.) um *etwas konkret Geplantes* zum Ausdruck zu bringen. (Sind noch keine festen Vereinbarungen oder Vorbereitungen getroffen, benutzt man "Going to"-Future.)

Beispiel: Sue and Simon are getting married next week. – Sue and Simon heiraten nächste Woche.

Exercises
Übungen

I. *Form 8 of Sutton Grammar School are going to have a party tomorrow, but they haven't prepared anything yet. Write down what they are going to do. Use "going to"-Future.*

   Die Klasse 8 der Sutton Grammar School hat morgen eine Party, aber sie haben noch nichts vorbereitet. Schreibe auf, was sie alles machen werden. Benutze das "Going-to"-Futur!

   Beispiel: *The party / to start / at 7 p.m.*
   The party is going to start at 7 p.m.

1. The girls / to serve tea and biscuits / first
2. Tom / to make a short speech / at 7.15 p.m.
3. He / to welcome / the guests of the German exchange programme
4. He / to give / a book about Sutton as a present to the speaker of the German class
5. At 7.30 p.m. / the disco / to start
6. The dancing club / to perform / new American dances
7. Then / most of the students / to dance
8. At 9 p.m. / there / to be a break
9. They / to show a film / about school life in England to inform their German guests.
10. Afterwards / they / to answer questions asked by the German students.

II. Use the correct Future form.
Benutze die richtige Futurform!

1. There are a lot of clouds. It (to rain) soon.
2. The train to London (to leave) at 5 p.m.
3. Next Saturday the band "The Black Spiders" (to be) on stage.
4. What (to happen) if the party wins the election?
5. This time next week we (to lie) on the beach in Rimini.
6. Our best player is ill. Our team (to lose) the match next Friday.
7. If I meet him, I (to tell) him.
8. We have just decided that we (to go) to Spain for Christmas.
9. He has never worked in his life, so he (not/to get) any pension now.
10. Judy (to have a party). She has already invited all her friends.
11. We don't have to discuss this problem now because I (to see) you tomorrow afternoon.
12. Linda (to be) late today. There has been such heavy traffic on the M 25.
13. I have to hurry because my plane (to leave) in 1 hour.
14. (you/to visit) us tomorrow?
15. In 10 years from now we (probably/to be) rich.
16. Jerome (never/to marry) Sheila if she doesn't stop talking so much.
17. Look at this tree. It (to fall) on the house during the next thunderstorm.
18. Grandfather (never/to travel) by plane.
19. We (to write) a test tomorrow. It has been announced for over a week now.
20. The new job (to be) hard for him, but I'm sure he (to get) used to it soon.

Future II Simple
Futur II/Zukunft II

regelmäßiges Verb

Bejahter Satz	Verneinter Satz	Fragesatz
I will* have worked.	I won't** have worked.	Will I have worked?
You will have worked.	You won't have worked.	Will you have worked?
He will have worked.	He won't have worked.	Will he have worked?
She will have worked.	She won't have worked.	Will she have worked?
It will have worked.	It won't have worked.	Will it have worked?
We will have worked.	We won't have worked.	Will we have worked?
You will have worked.	You won't have worked.	Will you have worked?
They will have worked.	They won't have worked.	Will they have worked?

Beispiel-formen

*will = 'll **won't = will not

unregelmäßiges Verb

Bejahter Satz	Verneinter Satz	Fragesatz
I will* have gone.	I won't** have gone.	Will I have gone?
You will have gone.	You won't have gone.	Will you have gone?
He will have gone.	He won't have gone.	Will he have gone?
She will have gone.	She won't have gone.	Will she have gone?
It will have gone.	It won't have gone.	Will it have gone?
We will have gone.	We won't have gone.	Will we have gone?
You will have gone.	You won't have gone.	Will you have gone?
They will have gone.	They won't have gone.	Will they have gone?

Die Bildung des Future II Simple:

Bildung

regelmäßige Verben: "will" + "have" + 1. Verbform + "-ed"

Beispiel: I will have finished.

Rechtschreibbesonderheiten beim Anhängen von "-ed" siehe S. 27.

unregelmäßige Verben: "will" + "have" + 3. Verbform

Beispiel: I will have eaten

Future II wird verwendet

Anwendung

bei Handlungen, die zu einem bestimmten Zeitpunkt der Zukunft *geschehen sein werden*. Dieser Zeitpunkt wird meist durch eine entsprechende Zeitbestimmung wie

by ...	– (spätestens) bis
in (ten minutes)	– in (zehn Minuten)
next (month)	– nächsten (Monat)

oder durch eine zweite Handlung, eingeleitet durch "by the time ...", gekennzeichnet.

Beispiel: By tomorrow he will have done everything. – Bis morgen wird er alles gemacht haben.

By the time Mary gets home her mother will have finished ironing. – Bis Mary nach Hause kommt, wird ihre Mutter die Bügelwäsche schon erledigt haben.

---

*will = 'll **won't = will not*

Future II Continuous

Futur II / Zukunft II Verlaufsform

Beispiel-
formen

Bejahter Satz	Verneinter Satz	Fragesatz
I will* have been working.	I won't** have been working.	Will I have been working?
You will have been working.	You won't have been working.	Will you have been working?
He will have been working.	He won't have been working.	Will he have been working?
She will have been working.	She won't have been working.	Will she have been working?
It will have been working.	It won't have been working.	Will it have been working?
We will have been working.	We won't have been working.	Will we have been working?
You will have been working.	You won't have been working.	Will you have been working?
They will have been working.	They won't have been working.	Will they have been working?

Die Bildung des Future II Continuous:

"will" + "have" + "been" + 1. Verbform + "-ing"

Beispiel: I will have been waiting.

Rechtschreibbesonderheiten beim Anhängen von "-ing" siehe S. 21.

Bildung

Future II Continuous wird selten benutzt.

Es drückt wie Future II Simple Vorzeitigkeit gegenüber einem bestimmten Zeitpunkt der Zukunft aus, betont darüber hinaus aber die *ununterbrochene Dauer* des Vorgangs.

Beispiel: By the end of March I will have been working in this firm for 2 years.
Ende März arbeite ich schon 2 Jahre in dieser Firma.

Beachte: Im Deutschen wird stattdessen Präsens (Gegenwart) verwendet: „arbeite" für "will have been working".

Anwendung

*will = 'll **won't = will not

Exercises

Übungen

I. *The Pools are going to go on holiday next Friday. Write down what they will have done before they leave.*
   Die Pools fahren nächsten Freitag in Urlaub. Schreibe auf, was sie getan haben werden, bevor sie abfahren!
   Beispiel: *to shut the windows*
   They will have shut the windows.

1. to ask their neighbours to keep an eye in their house
2. to give the key to Aunt Mary
3. to take the cat to a pets' home
4. to check the shed door
5. to do all the washing
6. Mrs Pool / to do all the ironing
7. Mr Pool / to check the car
8. to pack the suitcases
9. to buy maps for their route
10. to inform themselves about the country they are going to
11. to water the flowers
12. to pull out the TV plug
13. to turn off the main water tap
14. to put a new film in the camera
15. to take their valuables to the bank

II. *Form sentences using Future II Continuous.*
   Bilde Sätze, in denen du Futur II Verlaufsform benutzt!
1. By 7 o'clock / he / to sleep for 10 hours
2. Next month / they / to build / this house for 6 months
3. The dancers / to practise for the show for 4 weeks next weekend
4. In 2005 / we / to live in our house for 10 years
5. Next year / they / to play / "The Mousetrap" for 45 years
6. By next Saturday / Jack / to stay with us for 2 weeks
7. By the end of the year / I / to go to this school for 5 years
8. By the end of the term / Simon / to play for this club for 2 years
9. By 7 o'clock my father / to repair / his car / for 5 hours
10. By the end of our journey / we / to travel / for 12 hours

Conditional I Simple
Konditional I

Beispiel-
formen

Bejahter Satz	Verneinter Satz	Fragesatz
I would* go.	I wouldn't** go.	Would I go?
You would go.	You wouldn't go.	Would you go?
He would go.	He wouldn't go.	Would he go?
She would go.	She wouldn't go.	Would she go?
It would go.	It wouldn't go.	Would it go?
We would go.	We wouldn't go.	Would we go?
You would go.	You wouldn't go.	Would you go?
They would go.	They wouldn't go.	Would they go?

Die Bildung des Conditional I Simple:

"would" + 1. Verbform

Beispiel: He would come.

Beachte: Die Kurzform "'d" für "would" ist identisch mit der Kurzform "'d" für "had". Man kann nur durch die nachfolgende Form unterscheiden, ob "would" oder "had" gemeint ist:

Nach "would" folgt 1. Verbform.

Bildung

Beispiel: I'd go.

Nach "had" folgt 3. Verbform.

Beispiel: I'd gone.

Conditional I wird verwendet

▶ in den *Hauptsätzen der Bedingungssätze (If-Sätze) vom Typ II* (Improbable Condition – unwahrscheinliche Bedingung, siehe S. 132 ff).

In den entsprechenden Nebensätzen steht Past Tense (Imperfekt).

Anwendung

Beispiel: <u>I would make a journey</u>   <u>if I won in a lottery.</u>

          Conditional I   Past Tense

          Ich würde eine Reise machen, wenn ich in der Lotterie gewänne.

▶ in der *indirekten Rede,* wenn das einleitende Verb in einer Zeit der Vergangenheitsgruppe steht und in der direkten Rede Future I (Futur I) gebraucht wurde. (Siehe auch Kapitel "Reported Speech – Indirekte Rede", S. 86 ff).

Beispiel: Direkte Rede: Mary said: "I will visit London." – Mary sagte: „Ich werde London besuchen."

         Indirekte Rede: Mary said she would visit London. – Mary sagte, sie würde London besuchen.

---

*would = 'd **wouldn't = would not

▶ in *Hauptsätzen*. Es entspricht dann dem deutschen Konjunktiv (Möglich-keitsform) im Imperfekt oder einer Umschreibung mit „würde".

Beispiel: A cool lemonade would be nice. – Eine kühle Limonade wäre schön.

A long rest would do us good. – Eine lange Pause würde uns gut tun.

▶ um ein *typisches Verhalten in der Vergangenheit* auszudrücken.

Beispiel: She would go to the disco every Saturday. – Sie ging jeden Samstag in die Disco.

▶ um eine *Weigerung in der Vergangenheit* zum Ausdruck zu bringen (wouldn't).

Beispiel: I told him to come, but he wouldn't. – Ich sagte ihm, er solle kommen, aber er weigerte sich.

Conditional I Continuous
Konditional I Verlaufsform

Beispiel-formen

Bejahter Satz	Verneinter Satz	Fragesatz
I would* be going.	I wouldn't** be going.	Would I be going?
You would be going.	You wouldn't be going.	Would you be going?
He would be going.	He wouldn't be going.	Would he be going?
She would be going.	She wouldn't be going.	Would she be going?
It would be going.	It wouldn't be going.	Would it be going?
We would be going.	We wouldn't be going.	Would we be going?
You would be going.	You wouldn't be going.	Would you be going?
They would be going.	They wouldn't be going.	Would they be going?

Die Bildung des Conditional I Continuous:

Bildung

"would" + "be" + 1. Verbform + "-ing"

Beispiel: They would be leaving.

Rechtschreibbesonderheiten beim Anhängen von "-ing" siehe S. 21.

Conditional I Continuous wird verwendet

Anwendung

wie Conditional I Simple, wenn die *Dauer* eines Vorgangs betont werden soll.

Beispiel: I would be working if I weren't ill. –

Ich würde arbeiten, wenn ich nicht krank wäre.

---

*would = 'd **wouldn't = would not

Exercises
Übungen

I. *Put the verbs in brackets into Conditional I.*
   Setze die Verben in Klammern ins Konditional I!

1. If you wore your coat you (not/to fall) ill so often.
2. ... you (to mind) helping me?
3. I (to like) to introduce you to my uncle.
4. I (to learn) more if I were you.
5. If they lived in London they (to go out) quite regularly.
6. They called the assistant, but he (not/to listen).
7. ... you (to like) an orange-juice?
8. Mr Baker remarked that he (to get) a better job next month.
9. If Susan passed the exam, she (to be able to) work in her uncle's firm.
10. What ... you (to do) if you were in my situation?
11. ... you (to open) the window, please?
12. Only a miracle (to help) him.
13. Some new friends (to make) him feel at home here.
14. If I had enough money I (to buy) that car at once.
15. She tried to open the suitcase, but it (not/to open).

II. *Translate the following sentences.*
   Übersetze die folgenden Sätze!

1. Ich hätte gerne ein Doppelzimmer mit Dusche bestellt.
2. Möchtest du noch einen Tee?
3. Würdest du bitte die Briefe so schnell wie möglich zur Post bringen?
4. Früher ging mein Vater jeden Sonntag in seinen Club.
5. Die Gangster befahlen ihm den Tresor zu öffnen, aber er weigerte sich.
6. Wenn ich du wäre, würde ich ihn sofort anrufen.
7. Würde es dir etwas ausmachen, wenn ich eine Stunde später käme?
8. Herr Ober, wir würden gerne bezahlen.
9. Würdest du bitte morgen Abend bei mir vorbeikommen?
10. Er sagte, er würde nächste Woche nach New York fliegen.

Conditional II Simple

Konditional II

regelmäßiges Verb

Bejahter Satz	Verneinter Satz	Fragesatz
I would* have worked.	I wouldn't** have worked.	Would I have worked?
You would have worked	You wouldn't have worked	Would you have worked?
He would have worked.	He wouldn't have worked.	Would he have worked?
She would have worked.	She wouldn't have worked.	Would she have worked?
It would have worked.	It wouldn't have worked.	Would it have worked?
We would have worked.	We wouldn't have worked.	Would we have worked?
You would have worked.	You wouldn't have worked.	Would you have worked?
They would have worked.	They wouldn't have worked.	Would they have worked?

unregelmäßiges Verb

Bejahter Satz	Verneinter Satz	Fragesatz
I would* have gone.	I wouldn't** have gone.	Would I have gone?
You would have gone.	You wouldn't have gone.	Would you have gone?
He would have gone.	He wouldn't have gone.	Would he have gone?
She would have gone.	She wouldn't have gone.	Would she have gone?
It would have gone.	It wouldn't have gone.	Would it have gone?
We would have gone.	We wouldn't have gone.	Would we have gone?
You would have gone.	You wouldn't have gone.	Would you have gone?
They would have gone.	They wouldn't have gone.	Would they have gone?

Die Bildung des Conditional II Simple:

regelmäßige Verben: "would" + "have" + 1. Verbform + "-ed"

Beispiel: I would have liked.

Rechtschreibbesonderheiten beim Anhängen von "-ed" siehe S. 27.

Zur Verwechselungsgefahr bei Verwendung der Kurzform "'d" für "would" siehe S. 63.

---

*would = 'd **wouldn't = would not*

unregelmäßige Verben: "would" + "have" + 3. Verbform
Beispiel: I would have gone.

Conditional II Simple wird verwendet

Anwendung

▶ in den *Hauptsätzen der Bedingungssätze (If-Sätze) vom Typ III* (Impossible Condition – unmögliche Bedingung, siehe S. 135 f.). In den entsprechenden Nebensätzen steht Past Perfect (Plusquamperfekt).

Beispiel: <u>If he had worked harder,</u>   <u>he would have succeeded.</u>

             Past Perfect   Conditional II

     Wenn er härter gearbeitet hätte, hätte er Erfolg gehabt.

▶ in der *indirekten Rede,* wenn das einleitende Verb in einer Zeit der Vergangenheitsgruppe steht und in der direkten Rede a) Future II (Futur II) oder b) in If-Sätzen Conditional I (Konditional I) gebraucht wurde.

Beispiel: a) Direkte Rede: He said: "I will have worked ..." – Er sagte: „Ich werde gearbeitet haben ..."

          Indirekte Rede: He said he would have worked ... – Er sagte, er würde gearbeitet haben ...

  b)   Direkte Rede: He said: "If it rained we would stay in." – Er sagte: „Wenn es regnete, blieben wir zu Hause."

          Indirekte Rede: He said if it had rained, they would have stayed in. – Er sagte, wenn es geregnet hätte, wären sie zu Hause geblieben.

▶ in *Hauptsätzen,* wie Konditional I, aber in Bezug auf die *Vergangenheit* (entspricht einem deutschen Konjunktiv II oder einer Umschreibung mit „würde".

Beispiel: I would have gone anyway. – Ich wäre sowieso gegangen.

     A cool lemonade would have been nice. – Eine kühle Limonade wäre schön gewesen.

Conditional II Continuous
Konditional II Verlaufsform

Beispiel-formen

Bejahter Satz	Verneinter Satz	Fragesatz
I would* have been going.	I wouldn't** have been going.	Would I have been going?
You would have been going.	You wouldn't have been going.	Would you have been going?
He would have been going.	He wouldn't have been going.	Would he have been going?
She would have been going.	She wouldn't have been going.	Would she have been going?
It would have been going.	It wouldn't have been going.	Would it have been going?
We would have been going.	We wouldn't have been going.	Would we have been going?
You would have been going.	You wouldn't have been going.	Would you have been going?
They would have been going.	They wouldn't have been going.	Would they have been going?

Bildung

Die Bildung des Conditional II Continuous:
"would" + " have" + "been" + 1. Verbform + "-ing"
Beispiel: I would have been waiting.
Rechtschreibbesonderheiten beim Anhängen von "-ing" siehe S. 21.
Zur Verwechslungsgefahr bei Verwendung der Kurzform "'d" für "would" siehe S. 63.

Anwendung

Conditional II Continuous wird verwendet
wie Conditional II Simple, wenn die *Dauer* eines Vorgangs betont werden soll.
Beispiel: I would have been working for 2 hours if I hadn't been ill. – Ich hätte 2 Stunden gearbeitet, wenn ich nicht krank gewesen wäre.

---

*would = 'd **wouldn't = would not

Exercises

Übungen

I. *Put the verbs in brackets into Conditional II.*
   Setze die Verben in Klammern ins Konditional II!

1. I (to go) to see him at once if I had known about the accident.
2. ... you (to do) this for me if I had asked you?
3. I (to do) it anyway.
4. He said by the 3rd of August he (to stay) in New England for 3 weeks.
5. If the police had come at once, they (to catch) the thief.
6. If the weather had been fine, we (to go) swimming.
7. He (never/to ask) me this question.
8. A long walk (to do) us good.
9. If I only had seen, I (to stop) it.
10. If you had gone there, you (to meet) him.
11. You should have asked Mr Hide. He (to be glad) to be able to help you.
12. Holidays in the South (to be) better for him.
13. That (to be) awfully nice of him.
14. I hoped they (to finish) before their parents got back home.
15. If they had found the person earlier, they (to be able to) save his life.
16. Without a special document we (not to be allowed) to enter.
17. Without a life jacket he (to be drowned).
18. I (to like) to visit Madame Tussaud's, but we hadn't got enough time.
19. My mother (to buy) the pullover for me, but they hadn't got it in the right colour.
20. Mrs Shutter (to paint) the living-room herself, but she broke her leg.

Die Tabelle auf den nächsten Seiten gibt eine Übersicht der Zeiten im Aktiv.

Die Zeiten – Aktiv – Tabellarische Übersicht

English Terms	Deutsche Begriffe	Lateinische Bezeichnung	Beispiel-formen	Bildungsweise	Anwendung	Signalwörter
Present Tense Simple	einfache Gegenwart	Präsens	I work he works	1. Verbform, bei he, she, it + "-(e)s"	▲ bei Dauerzuständen ▲ bei regelmäßig wiederholten Vorgängen in der Gegenwart ▲ bei allgemein gültigen Feststellungen ▲ bei zukünftigem Geschehen, das durch Fahrplan, Programm etc. bereits festgelegt ist ▲ bei nacheinander geschehenden Handlungen	often, seldom, always, never, sometimes, every, normally, usually, occasionally
Present Tense Continuous	Verlaufsform Gegenwart	Präsens Verlaufsform	I am working he is working	am/are/is + 1. Verbform + "-ing"	▲ bei momentanen Handlungen ▲ bei zukünftigen, bereits vereinbarten Handlungen ▲ bei wiederholt geschehenden Handlungen eines begrenzten Zeitraums	just, just now, now, right now, at the moment, Look!, Listen!, next …, the following
Past Tense Simple	einfache Vergangenheit	Imperfekt oder Präteritum	I worked he worked	*regelmäßige Verben:* 1. Verbform + "-ed"/*unregelmäßige Verben:* 2. Verbform	▲ bei einmaligen oder wiederholten oder aufeinander folgenden Vorgängen, die in der Vergangenheit angefangen haben und abgeschlossen sind	yesterday, … ago, in 1960, the other day, the day before, last …
Past Tense Continuous	Verlaufsform Vergangen-heit	Imperfekt/ Präteritum Verlaufsform	I was working he was working	was/were + 1. Verbform + "-ing"	▲ um den Ablauf einer Handlung zu einem bestimmten Zeitpunkt/in einem bestimmten Zeitraum der Vergangenheit zu bezeichnen ▲ bei gleichzeitigen Vorgängen in der Vergangenheit	oft: while, when

Die Zeiten – Aktiv – Tabellarische Übersicht

English Terms	Deutsche Begriffe	Lateinische Bezeichnung	Beispielformen	Bildungsweise	Anwendung	Signalwörter
Present Perfect Simple	einfache vollendete Gegenwart	Perfekt	I have worked he has worked	have/has + *regelmäßige Verben*: 1. Verbform + "-ed" *unregelmäßige Verben*: 3. Verbform	▶ für Vorgänge, die in der Vergangenheit anfingen und bis in die Gegenwart reichen ▶ für Vorgänge, die in der Vergangenheit anfingen und gerade erst abgeschlossen sind ▶ für Vorgänge, deren Auswirkungen bis in die Gegenwart reichen ▶ für Vorgänge, die einmal, mehrmals, nie vor dem Zeitpunkt des Sprechens passierten, jedoch ohne Zeitangabe der Vergangenheit	just, already, since, for, till now, up to now, up to the present, so far, never, ever, not yet, this morning*, this year*
Present Perfect Continuous	Verlaufsform vollendete Gegenwart	Perfekt Verlaufsform	I have been working, he has been working	have/has + been + 1. Verbform + "-ing"	▶ für Handlungen, die in der Vergangenheit begannen und noch andauern (die Dauer dieser Handlung wird betont) ▶ um auszudrücken, dass eine noch nicht weit zurückliegende Handlung zu unbeabsichtigten Folgen in der Gegenwart geführt hat	oft: all ..., the whole ..., how long, since, for
Past Perfect Simple	einfache vollendete Vergangenheit oder Vorvergangenheit	Plusquamperfekt	I had worked he had worked	had + *regelmäßige Verben*: 1. Verbform + "-ed" *unregelmäßige Verben*: 3. Verbform	▶ für Handlungen, die zu einem bestimmten Zeitpunkt der Vergangenheit abgeschlossen waren ▶ für Handlungen, die vor einem bestimmten Zeitpunkt der Vergangenheit begannen und bis zu diesem oder über diesen hinaus andauerten	

*wenn noch nicht vorüber

Die Zeiten – Aktiv – Tabellarische Übersicht

English Terms	Deutsche Begriffe	Lateinische Bezeichnung	Beispielformen	Bildungsweise	Anwendung	Signalwörter
Past Perfect Continuous	Verlaufsform vollendete Vergangenheit/Vorvergangenheit	Plusquamperfekt Verlaufsform	I had been working he had been working	had + been + 1. Verbform + "-ing"	▶ für Handlungen, die vor einem bestimmten Zeitpunkt der Vergangenheit begannen und bis zu diesem andauerten oder kurz vor diesem beendet waren	
Future I ("Will"-Future) Simple	einfache Zukunft I	Futur I	I will work he will work	will + 1. Verbform	▶ um zukünftiges Geschehen auszudrücken, das der Sprecher nicht beeinflussen kann ▶ um einen Entschluss auszudrücken, der spontan im Moment des Sprechens gefasst wird ▶ im Hauptsatz eines If-Satzes Typ I ▶ bei Vermutung von zukünftigem Geschehen	next ..., the following, in 2007, in 6 days, in 2 weeks, in 3 months, in 4 years, tomorrow, the day after tomorrow, etc.
Future I ("Will"-Future) Continuous	Verlaufsform Zukunft I	Futur I Verlaufsform	I will be working he will be working	will be + 1. Verbform + "-ing"	▶ für Vorgänge, die zu einem bestimmten Zeitpunkt/in einem bestimmten Zeitraum der Zukunft gerade ablaufen werden ▶ für zukünftige Vorgänge, die für ganz sicher oder selbstverständlich gehalten werden	next ..., the following, in 2007, in 6 days, in 2 weeks, in 3 months, in 4 years, tomorrow, the day after tomorrow, etc.
Future I ("Going to"-Future)	Zukunft I	Futur I	I am going to work he is going to work	am/are/is + going to + 1. Verbform	▶ für eine logische Schlussfolgerung ▶ um eine Absicht auszudrücken, die zum Zeitpunkt des Sprechens bereits besteht	

Die Zeiten – Aktiv – Tabellarische Übersicht

English Terms	Deutsche Begriffe	Lateinische Bezeichnung	Beispielformen	Bildungsweise	Anwendung	Signalwörter
Future II Simple	einfache Zukunft II	Futur II	I will have worked he will have worked	will have + regelmäßige Verben: 1. Verbform + "-ed" unregelmäßige Verben: 3. Verbform	▶ für Handlungen, die zu einem bestimmten Zeitpunkt der Zukunft geschehen sein werden	oft: by ..., in ..., next ..., etc.
Future II Continuous	Verlaufsform Zukunft II	Futur II Verlaufsform	I will have been working he will have been working	will have been + 1. Verbform + "-ing"	▶ wie Future II Simple, betont jedoch die ununterbrochene Dauer	
Conditional I Simple		einfaches Konditional I	I would work he would work	would + 1. Verbform	▶ in Hauptsätzen beim If-Satz Typ II ▶ in der indirekten Rede (backshift von Future I) ▶ in Hauptsätzen wie deutscher Konjunktiv („würde") ▶ für typisches Verhalten/Weigerung in der Vergangenheit	
Conditional I Continuous		Konditional I Verlaufsform	I would be working he would be working	would be + 1. Verbform + "-ing"	▶ wie Conditional I Simple, nur die Dauer wird betont	

Die Zeiten – Aktiv – Tabellarische Übersicht

English Terms	Deutsche Begriffe	Lateinische Bezeichnung	Beispielformen	Bildungsweise	Anwendung	Signalwörter
Conditional II Simple		einfaches Konditional II	I would have worked he would have worked	would have + *regelmäßige Verben:* 1. Verbform + "-ed" *unregelmäßige Verben:* 3. Verbform	▲ in Hauptsätzen beim If-Satz Typ III ▲ in der indirekten Rede (backshift von Future II) ▲ in Hauptsätzen wie Conditional I, jedoch in Bezug in die Vergangenheit	
Conditional II Continuous		Konditional II Verlaufsform	I would have been working he would have been working	would have been + 1. Verbform + "-ing"	▲ wie Conditional II Simple, nur die Dauer wird betont	

Final Test: Active Voice

Abschlusstest: die Zeiten – Aktiv

I. *Put the verbs in brackets into the correct tense.*
Setze die Verben in Klammern in die richtige Zeit!

1. When he (to come) home last night, he (to find out) that his brother (already/to clean) the flat.
2. The boss (cannot) believe what he (to see) yesterday morning when he (to enter) the office.
3. Everyone (to play cards) and nobody (to work) when he came in.
4. As a child he (not to eat) his soup under any circumstances.
5. 2 weeks from today he (to be) away for 2 years.
6. Joan (not/to come) home since she (to leave) a year ago.
7. Jack (to tell) me last Monday that he (to look) after our cat while we (to travel) around England the following week.
8. Why . . . the sun always (to rise) in the East?
9. I (to sit) here all morning and not a single worker (to arrive) up to now.
10. Why . . . workers nowadays never (to come) when they (to promise) to?
11. James (to like) to go on holiday next Christmas, but Lord Nobleton (not to allow) him to go.
12. Before Mary (to accept) her new job, she (to work) for General Motors for 15 years.
13. . . . you ever (to visit) the Great Bazaar in Istanbul?
14. Yes, I (to be) there last October and I (to like) to go there again next year.
15. We (to see) Mr Smithers only once up to then, but we (to recognize) him at once when he (to come) in last night.
16. My husband (not/to sleep) well for almost a year now; so he (to get up) every night.
17. While the doctor (to examine) the patient, the nurse (to prepare) the injection.
18. I (never/to remember) him if he (not/to help) me last summer.
19. There (to be) so many clouds in the sky today that I (to be) sure it (to rain).
20. Why . . . you (not/to tell) me last Friday that you (never/to see) the Eiffel Tower before you (to come) to Paris?

II. *Translate the following sentences.*
Übersetze die folgenden Sätze!

1. Ich würde ihn gern besuchen, aber er hat mich seit 2 Wochen nicht mehr angerufen.
2. Als er vor 2 Jahren erstmals nach 10 Jahren wieder nach Deutschland kam, wusste er nicht mehr, dass wir auf der rechten Straßenseite fahren.
3. Als wir das letzte Mal in der Fabrik waren, arbeiteten alle sehr schwer.
4. Wenn ich nicht schon so oft in England gewesen wäre, wäre ich gerne noch einmal nach London gefahren.
5. Als wir letzten Freitag im Theater waren, trafen wir einen alten Freund, den wir schon 2 Jahre lang nicht mehr gesehen hatten.
6. Nächstes Jahr im Oktober werden wir 20 Jahre verheiratet sein.
7. Wir wohnen jetzt seit 7 Jahren in dieser Wohnung. Heute ist sie nicht mehr so schön, wie sie war, als wir einzogen.
8. In den letzten 2 Jahren war Virginia ständig krank.
9. Nachdem Sepp 5 Jahre in den USA gelebt hatte, war er froh, dass er endlich nach Bayern zurückkehren durfte.
10. Wenn Mr O'Neill regelmäßig sein Geld gespart hätte, dann wäre er heute Millionär.
11. Nachdem Ian letztes Jahr im Urlaub beraubt worden war, sagte er, er würde nie mehr nach Europa kommen.
12. Während seines letzten Aufenthaltes hatten Diebe ihm seine goldene Armbanduhr gestohlen, die sein Großvater ihm vor Jahren gegeben hatte.
13. Aaron wollte nicht mehr nach Hause gehen, weil er sich vor seinem Vater fürchtete.
14. Ich kann dich morgen leider nicht besuchen, denn von 10 bis 12 Uhr spiele ich Tennis.
15. Als der Filmstar zur Tür hereinkam, starrten sie alle an, also ob sie noch nie eine Schauspielerin gesehen hätten.
16. Oliver lernt gerade Englisch, obwohl er Grammatik hasst.
17. Mr Morris spielt jeden Samstag mit seinem Sohn Fußball, aber diesen Samstag spielt er nicht, weil er sich letzte Woche verletzt hatte.
18. Er war noch nie in seinem Leben im Ausland, aber an Weihnachten wird er nach Rio fliegen.
19. Als die Feuerwehr ankam, brannte bereits das ganze Haus, obwohl alle versucht hatten das Feuer zu löschen (to extinguish).
20. Ich wäre als Kind gerne ans Meer gefahren, aber meine Eltern fuhren jedes Jahr in die Berge.

The Tenses Passive Voice

Tempora – Passiv/die Zeiten – Leideform

Im Passiv wird die Person oder das Ding, mit der/mit dem etwas geschieht, zur Hauptsache. Diese „leidende" Person oder dieses „leidende" Ding wird Subjekt.

Beispiel: *Aktiv:* Die Polizei fängt den Dieb. – The police catch the thief.

Passiv: Der Dieb wird gefangen (von der Polizei). – The thief is caught (by the police).

(Der Dieb ist die „leidende" Person.)

Der Begriff **Leideform** ist etwas irreführend. Das „Leiden" kann sehr wohl etwas Erfreuliches sein.

Beispiel: *Passiv:* Der Schüler wird gelobt. – The student is praised.

(„Der Schüler" ist die „leidende" Person.)

Die Bildung der Passive Voice:

Im Deutschen wird das Passiv mit einer Form von „werden" und dem Partizip Perfekt (Mittelwort der Vergangenheit, z. B. gefahren, getan, gebaut, gesehen) gebildet.

Beispiel: Er **wurde** zum Bahnhof **gebracht.**

Form von	Partizip
„werden"	Perfekt

Bildung

Im Englischen wird das Passiv mit einer Form von "to be" (also „sein" statt „werden") und dem Past Participle (Partizip Perfekt/Mittelwort der Vergangenheit) gebildet.

Beispiel: *regelmäßiges Verb:* Paul **is** **punished.**

Form	Past
von	Participle*
"to be"	

unregelmäßiges Verb: Paul **is** **driven.**

Form	Past
von	Participle*
"to be"	

Bei regelmäßigen Verben endet das Past Participle auf "-ed". Bei unregelmäßigen Verben ist es die 3. Verbform.

Die Formen von "to be" richten sich nach der Zeit und der Person.

Formen

Simple Forms	
Present Tense (Präsens/Gegenwart)	am/are/is
Past Tense (Imperfekt oder Präteritum/Vergangenheit)	was/were
Present Perfect (Perfekt/vollendete Gegenwart)	have/has been
Past Perfect (Plusquamperfekt/Vorvergangenheit)	had been
Future I (Futur I/Zukunft I)	will be
Future II (Futur II/Zukunft II)	will have been
Conditional I (Konditional I)	would be
Conditional II (Konditional II)	would have been

Continuous Forms (Verlaufsformen):	
Present Tense	am/are/is being
Past Tense	was/were being
Die anderen Continuous-Formen werden im Passiv nicht verwendet.	

Die Zeiten – Passiv – Tabellarische Übersicht	
Zeiten	**Beispielformen**
Present Tense Simple (Präsens/Gegenwart)	I am driven you are driven he, she, it is driven we are driven you are driven they are driven
Present Tense Continuous (Präsens/Gegenwart Verlaufsform)	I am being driven you are being driven he, she, it is being driven we are being driven you are being driven they are being driven
Past Tense Simple (Imperfekt oder Präteritum/Vergangenheit)	I was driven you were driven he, she, it was driven we were driven you were driven they were driven

Zeiten	Beispielformen
Past Tense Continuous (Imperfekt oder Präteritum/ Vergangenheit Verlaufsform)	I was being driven you were being driven he, she, it was being driven we were being driven you were being driven they were being driven
Present Perfect (Perfekt/vollendete Gegenwart)	I have been driven you have been driven he, she, it has been driven we have been driven you have been driven they have been driven
Past Perfect (Plusquamperfekt/ Vorvergangenheit)	I had been driven you had been driven he, she, it had been driven we had been driven you had been driven they had been driven
Future I (Futur I/Zukunft I)	I will be driven you will be driven he, she, it will be driven we will be driven you will be driven they will be driven
Future II (Futur II/Zukunft II)	I will have been driven you will have been driven he, she, it will have been driven we will have been driven you will have been driven they will have been driven
Conditional I (Konditional I)	I would be driven you would be driven he, she, it would be driven we would be driven you would be driven they would be driven
Conditional II (Konditional II)	I would have been driven you would have been driven he, she, it would have been driven we would have been driven you would have been driven they would have been driven

Transforming Active into Passive

Die Umwandlung von Aktiv in Passiv

Beispiel: Aktiv:

	Mrs Cooper	**opened**	**the tin**
(Past Tense)	(Subjekt)	(Prädikat)	(Objekt)
	Frau Cooper	öffnete	die Dose.

Passiv:

	The tin	**was opened**	**by Mrs Cooper.**
(Past Tense)	(Subjekt)	(Prädikat)	(Objekt)
	Die Dose wurde von Frau Cooper geöffnet.		

Beachte: Bei der Umwandlung eines Aktivsatzes in einen Passivsatz (oder umgekehrt) werden Subjekt (die handelnde Person/das handelnde Ding) und Objekt (die Person oder das Ding, mit der/dem etwas geschieht) vertauscht. Die Zeit wird jedoch beibehalten.

An Active Sentence with a Personal Pronoun as Object
Ein Aktivsatz mit einem Personalpronomen/persönlichen Fürwort als Objekt

Beispiel: Aktiv: Mr Morris took him to the airport.

Passiv: He was taken to the airport by Mr Morris.

Da Subjekt und Objekt vertauscht werden, ändert sich in der Folge auch der Fall des Personalpronomens.

me ↔ I	us ↔ we
him ↔ he	them ↔ they
her ↔ she	

Die Pfeile gelten in beiden Richtungen, da ein Personalpronomen als Subjekt des Aktivsatzes zum Objekt des Passivsatzes wird und dabei ebenfalls den Fall ändert.

Beispiel: Aktiv: He took Peter to hospital.

Passiv: Peter was taken to hospital by him.

Beachte: Lass dich nicht vom Deutschen in die Irre führen!

Beispiel: Uns wurde gesagt, ...

We were told ...

An Active Sentence with Two Objects
Ein Aktivsatz mit zwei Objekten

Ein Aktivsatz mit zwei Objekten liefert zwei Passivsätze. Beide Objekte können nämlich Subjekt des Passivsatzes werden.

Das Verb
Tempora – Passiv

Beispiel: Aktiv:

The lady	**showed**	**us**	**the castle.**
Die Dame	**zeigte**	**uns**	**das Schloss.**
Subjekt	Prädikat	Objekt 1	Objekt 2

Passiv: **We** were shown the castle by the lady.

Uns wurde das Schloss von der Dame gezeigt.

Subjekt 1

The castle was shown to us by the lady.

Das Schloss wurde uns von der Dame gezeigt.

Subjekt 2

Beachte: Das indirekte Objekt wird mit "to" angeschlossen.

By-Agent – Das präpositionale Objekt mit "by"

Am Ende eines Passivsatzes kann der Handlungsträger (derjenige, von dem etwas gemacht wird) genannt werden. Im Deutschen geschieht das durch die Präposition (Verhältniswort) „von", im Englischen durch die Präposition "by".

Beispiel: The box was opened **by** Mr Cooper.

Die Schachtel wurde **von** Mr Cooper geöffnet.

Dieser Handlungsträger wird jedoch nur genannt, wenn er für die Aussage von Bedeutung ist. Ein unpersönlicher, anonymer Handlungsträger (wie z.B. somebody, people etc.) wird weggelassen.

Beispiel: Aktiv: Someone opened the box.

Passiv: The box was opened (by someone).

Exercises
Übungen

I.   *Put into the Passive Voice. (2) means 2 possibilities.*
   Setze ins Passiv! „(2)" bedeutet 2 Möglichkeiten.

1. Simon bought a motorbike last week.
2. The boyscouts helped the old lady.
3. Mrs Scott will type the letters tomorrow.
4. The boys are repairing the bike.
5. The best student will win the prize.
6. In Austria the people speak German.
7. The thieves had stolen a hundred radios and TVs before the police caught them.
8. The grocer will send us the drinks tonight. (2)
9. They don't sell books any longer.

10. The nurse has told the children a good story. (2)
11. The firm fired the lazy workers.
12. Some days ago our dog bit the postman.
13. Dunlop invented the tyre.
14. After they had mended the engine, they were able to continue their journey.
15. The porters have already carried the suitcases to the taxi.
16. The church gave free soup to the poor. (2)
17. My sister has given me the necklace as a present. (2)
18. The students were making good efforts.
19. They didn't publish the newspaper any longer.
20. The Royal family uses Buckingham Palace as a city residence.

II. *Put into the Active Voice.*
   Setze ins Aktiv!
1. The burglary was discovered by the police.
2. English is spoken in many countries.
3. Mr Carter will be elected.
4. The Tower of London is used as a museum nowadays.
5. This house will be pulled down next year.
6. The old trunk had not been opened before.
7. When Mary came home, the washing-up had already been done by her husband.
8. The meat was being prepared by the cook.
9. Bad weather has been announced by the weather forecast.
10. The Rolls Royce was sold by the Duke.
11. The aerial has been put on the roof by the electrician.
12. This book will be translated by me.
13. The jewellery has been stolen by clever thieves.
14. The town was completely destroyed by an earthquake.
15. The plants have already been watered by Mrs Cool.

III. *Translate the following sentences.*
   Übersetze die folgenden Sätze!
1. Nächstes Jahr wird das neue Einkaufszentrum eröffnet.
2. Der Preis wurde uns letzte Woche überreicht.
3. Vor 2 Jahren wurde die Diskothek geschlossen, aber sie wird bald wieder von dem neuen Eigentümer eröffnet werden.
4. Das einsame Dorf war niemals zuvor von einem Fremden betreten worden.
5. Bevor er nach London kam, war ihm von seiner Firma ein Haus gemietet worden.

The Passive Infinitive – Present Tense Form

Der Infinitiv Passiv – Präsensform/die Grundform der Leideform – Gegenwartsform

Die Bildung der Present Tense Form

regelmäßige Verben: "(to) be" + 1. Verbform + "-ed"

   Beispiel: (to) be invited – eingeladen werden   *Bildung*

unregelmäßige Verben: "(to) be" + 3. Verbform

   Beispiel: (to) be shown – gezeigt werden

   Beispielsatz: This letter must be written at once.
   Dieser Brief muss sofort geschrieben werden.

Zur Anwendung des Infinitiv Passiv Präsens siehe unter Infinitiv Passiv Perfekt.   *Anwendung*

The Passive Infinitive – Present Perfect Form

Der Infinitiv Passiv – Perfektform/die Grundform der Leideform – vollendete Gegenwartsform

Die Bildung der Present Perfect Form:

regelmäßige Verben: "(to) have been" + 1. Verbform + "-ed"   *Bildung*

   Beispiel: (to) have been invited – eingeladen worden sein

   Beispielsatz: This ought to have been discussed earlier. – Das sollte früher diskutiert worden sein. (Das hätte früher diskutiert werden sollen.)

unregelmäßige Verben: "(to) have been" + 3. Verbform

   Beispiel: (to) have been shown – gezeigt worden sein

Beachte: Die Perfektform des Infinitiv Passiv wird benutzt um die Beziehung zur Vergangenheit zum Ausdruck zu bringen. Im Deutschen verwendet man stattdessen oft die Präsensform des Infinitivs, ein Hilfsverb übernimmt dann den Bezug zur Vergangenheit.

Die Verwendung des Passive Infinitive:

▶ Anders als im Deutschen wird der Infinitiv Passiv benutzt nach *"to be"* (sein), *"to leave"* (hinter-, zurück-, übrig, offen lassen etc.), *"to remain"* (bleiben).

Beispiel: "to be": The glasses were not to be found. – Die Brille war nicht zu finden.

"to leave": His letter leaves much to be discussed. – Sein Brief lässt viele Fragen offen.

"to remain": Much remains to be done. – Viel bleibt (noch) zu tun.

▶ Anstelle eines *Relativsatzes mit passivischem Sinn* dient der Infinitiv Passiv als Verkürzung (siehe Infinitiv S. 120).

Beispiel: This is a question to be answered.

This is a question <u>**which must be answered.**</u> – Das ist eine Frage, die
                            Relativsatz   beantwortet werden
                                                       muss.

▶ Der Infinitiv Passiv ohne "to" steht in Sätzen mit passivischem Sinn *nach Hilfsverben* wie: must, can, could, will, would, shall, should;
mit "to" *nach Hilfsverben* wie: ought to, to have to

Beispiel: This can be explained. – Das kann erklärt werden.
This ought to be done. – Das sollte getan werden.

Exercises

Übungen

I. Put into the Passive Voice.
   Setze ins Passiv!
1. We must mend the roof.
2. They should clean the windows at least twice a month.
3. Nobody can answer this question.
4. They ought to do their homework properly.
5. Children should consult the dentist regularly.
6. The members of the committee couldn't solve the problems.
7. The children mustn't enter this room.
8. The students may open the presents after dinner.
9. The secretary should write the letters.
10. We will choose the best.

II. Shorten the following sentences.
   Verkürze die folgenden Sätze!
1. They have decided about the methods which should be used.
2. There was no time which could be lost.

84

3. There were a lot of problems which had to be solved.
4. There are a lot of letters which should be written.
5. We have a lot of relatives who should be visited.

III. Translate the following sentences.
   Übersetze die folgenden Sätze!
1. Sie ist wirklich zu bedauern (to pity).
2. Es sind noch viele Reparaturen zu erledigen.
3. Die Briefe müssen heute noch zur Post gebracht werden.
4. Es bleibt nur noch wenig zu sagen.
5. Diese Dose darf nicht neben offenes Feuer gestellt werden.
6. Dieses Buch lässt noch viele Fragen unbeantwortet.
7. Es muss sofort nach ihm geschickt werden.
8. Das sollte bis morgen erledigt sein.
9. Die Schlüssel konnten nirgendwo gefunden werden.
10. Diese Frage hätte früher gestellt werden müssen.

Final Test: Passive Voice

Abschlusstest: die Zeiten – Passiv

Test

I. Put into the Passive Voice. (2) means 2 possibilities.
   Setze ins Passiv! „(2)" bedeutet 2 Möglichkeiten.
1. A thunderstorm destroyed most of the houses.
2. Nobody understood the explanations.
3. We have to pay the bills.
4. Our hostess offered us tea and biscuits. (2)
5. We had to learn the poem by heart.
6. Uncle Richard feeds the cat every morning.
7. Lions like meat.
8. Tolstoi wrote "War and Peace".
9. Some scientists discovered the Egyptian grave last year.
10. Sam told her the secret. (2)
11. People built the castle in the 17th century.
12. You can visit the Museum of London every day except Mondays.
13. Some weeks ago the boss gave Mr Smith notice.
14. They hadn't looked after the dog properly before it got ill.
15. The housewife hadn't tried the recipe before.
16. You mustn't touch this old vase.
17. Nobody has shown me the document. (2)
18. Will you answer her letter?
19. The friendly gentleman showed us the way. (2)
20. The radio station is just broadcasting an interesting radio play.

II. *Transform the sentences from Passive Voice into Active Voice.*
   Wandle Passiv in Aktiv um!
1. The discovery was made yesterday.
2. Two people were killed by a careless driver.
3. This bed hasn't been slept in.
4. They were being laughed at.
5. I was given the opportunity by my boss.
6. The machine is driven by electricity.
7. He was being helped by his son.
8. The books were written by the same author.
9. The population had been warned by the police.
10. He had been rescued by the mountain rescue team.

III. *Translate the following sentences.*
   Übersetze die folgenden Sätze!
1. Solche Sachen sollten abgeschafft werden.
2. Es wird berichtet, dass er ernsthaft verletzt ist.
3. Der Fehler konnte nicht gefunden werden.
4. Solche Hüte werden meist von Eingeborenen getragen.
5. Die vermisste Geldbörse wurde von einem kleinen Jungen gefunden.
6. Vor einigen Jahren wurde die Bevölkerung evakuiert, eine Talsperre errichtet und das Dorf überflutet.
7. Von ihm wird gesagt, dass er intelligent sei.
8. Die Heizung muss vor dem Winter repariert werden.
9. Der Keller sollte aufgeräumt werden.
10. Man überreichte ihm einen Preis.

Reported Speech

Indirekte Rede

Die indirekte Rede unterliegt im Englischen ganz bestimmten Regeln.
Die Zeit in der indirekten Rede hängt von zwei Faktoren ab:

▶ von der Zeit des Einleitungssatzes (he says, she asked, ...);
▶ von der Zeit, die in der direkten Rede benutzt wurde.

No Backshift

Keine Zeitveränderung

Steht der Einleitungssatz in einer *Zeit der Gegenwartsgruppe* (Present Tense, Present Perfect, Future I), so wird die Zeit, die in der direkten Rede steht, beibehalten. Pronomen (Fürwörter) werden dem Sinn entsprechend verändert und die Verbform wird der Person angepasst (z. B. I have → he has).

Beispiel: *Direkte Rede:*   **He says,**   **"I worked in London."**

                Einleitungssatz   direkte Rede

                Present Tense   Past Tense

                Einleitungssatz   indirekte Rede

Indirekte Rede: **He says**   **that he worked in London**

Das Past Tense der direkten Rede wird also übernommen, da der Einleitungssatz im Present Tense steht.

Grundregel

Backshift

Zeitveränderung

Steht der Einleitungssatz in einer *Zeit der Vergangenheitsgruppe* (Past Tense, Past Perfect, Future II, Conditional), so wird die Zeit, die in der direkten Rede stand, folgendermaßen verändert:

Grundregel

Direkte Rede	Indirekte Rede
Present Tense He said, "I go ..."	**→ Past Tense** He said that he went ...
Past Tense He said, "I went ..."	**→ Past Perfect** He said that he had gone ...
Present Perfect He said, "I have gone ..."	**→ Past Perfect** He said that he had gone ...
Future I He said, "I will go ..."	**→ Conditional I** He said that he would go ...
Future II He said, "I will have gone ..."	**→ Conditional II** He said that he would have gone ...

Die gleichen Veränderungen gelten für Continuous Forms (ing-Formen/Verlaufsformen), wenn der Einleitungssatz der indirekten Rede in einer Zeit der Vergangenheitsgruppe steht.

Beispiel: *Direkte Rede:*

He said, "I am working . . ." (Present Tense Continuous)

Indirekte Rede:

He said that he was working. (Past Tense Continuous)

Pronomen werden dem Sinn entsprechend verändert und die neue Verbform wird der neuen Person angepasst.

Exceptions: No Backshift
Ausnahmen: keine Zeitveränderung

▶ Obwohl der Einleitungssatz in einer Zeit der Vergangenheitsgruppe steht, tritt keine Zeitveränderung ein, wenn die Aussage *allgemein gültig* ist (a) oder zum Zeitpunkt der Wiedergabe *noch zutrifft* (b).

Beispiel zu (a): *Direkte Rede:*   He said, "Berlin is the capital of Germany."

Indirekte Rede: He said that Berlin is the capital of Germany.

Beispiel zu (b): *Direkte Rede:*   He said, "My mother is in hospital."

Indirekte Rede: He said that his mother is in hospital.

▶ Past Perfect, Conditional I und II, should, ought to, might, used to, had better werden nicht verändert.

Beispiel: *Direkte Rede:*   He said, "I had gone . . ."

Indirekte Rede: He said that he had gone.

Backshift in Connection with Modal Auxiliaries
Zeitveränderung bei den modalen Hilfsverben

Manche Modal Auxiliaries (modale Hilfsverben) werden nur in bestimmten Fällen verändert, auch wenn der Einleitungssatz in einer Zeit der Vergangenheitsgruppe steht.

▶ *"Could"* wird nur verändert, wenn es einer deutschen Indikativform (konnte) entspricht.

Beispiel: *Direkte Rede:*   He said, "I could read when I was 5."

Indirekte Rede: He said that he had been able to read . . .

Beachte: Da "can" nicht alle Zeiten bilden kann, benötigt man Formen des Ersatzverbs "to be able to" (siehe auch Kapitel "Auxiliary Verbs – Hilfsverben", S. 95 ff.).

▶ *"Must"* wird nur verändert, wenn es zum Ausdruck einer Notwendigkeit dient, die zum Zeitpunkt der Wiedergabe nicht mehr besteht.

Beispiel: *Direkte Rede:* He said, "I must take the medicine."

Indirekte Rede: He said that he had to take the medicine. (Er muss sie zum Zeitpunkt der Wiedergabe nicht mehr nehmen.)

Beachte: Da "must" nicht alle Zeiten bilden kann, benötigt man Formen des Ersatzverbs "to have to" (siehe auch Kapitel "Auxiliary Verbs – Hilfsverben", S. 101).

▶ *"Mustn't"* (nicht dürfen) wird nur verändert, wenn das Verbot zum Zeitpunkt der Wiedergabe nicht mehr gilt. Dann wird es durch "wasn't/weren't allowed to oder "shouldn't" ersetzt.

Beispiel: *Direkte Rede:* The doctor said, "You mustn't get up."

Indirekte Rede: The doctor said that he shouldn't get up. (Jetzt darf er aber wieder aufstehen.)

▶ *"Needn't* (nicht müssen/brauchen) wird nur verändert, wenn die Nichtverpflichtung, die durch "needn't" ausgedrückt wird, zum Zeitpunkt der Wiedergabe nicht mehr gilt.

Beispiel: *Direkte Rede:* The teacher said, "You needn't do your homework, because it's your birthday."

Indirekte Rede: The teacher said that I didn't have to do my homework, because it was my birthday.

Beachte: Da "needn't" nicht alle Zeiten bilden kann, benötigt man Formen des Ersatzverbs "not to have to" (siehe auch Kapitel "Auxiliary Verbs – Hilfsverben", S. 101 f.).

Changes in Time and Place Expressions
Veränderungen von Zeit- und Ortsangaben

Steht der Einleitungssatz in einer Zeit der Vergangenheitsgruppe oder treffen aufgrund der veränderten Sprechsituation Zeit- und Ortsangaben nicht mehr zu, so müssen die Zeitangaben sinngemäß angepasst werden.

Beispiel: *Direkte Rede:* He said, "Yesterday I went to the cinema."

Indirekte Rede: He said he had gone to the cinema the day before.

Wie die Zeitangaben im Einzelfall zu verändern sind, zeigt die Tabelle auf der folgenden Seite:

Grund-regel

Direkte Rede	Indirekte Rede
today	that day
yesterday	the day before
... days ago (etc.)	... days before (etc.)
last week (etc.)	the week before (etc.)
next year (etc.)	the following year (etc.)
now	then
tomorrow	the next/following day
here	there
this (Demonstrativpronomen)	that
these	those

Different Sentence Types in Reported Speech
Verschiedene Satzarten in der indirekten Rede

Statements – Aussagesätze

Grund-
regel

Ein Aussagesatz wird in der indirekten Rede mit *"that"* eingeleitet. Das "that" kann jedoch auch weggelassen werden.

Beispiel: *Direkte Rede:*   He said, "I work in London."

Indirekte Rede: He said (that) he worked in London.

Questions – Fragesätze

Grund-
regel

Ein Fragesatz wird in der indirekten Rede mit dem entsprechenden *Fragewort* (z. B. when, where etc.) eingeleitet, wenn in der direkten Rede ein Fragewort enthalten war.

Beispiel: *Direkte Rede:*   He asked, "Where do you live?"

Indirekte Rede: He asked where I lived.

Ein Fragesatz ohne Fragewort wird in der indirekten Rede mit *"if"* oder *"whether"* (ob) eingeleitet.

Beispiel: *Direkte Rede:*   He asks, "Will he come tomorrow?"

Indirekte Rede: He asks if/whether he will come tomorrow.

Beachte: Die Umschreibung mit "do" fällt im indirekten Fragesatz weg, es sei denn, es handelt sich um einen verneinten Fragesatz in der Gegenwart (Present Tense Simple). Die Satzstellung im indirekten Fragesatz ist wie im Aussagesatz.

Commands – Befehle

Ein indirekter Befehl wird durch *"to"* oder *"not to"* + *Infinitiv* (Grundform) gebildet. Indirekte Befehle fallen nicht unter die Regeln der Zeitverschiebung, egal in welcher Zeit der Einleitungssatz steht.

Beispiel: *Direkte Rede:* The teacher tells the students, "Don't talk!"
         Indirekte Rede: Sue told him to close the window.
         Direkte Rede: The teacher tells the students, "Don't talk!"
         Indirekte Rede: The teacher tells the students not to talk.

*Grund-
regel*

Mixed Exercises for Reported Speech
Gemischte Übungen zur indirekten Rede

Übungen

I. *Put into reported speech.*
   Setze in die indirekte Rede!

Statements

1. My sister tells me, "I have got a good report."
2. The boss says, "On Saturday you will all have to come in."
3. "It's going to rain", the speaker says.
4. Mother says, "If the weather is fine, we can have a picnic."
5. She tells me, "The Millers moved house last week."

Questions

1. The caretaker wants to know, "Who broke this window?"
2. "When will he arrive?" Grandma asks.
3. "Where do you do your weekly shopping?" the new neighbour asks.
4. The teacher wants to know, "Have you ever been to Hong Kong?"
5. The inspector asks, "Where were you between 6 p.m. and 8 p.m. last Monday?"

Commands

1. "Don't go out so often." father tells me.
2. The teacher tells me, "Copy this till tomorrow."
3. The old lady tells her young neighbour, "Don't turn your radio on so loud after 10 p.m.!"
4. "Be careful." the guide tells the visitors.
5. "Do not iron this blouse." the label tells us.

II. Put into reported speech. Mind the change of tenses and the changes in time and place.

Setze in die indirekte Rede! Achte auf Zeitveränderungen und Veränderungen von Orts- und Zeitangaben!

Statements

1. The announcer said, "Many houses were destroyed by the thunderstorm, so that the inhabitants were taken to a school building in the next village."
2. My friend told me, "I'll join the school orchestra as soon as possible."
3. Our teacher told us, "Next Monday we'll have a meeting for the parents. The headmaster wants to know how many of the parents will come."
4. "They have been living in this town for many years and I think they will stay here for the next few years," my brother said.
5. Grandmother told me, "When I was young, we used to walk to school.
6. The teacher said, "You'll have to hand in the papers tomorrow, because I'm going to correct them over the weekend."
7. My father remarked, "Somebody seems to be in the living-room, I've just heard a strange noise."
8. Susan said to her brother, "Next week we'll celebrate our parents' anniversary, I'm planning to buy something really nice for them."
9. The photographer said, "When I took these photos I didn't know they were going to become such an important proof."
10. My Indian classmate told me, "In India parents often choose the future husband for their daughter and sometimes they haven't even met before the wedding."

Questions

1. Maud's parents asked, "When are you going to work harder at school?"
2. The stranger asked, "Can you tell me the way to the station?"
3. The boss asked his employee, "Will you be able to finish these papers till the end of the month?"
4. The teacher asked, "Who can tell me where we stopped last lesson?"
5. "For how long have you been a member of the boyscouts?" the new boy wanted to know.
6. The quizmaster asked, "Where and when was Shakespeare born and what are his most famous plays?"
7. Mother asked, "How did you do your maths homework before Dad bought you the calculator?"
8. Mrs Sims asked my mother, "Can you look after my cat while I'm on holiday?"
9. Grandmother asked my mother, "Why do young people always speak so quickly?"
10. "Did Mr Baker call while I was out?" the doctor wanted to know.

Das Verb
Indirekte Rede

Commands

1. The hairdresser told me, "Don't use the hairdrier too often."
2. The inspector told the policeman, "Find out what happened last night."
3. Sue told her little brother, "Don't be so rude."
4. "Mind the gap." the announcer in the underground station told the passengers.
5. "Stop talking at once." the teacher told Bob.
6. The sign told he visitors, "Don't feed the animals."
7. "Take two tablets every morning before breakfast." the doctor told me.
8. The vet told me, "See me again next Tuesday."
9. The parents told the children, "Don't play with the video while we are away."
10. The teacher told us, "Finish the essay till next week."

III. Put into reported speech. Mind the changes and the type of sentence. Be careful with the auxiliary verbs.
Setze in die indirekte Rede! Achte auf die Veränderungen und den Satztyp! Vorsicht bei den Hilfsverben!

1. The headmaster told me, "Since you were elected, the school magazine has very much improved. I even enjoyed the article about myself."
2. The Hut family told us, "Our holidays were terrible this year. We only got one hotel room instead of the two we had booked."
3. The teacher told us, "Water boils at 100 °C."
4. He said, "My parents are on holiday." (They are still away.)
5. The doctor told me, "You mustn't drink coffee or smoke." (He is still not allowed to.)
6. The interviewer wanted to know, "When did your pop career start and what are your plans for the future?"
7. One TV reporter said, "Years ago the Thames was so polluted that no fish could live in it."
8. When I went to the interview for the new job I was asked, "Why have you been out of work for 6 months? Are you not willing to work in a different job than the one you had before?
9. The pilot said, "That was a near miss. I suddenly saw a plane right in front of me and there was nothing I could do."
10. The student asked me, "Can you help me please? I've been trying to solve this problem for 20 minutes now."
11. The stewardess told us, "Fasten your seatbelts and stop smoking."
12. The notice said, "Anybody who finds the necklace and takes it to the lost property office will get a reward of £ 50."
13. The teacher asked the new student, "Where did you live before and which school did you do to?"

14. The speaker said, "100 years ago people thought women should look after their children and the house and ought not to take an active part in politics."
15. Mrs Moore said, "I was driving along a lonely country road when suddenly a shining circulating object landed right in front of me. I'm sure it was a UFO."
16. The reporter wanted to know, "How did you feel when your team won the match yesterday?"
17. The politician promised, "If we win the next election, we'll change everything."
18. My friend said, "I called you at 5 o'clock but you didn't answer the phone, so I couldn't tell you about the ticket."
19. The weather forecast announced, "There will be little rain in some parts of England in the morning but during the day it'll get dry and sunny."
20. He asked me, "Can you lend me £ 15? I've forgotten my purse, but I'd like to buy this CD."

Final Test: Reported Speech

Abschlusstest: indirekte Rede

I. *Put into reported speech.*
Setze in die indirekte Rede!
1. The student said, "When the teacher asked me, I was so nervous that I couldn't answer although I knew the correct answer."
2. The teacher asked us, "Put these 20 sentences into reported speech and learn the new words."
3. The announcement says, "Due to bad weather conditions the flight to Boston will be delayed."
4. The receptionist asked, "Would you like a room with a bath or with a shower?"
5. The secretary asked her boss, "Do you want me to phone Moneymaker Ltd. at once?"
6. My aunt says, "Your mother phoned half an hour ago and wanted to know if you were in."
7. The host family asked Peter, "Have you ever been to England before or is this your first visit?"
8. The guide told us, "This castle belongs to the Duke and it has been open to the public since 1980."
9. Carol asks Sabine, "Have you received the postcard I wrote you from Spain?"
10. The teacher explained, "When we go to France, you'll all have to look after your luggage yourselves."

II. *Now try it the other way round. Put into direct speech.*
Nun versuche es andersherum! Setze in die direkte Rede!

1. The shop assistant asked me if I preferred to wait for the alteration or if they should send it to me.
2. My neighbour told me that somebody had been at the door.
3. The ticket collector told us we had the wrong ticket and couldn't take that bus.
4. He asked me when Mrs Kelly would arrive and if he should pick her up.
5. The trainer told the boys to be at the stadium at 8 o'clock.
6. I asked the waitress if they would accept cheques.
7. Grandfather wants to know when dinner is ready.
8. I told him that I had never been abroad before but I would like to go to England.
9. The newspaper said that the concert had been the most interesting part of the programme.
10. The landlord said that I could move in right away.

Auxiliary Verbs

Hilfsverben

Die Gruppe der Hilfsverben lässt sich grammatisch in zwei Kategorien unterteilen:

▶ die **vollständigen Hilfsverben (primary auxiliaries):** to be, to do, to have;
▶ die **unvollständigen, modalen Hilfsverben (modal auxiliaries),** die nur eine oder zwei Formen bilden können: can, must, may/might, will/would, shall/ should, need, ought to, used to.

Primary Auxiliaries

Vollständige Hilfsverben

Die vollständigen Hilfsverben "to be", "to do", "to have" können sowohl als Hilfsverb als auch als Vollverb benutzt werden. Einen Überblick über die Formen geben die folgenden Seiten.

To be – sein
Present Tense (Präsens/Gegenwart):

Formen

Bejahter Satz	Verneinter Satz
I am (I'm)	I am not (I'm not)
you are (you're)	you are not (you aren't)
he is (he's)	he is not (he isn't)
she is (she's)	she is not (she isn't)
it is (it's)	it is not (it isn't)
we are (we're)	we are not (we aren't)
you are (you're)	you are not (you aren't)
they are (they're)	they are not (they aren't)

Past Tense (Imperfekt oder Präteritum/Vergangenheit):

Bejahter Satz	Verneinter Satz
I was	I was not (I wasn't)
you were	you were not (you weren't)
he was	he was not (he wasn't)
she was	she was not (she wasn't)
it was	it was not (it wasn't)
we were	we were not (we weren't)
you were	you were not (you weren't)
they were	they were not (they weren't)

Present Participle (ing-Form/Partizip Präsens/Mittelwort der Gegenwart): being
Past Participle (Partizip Perfekt/Mittelwort der Vergangenheit): been
Stammformen: to be (am/are/is) – was/were – been

Funktionen

▶ Als *Hilfsverb* hilft "to be" zusammengesetzte Zeiten zu bilden.
  a) "To be" + ing-Form ergibt die verschiedenen Continuous-Formen (Verlaufsformen).
  Beispiel: I am going (Present Tense Continuous)
  b) "To be" + 3. Verbform ergibt Passiv.
  Beispiel: It was opened (Past Tense – Passive Voice)
▶ Als *Vollverb* ist "to be" ein Zustandsverb oder ein Beziehungsverb. Es drückt einen Zustand, eine Eigenschaft oder eine Beziehung aus und tritt nur in der Simple-Form auf.
  Beispiel: He is a teacher.
              She is nice.
              They are my friends.

▶ *"There"* + *"to be"* drückt aus, dass etwas vorhanden ist.

Beispiel: There are three books on the desk. – Auf dem Tisch gibt es drei Bücher. ("There" + "to be" – es gibt.)

▶ *"To be"* + *Infinitiv mit "to"* drückt aus, dass etwas geschehen soll.

Beispiel: The meeting is to take place in August. – Das Treffen soll im August stattfinden. ("To be" + Infinitiv mit "to" – sollen.)

To do – tun
Present Tense (Präsens/Gegenwart):

Bejahter Satz	Verneinter Satz
I do	I do not (I don't)
you do	you do not (you don't)
he does	he does not (he doesn't)
she does	she does not (she doesn't)
it does	it does not (it doesn't)
we do	we do not (we don't)
you do	you do not (you don't)
they do	they do not (they don't)

Past Tense (Imperfekt oder Präteritum/Vergangenheit):

Bejahter Satz	Verneinter Satz
I did	I did not (I didn't)
you did	you did not (you didn't)
he did	he did not (he didn't)
she did	she did not (she didn't)
it did	it did not (it didn't)
we did	we did not (we didn't)
you did	you did not (you didn't)
they did	they did not (they didn't)

Present Participle (ing-Form/Partizip Präsens/Mittelwort der Gegenwart): doing
Past Participle (Partizip Perfekt/Mittelwort der Vergangenheit): done
Stammformen: to do – did – done

Die Funktionen von "to do":

▶ "To do" kann *Vollverb* sein und hat dann die Bedeutung „tun", „machen", „erledigen" etc.

Beispiel: I do the washing-up. – Ich erledige den Abwasch.

► "To do" als *Hilfsverb* kann zur *Betonung und Hervorhebung* einer Aussage dienen.

Beispiel: I did see the UFO. – Ich habe das UFO (bestimmt) gesehen.

► "To do" als *Hilfsverb* wird in *Kurzantworten* (siehe S. 114) und Frageanhängseln (siehe S. 112 f.) benutzt, falls kein anderes Hilfsverb vorhanden ist.

Beispiel: You like parties, don't you? Oh yes, I do.

► "To do" als *Hilfsverb* wird zur Bildung von *Fragesätzen* und *verneinten Sätzen* benutzt, falls kein anderes Hilfsverb vorhanden ist (Umschreibung mit "do" siehe S. 108 f.).

Beispiel: Do you like parties? I don't like.

To have – haben
Present Tense (Präsens/Gegenwart):

Bejahter Satz	Verneinter Satz
I have (I've)	I have not (I haven't)
you have (you've)	you have not (you haven't)
he has (he's*)	he has not (he hasn't)
she has (she's)	she has not (she hasn't)
it has (it's)	it has not (it hasn't)
we have (we've)	we have not (we haven't)
you have (you've)	you have not (you haven't)
they have (they've)	they have not (they haven't)

Past Tense (Imperfekt oder Präteritum/Vergangenheit):

Bejahter Satz	Verneinter Satz
I had (I'd**)	I had not (I hadn't)
you had (you'd)	you had not (you hadn't)
he had (he'd)	he had not (he hadn't)
she had (she'd)	she had not (she hadn't)
it had (it'd)	it had not (it hadn't)
we had (we'd)	we had not (we hadn't)
you had (you'd)	you had not (you hadn't)
they had (they'd)	they had not (they hadn't)

---

* *"'s" kann Abkürzung sein für "is" oder für "has". Folgt eine ing-Form, kann es nur für "is" stehen, folgt eine 3. Verbform, kann es nur für "has" stehen. Beispiel: He's reading a book. (He is reading a book.)*
He's eaten a steak. (He has eaten a steak.)

** *"'d" kann Abkürzung sein für "would" und "had". Folgt ein Infinitiv, kann es nur für "would" stehen, folgt eine 3. Verbform, kann es nur für "had" stehen. Beispiel: I'd like a hamburger. (I would like . . .) I'd seen the man. (I had seen . . .)*

Present Participle (ing-Form/Partizip Präsens/Mittelwort der Gegenwart): having

Past Participle (Partizip Perfekt/Mittelwort der Vergangenheit): had

Stammformen: to have – had – had

Die Funktionen von "to have":

▶ Als *Hilfsverb* hilft "to have" in Verbindung mit einer 3. Verbform Present Perfect, Past Perfect, Future II und Conditional II zu bilden.

Beispiel: I have seen (Present Perfect)

I had made (Past Perfect)

▶ Als *Vollverb* bedeutet "to have" „haben", „besitzen". Oft wird im britischen Englisch dann "have got" verwendet, sodass eine Umschreibung mit „do" bei Fragen und verneinten Sätzen wegfällt.

Beispiel: I have (got) a car.

I haven't got a car.

Have you got a car?

▶ "To have" kommt *zusammen mit Nomen in einigen Ausdrücken* vor, die sich wie Tätigkeitsverben (Vollverben) verhalten. Sie können also Continuous Forms (Verlaufsformen) bilden, Fragen und verneinte Sätze werden mit "do" umschrieben. Zu diesen Ausdrücken gehören:

to have a party	– eine Party geben
to have a bath	– baden
to have a shower	– duschen
to have a walk	– spazieren gehen
to have breakfast	– frühstücken
to have lunch	– Mittag essen
to have dinner	– Abend essen
to have fun	– sich vergnügen
to have a laugh	– lachen
to have a look	– anschauen

▶ *"To have" + Objekt + 3. Verbform* bildet ein Vollverb in der Bedeutung „veranlassen, dass etwas getan wird".

Beispiel: I have my car repaired. – Ich lasse mein Auto reparieren.

(Siehe auch Kapitel "The German Verb ‚lassen' and its English Equivalents", S. 138 f.)

Modal Auxiliaries

Modale/unvollständige Hilfsverben

Anders als im Deutschen werden die unvollständigen Hilfsverben im Englischen nur als Hilfsverben (nicht als Vollverben) benutzt.

Beispiel: Er <u>muss</u> ins Büro. – He <u>**must**</u>   <u>**go**</u> to the office.

              Vollverb   Hilfsverb   Vollverb

Nur "need" kann als Vollverb benutzt werden.

Beispiel: I need a new car. – Ich brauche ein neues Auto.

Die unvollständigen Hilfsverben heißen „unvollständig", da sie nur eine Präsensform oder eine Präsens- und Imperfektform bilden können. Fehlende Formen und Infinitiv werden durch bedeutungsverwandte Verben und Ausdrücke umschrieben.

Can (to be able to) – können

Formen

Formen von "can":

\+ can/could

– cannot (can't)/could not (couldn't)

"Can" kann also nur Präsens (Present Tense) und Imperfekt (Past Tense) bilden. Für alle anderen Zeiten (auch für Futur!) benötigt man ein Ersatzverb: to be able to.

Formen des Ersatzverbs:

to be (am/are/is) able to – was/were able to – been able to

Beispiel: I will be able to speak French in a few years. – Ich werde in ein paar Jahren Französisch sprechen können.

Funktionen

Funktionen von "can":

▶ "Can" drückt eine *Fähigkeit* oder – in der Verneinung – eine *Unfähigkeit* aus.

   Beispiel: He can speak English. – Er kann (ist fähig) Englisch (zu) sprechen.

▶ "Can" drückt eine *Erlaubnis* oder – in der Verneinung – ein Verbot aus.

   Beispiel: You can have my car. – Du kannst (hast die Erlaubnis) mein Auto (zu) haben.

▶ "Can" drückt eine *Möglichkeit* oder – in der Verneinung – eine *Unmöglichkeit* aus.

   Beispiel: That can't be the right number. – Das kann nicht (kann unmöglich) die richtige Nummer sein.

▶ "Can" drückt eine *Annahme* aus.

   Beispiel: Can the book be on the table? – Kann das Buch auf dem Tisch liegen? (Ich nehme an, dass es auf dem Tisch liegt.)

► "Can" in Fragen drückt eine *Bitte* aus.

    Beispiel: Can I open the window? – Kann ich (bitte) das Fenster öffnen?

► "Can't" in Fragen drückt einen *Vorschlag* aus.

    Beispiel: Can't we go swimming? – Können wir nicht schwimmen gehen?

    (Was hältst du von dem Vorschlag schwimmen zu gehen?)

Must (to have to) – müssen
Formen von "must":

Formen

+ must

– need not (needn't)

"Must" besitzt also nur eine Präsensform (Present Tense). Für alle anderen Zeiten benötigt man ein Ersatzverb: to have to.

Formen des Ersatzverbs:

to have to – had to – had to

Beachte: "Must" hat zwar eine verneinte Form "must not (mustn't)", jedoch bedeutet diese „nicht dürfen". Will man „nicht müssen" ausdrücken, so heißt es "need not (needn't)" oder "do not (don't) have to"!

Funktionen von "must":

► "Must" drückt eine *Notwendigkeit,* "needn't" das Fehlen einer Notwendig-keit aus.

Funktionen

    Beispiel: You must work harder. – Du musst härter arbeiten. (Es ist notwen-dig, dass du härter arbeitest.)

    You needn't answer. – Du musst nicht antworten. (Es ist nicht notwendig, dass du antwortest.)

► "Must" drückt eine *Annahme* oder eine *Schlussfolgerung* aus.

    Beispiel: She looks quite old. She must be about 60. – Sie sieht ziemlich alt aus. Sie muss so um die 60 sein. (Ich nehme an, dass sie um die 60 ist.)

► "Must" drückt einen eindringlichen *Ratschlag,* eine *Aufforderung* aus.

    Beispiel: You must see the dentist. – Du musst (solltest wirklich) zum Zahnarzt gehen.

Need – brauchen
Formen von "need":

Formen

+ need

– needn't

"Need" dient zur Verneinung von "must" und hat daher auch das gleiche Ersatzverb: to have to.

Formen des Ersatzverbs:
to have to – had to – had to

Funktionen von "need":

Funktionen

▶ "Need" als *Vollverb* drückt „brauchen", „benötigen" aus. Verneinung und Frage werden mit "do" umschrieben. "Need" als Vollverb kann alle Zeiten bilden.

Stammformen: to need – needed – needed.

Beispiel: I need a bigger flat. – Ich brauche (benötige) eine größere Wohnung.

I don't need a bigger flat. – Ich brauche (benötige) keine größere Wohnung.

I will need a bigger flat. – Ich werde eine größere Wohnung brauchen (benötigen).

▶ "Need" (brauchen, müssen, nötig haben) existiert als *Hilfsverb in Präsensfragen* (Present Tense questions). Es wird eine verneinte Antwort erwartet.

Beispiel: Need I go at once? – Muss ich sofort gehen?

No, you needn't. – Nein, das brauchst du nicht.

▶ "Need" wird außerdem in der *verneinten Präsensform* (negative Present Tense) als *Hilfsverb* verwendet.

Beispiel: You needn't get up so early. – Du brauchst nicht so früh aufzustehen.

May (to be allowed to) – dürfen

Formen

Formen von "may":

+ may/might
– may not/might not (mightn't)

"May" hat nur eine Präsensform (Present Tense). Die Imperfektform (Past Tense) "might" drückt nicht Vergangenheit, sondern Unsicherheit aus. Man benötigt also für alle Zeiten – außer Präsens – ein Ersatzverb: to be allowed to.

Formen des Ersatzverbs:
to be (am/are/is) allowed to – was/were allowed to – been allowed to

Beispiel: I was allowed to go to the cinema. (Past Tense) – Ich durfte ins Kino gehen.

Funktionen von "may":

Funktionen

▶ "May" drückt eine *Erlaubnis* oder – in der Verneinung – ein *Verbot* aus.

Beispiel: You may (not) go out. – Du darfst (nicht) hinausgehen.

▶ *Fragen* mit "may" und "might" bitten um eine *Erlaubnis*, wobei "might" äußerst höflich klingt.

102

Beispiel: May (might) I open the parcel? – Darf (dürfte) ich das Paket öffnen?

▶ "May" und "might" drücken eine *Annahme* aus, wobei "might" den Aspekt des Unsicheren betont.

Beispiel: It may rain. – Vielleicht regnet es.

It might rain. – Es könnte sein, dass es regnet.

▶ "Might" in Aussagesätzen drückt eine *Aufforderung* mit dem Unterton der Verärgerung aus.

Beispiel: You might be in time. – Du könntest (auch einmal) pünktlich sein.

Shall – sollen
Formen von "shall":

+ shall

– shall not (shan't)

Formen

Funktionen von "shall":

▶ Fragen mit "shall" (nur bei "I" und "we") drücken ein *Angebot* oder einen *Vorschlag* aus.

Funktionen

Beispiel: Shall I do this for you? (Angebot) – Soll ich das für dich tun?

Shall we go to the disco? (Vorschlag) – Sollen wir in die Disco gehen?

▶ In Fragen mit "I" und "we" kann "shall" auch eine *Bitte um eine Anweisung* ausdrücken.

Beispiel: Where shall I put the glasses? – Wohin soll ich die Gläser stellen?

▶ "Shall" drückt ein *Versprechen* aus.

Beispiel: She shall get her share. – Sie soll ihren Anteil bekommen.

"Shall" in der 1. Person Singular und Plural Futur ist heute nicht mehr gebräuchlich.

Should/ought to – sollten
Formen von "should"/"ought to":

+ should/ought to

– should not (shouldn't)/ought not to (oughtn't to)

Formen

Funktionen von "should"/"ought to":

▶ "Should/ought to" drückt einen *Ratschlag* aus.

Funktionen

Beispiel: I should/ought to see the doctor. – Ich sollte zum Arzt gehen.

▶ "Should/ought to" drückt eine *Forderung* oder *Verpflichtung* aus.

Beispiel: He should be put in prison. (Forderung) – Er sollte ins Gefängnis gesteckt werden.

We should ask the old lady if we can help her. (Verpflichtung) – Wir sollten die alte Dame fragen, ob wir ihr helfen können.

▶ "Should/ought to" drückt eine *Wahrscheinlichkeit* aus.

Beispiel: They should be in New York now. – Sie müssten jetzt eigentlich in New York sein.

"Should" in der 1. Person Singular und Plural Konditional ist heute nicht mehr gebräuchlich.

Used to – pflegten (Gewohnheit)

Formen

Formen von "used to":

+ used to
– didn't use to oder used not to

"Used to" besitzt nur die Vergangenheitsform. Die Verneinung und die Frage werden gewöhnlich mit "do" umschrieben, im britischen Englisch können Frage und Verneinung jedoch auch ohne "do"-Umschreibung gebildet werden.

Beispiel: I used to go out very often. (Aussagesatz) – Ich pflegte sehr oft auszugehen.

I didn't use to go out very often.

oder I used not to go out very often. (Verneinung) – Ich pflegte nicht sehr oft auszugehen.

Did you use to go out very often?

oder Used you to go out very often? (Frage) – Pflegten Sie sehr oft auszugehen?

Funktionen von "used to":

Funktionen

"Used to" dient zum Ausdruck eines *früheren Zustandes* oder einer *früheren Gewohnheit*.

Beispiel: There used to be many trees there. – Hier gab es früher* viele Bäume.

Will – werden

Formen

Formen von "will":

+ will ('ll)
– will not (won't)

Funktionen von "will":

Funktionen

▶ "Will" dient zur Bildung der *Futurzeiten*.

Beispiel: I will come. (Future I) – Ich werde kommen.

Ich will have seen. (Future II) – Ich werde gesehen haben.

▶ "Will" drückt eine *Bitte* aus.

Beispiel: Will you please pass me the sugar? – Reich mir doch bitte den Zucker.

---

* Häufig entspricht "used to" dem deutschen „früher".

▶ "Will" drückt ein *Angebot* aus.
   Beispiel: Will you have another cup of tea? – Möchtest du noch eine Tasse Tee?

▶ "Will" drückt einen *Befehl* aus.
   Beispiel: Campers will leave the place tidy. – Camper haben den Platz ordentlich zu hinterlassen.

▶ "Will" drückt eine *Vermutung* aus.
   Beispiel: The phone is ringing. That will be my mother. – Das Telefon klingelt. Das wird (wahrscheinlich) meine Mutter sein.

▶ "Will" kann bei der 3. Person eine *Gewohnheit* oder *Neigung* ausdrücken.
   Beispiel: Mrs Sutton will sit there and talk for hours. – Mrs Sutton pflegt dort zu sitzen und stundenlang zu schwätzen.

▶ "Will not (won't)" drückt eine *Weigerung* aus.
   Beispiel: He made a mistake, but he won't admit it. – Er hat einen Fehler gemacht, aber er will es (einfach) nicht zugeben.

Would – würden

Formen von "would":

+ would ('d)
- would not (wouldn't)

Formen

Funktionen von "would":

Funktionen

▶ "Would" dient zur Bildung des *Konditionals*.
   Beispiel: I would go. (Conditional I) – Ich würde gehen.
   I would have gone. (Conditional II) – Ich wäre gegangen.

▶ "Would" drückt eine *höfliche Bitte* aus.
   Beispiel: Would you please open the window? – Würdest du bitte das Fenster öffnen?

▶ "Would" drückt ein *Angebot* aus.
   Beispiel: Would you like a cup of tea? – Möchtest du eine Tasse Tee?

▶ "Would" drückt ein *typisches Verhalten in der Vergangenheit* aus.
   Beispiel: She would telephone me every day. – Sie rief mich gewöhnlich jeden Tag an.

▶ "Would not (wouldn't)" drückt eine *Weigerung in der Vergangenheit* aus.
   Beispiel: She wouldn't listen. – Sie wollte (einfach) nicht zuhören.

Exercises

Übungen

I. *Susanne is a German pupil, but she will soon be moving to England with her parents. A lot of things will change then. Form sentences.*
Susanne ist eine deutsche Schülerin, aber bald wird sie mit ihren Eltern nach England umziehen. Vieles wird sich dann ändern. Bilde Sätze!
Beispiel: *must go to school by bus*
Susanne will have to go to school by bus.

1. must wear a school uniform
2. must stay in school till 5 o'clock
3. cannot have lunch with her family
4. can play games at school in the afternoon
5. mustn't leave the school premises
6. must attend the morning assembly
7. needn't do so much homework
8. to have very long holidays
9. must make new friends
10. cannot speak German in class

II. *100 years ago a lot of things were different. Form sentences.*
Vor 100 Jahren war vieles anders. Bilde Sätze!
Beispiel: *children/can play in the streets*
Children could play in the streets.

1. children/can swim in the river
2. many children/must work because the family/need the money
3. mothers/must do the washing by hand
4. women/may not take an active part in politics
5. students/must walk to school
6. fathers/cannot spend Saturdays with their families – they/must go to work
7. the air/to be cleaner
8. people/must spend their free time without TV
9. water/must be carried to the houses
10. girls/may not wear trousers

III. Bill likes to show off. Form sentences using the Present Perfect.
Bill gibt gerne an. Bilde Sätze, in denen du Perfekt benutzt!
Beispiel: *may go to the disco since I was 12*
I have been allowed to go to the disco since I was 12.

1. can read difficult books since I was 10
2. may go on holiday on my own for 3 years
3. to have a girlfriend for 1 year
4. never/need my father's help
5. never/must repeat a class so far
6. to be given my own money since I was 8
7. always/can do my homework alone
8. to be allowed to drive my father's car for 3 months now
9. never/to have to help my mother in the kitchen
10. to be able to work with a computer for 5 years

IV. Translate the following sentences.
Übersetze die folgenden Sätze!

1. Du brauchst mir nicht zu helfen, wenn du keine Zeit hast.
2. Du solltest jeden Tag 20 Vokabeln lernen.
3. Könntest du bitte deinen Bruder fragen, ob ich morgen kommen kann.
4. Wir mussten länger bleiben, weil wir das Klassenzimmer noch aufräumen mussten.
5. 1960 pflegte ein Arbeiter nur £ 1.20 pro Stunde zu verdienen.
6. Wohin soll ich die Bücher legen?
7. Könntest du mir einen Gefallen tun?
8. Du solltest wirklich nicht so viel trinken.
9. Seit wann kann Herr Pfeiffer so gut Englisch sprechen?
10. Ich kann morgen leider nicht kommen, weil ich meine Mutter zum Arzt fahren muss.
11. Der Motor sprang einfach nicht an.
12. Ich würde dir gerne helfen, wenn ich könnte.
13. Könnten wir nicht ins Kino gehen?
14. Es könnte sein, dass wir am Wochenende Tante Paula besuchen.
15. Möchten Sie ein Einzel- oder ein Doppelzimmer?
16. Du darfst das Päckchen nicht vor deinem Geburtstag öffnen.
17. Wenn Sie mir heute noch die Briefe tippen können, können Sie morgen früh eine Stunde später kommen.
18. Wann wirst du endlich einmal deine Hausaufgaben alleine machen können?
19. Seit er den Unfall hatte, kann er nicht mehr laufen.
20. Würdest du bitte beim Arzt anrufen und fragen, wann ich kommen kann.

Die Umschreibung mit "do" in Fragen und bei Verneinungen

Jeder Fragesatz und jeder verneinte Satz benötigt im Englischen ein *Vollverb (VV)*, z. B. go, see, eat etc., und ein *Hilfsverb (HV)*, z. B. must, can, will etc.

Beispiel: What **is** he **doing?**

        (HV)   (VV)

      He **cannot speak** French.

        (HV) (VV)

Ist kein bedeutungstragendes oder durch die Zeitform bedingtes Hilfsverb vorhanden, muss eine Form von "to do" benutzt werden. Da alle Zeiten außer Present Tense und Past Tense mit Hilfsverben gebildet werden, ist eine Umschreibung mit "do" auch nur bei diesen Zeiten erforderlich.

Beispiel: I like pizza.

Die Verneinung lautet: I **don't like** pizza.

                         (HV) (VV)

Die Frage lautet: **Do** you **like** pizza?

                         (HV)   (VV)

Beachte: Bei der Umschreibung mit "do" ist "do" der Träger von Person und Zeit. Das Vollverb steht im Infinitiv.

     Beispiel: He didn't go. (Past Tense)

               Does he go? (Present Tense; 3rd person singular)

"To do" kann auch Vollverb sein. In einem solchen Fall muss der verneinte Satz oder der Fragesatz dennoch mit "do" umschrieben werden. Der entsprechende Satz hat dann zwei Formen von "to do".

     Beispiel: I **do** my homework.

                        (VV)

Die Verneinung lautet: I **don't do** my homework.

                         (HV) (VV)

Die Frage lautet: **Do** you **do** your homework?

                         (HV)   (VV)

Ausnahmen von der Umschreibung mit "do":

▶ Eine Frage wird nicht mit "do" umschrieben, wenn das Fragewort nach dem *Subjekt* des Aussagesatzes fragt. Dies ist immer bei Fragen mit "who" („wer") der Fall (aber nicht bei "who" in der Bedeutung von „wen").

Beispiel: Who wrote this? Mrs Baker wrote this. ("Mrs B." ist Subjekt.)

Auch Fragen mit "which" können nach dem Subjekt fragen und werden dann nicht mit "do" umschrieben.

Beispiel: Which car goes fast?

The sports car goes fast. ("The sports car" ist Subjekt.)

▶ Fragen und verneinte Sätze, die eine Form von *"to be"* enthalten, werden nicht mit "do" umschrieben.

Beispiel: Aussage: This is my brother.

Verneinung: This is not my brother.

Frage: Is this my brother?

▶ In verneinten Sätzen wird nicht mit "do" umschrieben, wenn "not" nicht das Verb, sondern ein *anderes Wort verneint.*

Beispiel: Not everybody liked the book.

Exercises

Übungen

Übungen

I. *Form negative sentences.*

Bilde verneinte Sätze.

1. Bert can speak French fluently.
2. The children like vegetables.
3. I will be able to come tomorrow.
4. He phoned me yesterday.
5. He has always been a good student.
6. I could read and write when I was 5 years old.
7. He had known him before he came to England.
8. Sue is watching TV.
9. The neighbour's boy goes to school by bus.
10. You may open the letter.
11. He came too late yesterday.
12. The children are very polite.
13. The Millers spent their last holidays in Italy.
14. They always go to Italy.
15. I learn my vocabulary every day.
16. Mrs Burl was in London yesterday.
17. I have heard this before.
18. The accident happened at 5 o'clock.
19. You have to pay an entrance fee.
20. Mr Cut works in an office.

II. *Form questions so that the answers fit.*
Bilde Fragen, sodass die Antworten passen!

1. Where . . . ?
   I was born in New York.
2. When . . . ?
   I was born on the 2nd October, 1965.
3. Where . . . ?
   I live in Frankfurt.
4. How long . . . ?
   I have been living in Frankfurt for 6 years.
5. Where . . . ?
   I lived in Boston.
6. What . . . ?
   I am a secretary.
7. Where . . . ?
   I work in an office in Frankfurt.
8. Where . . . ?
   I went to school in New York and Boston.
9. Where . . . ?
   My parents live in New York.
10. How long . . . ?
    I have been working in this firm for 3 years.
11. . . . ?
    Yes, I like my job very much.
12. How many . . . ?
    I have two children.
13. Where . . . ?
    My children go to school in Frankfurt.
14. . . . ?
    Yes, my wife works in Frankfurt, too.
15. Where . . . ?
    I learned German at school.
16. What . . . ?
    In my free time I play tennis.
17. When . . . ?
    I start work at 7 o'clock in the morning.
18. When . . . ?
    I get home at 4 o'clock in the afternoon.
19. . . . ?
    Yes, I like German food very much.
20. What . . . ?
    My favourite German meal is „Sauerkraut".

III. Form questions. Start with the given interrogative pronouns.
   Bilde Fragen! Beginne mit den vorgegebenen Fragewörtern!

1. Last year they opened a new restaurant in Bond Street.
   a) when b) where c) what
2. The Carters live in London.
   a) who b) where
3. Every Saturday Pit plays football in Kingston.
   a) when b) who c) what d) where
4. Mr Cats goes to work by underground.
   a) who b) how
5. He has been working hard for this test for 3 months.
   a) who b) how long c) how
6. Charlie Chaplin started his career in London.
   a) where b) who
7. The students had to look up the new words in a dictionary.
   a) where b) who c) what
8. The accident happened at 4 o'clock at the corner of Main Street.
   a) what b) where c) when
9. We didn't go out because of the rain.
   a) why
10. We go to the cinema once a week.
    a) how often b) where ... to

IV. Form questions to which the underlined words are the answer.
   Bilde Fragen, sodass die unterstrichenen Wörter antworten!

1. I usually go to bed at 10 o'clock.
2. I haven't spoken to him for 1 week.
3. 2 weeks ago the famous actor died.
4. He got a brand new bicycle.
5. They built the department store in 1985.
6. She usually prepares dinner at 6 o'clock.
7. The butler led me to Blue Hall.
8. He stopped smoking years ago.
9. The secretary speaks three languages.
10. My sister moved last month.
11. Grandpa drinks a glass of wine every evening.
12. Years ago scientists discovered the grave.
13. He will arrive on Sunday.
14. We stayed at home because Sue was ill.
15. She learned typing at school.
16. The police arrested the burglar.
17. Our neighbours are just painting the house.

Translate the following sentences.
Übersetze die folgenden Sätze!

1. Meine Eltern gehen nicht sehr oft aus.
2. Siehst du das Gebäude dort drüben?
3. Fährst du immer noch mit dem Fahrrad zur Arbeit?
4. Ich wohne nicht in München.
5. Warum bist du gestern abend nicht gekommen?
6. Ich hatte keine Zeit.
7. Magst du Pizza?
8. Hast du gestern den Film im Fernsehen gesehen?
9. Ich kenne Herrn Meier nicht.
10. Wo arbeitet dein Vater?
11. Warum rufst du Mary nicht mal an?
12. Letzte Woche hat sie ihre kranke Tante nicht besucht.
13. Sie arbeitet nicht ordentlich.
14. Wann bist du gestern ins Bett gegangen?
15. Warum hast du mich letzte Woche nicht gefragt?

Question Tags
Frageanhängsel

Question Tags sind durch Komma abgetrennte Kurzanhängsel am Ende eines Satzes. Sie entsprechen etwa dem deutschen *„nicht wahr"*, d. h. der Sprecher erwartet von seinem Zuhörer eine Bestätigung.

Beispiel: Your daughter is 12 years old, isn't she? – Deine Tochter ist 12 Jahre alt, nicht wahr?

Die Bildung dieser Kurzanhängsel richtet sich nach drei Prinzipien:

Bildung

Prinzip 1:
Das *Subjekt* des Satzes wird in Form eines Pronomens im Kurzanhängsel wieder aufgegriffen.
Beispiel: Peter is a teacher, isn't **he**?

Prinzip 2:
a) Ist der *Satz verneint,* wird das Frageanhängsel nicht verneint.
   Beispiel: She **isn't** 12 years old, **is** she?
b) Ist der *Satz nicht verneint,* wird das Frageanhängsel verneint.
   Beispiel: She **is** 12 years old, **isn't** she?

Prinzip 3:

a) Ist ein *Hilfsverb* im Satz vorhanden, wird dieses im Frageanhängsel wieder benutzt.

Beispiel: You **can** speak French, **can't** you?

b) Ist *kein Hilfsverb* im Satz vorhanden, wird eine Form von "do" im Frageanhängsel benutzt. Die Form von "do" richtet sich nach der Zeit (Present Tense, Past Tense) und der Person (z. B. I, you, he, Mary, they etc.) des Satzes.

Beispiel: She **works** in London, **doesn't she**? (Present Tense, 3rd person singular)

You **went** to Spain, **didn't** you? (Past Tense, 2nd person singular)

Zu beachten ist:

▶ Kurzanhängsel von *Befehlen* weichen von den Prinzipien ab. Befehle (commands) haben als Kurzanhängsel "will you". *Ausnahmen*

Beispiel: Shut the door, will you?

▶ Wegen ihrer fast negativen Bedeutung haben *Sätze mit einschränkenden Adverbien* wie "hardly" (kaum), "rarely" (selten), "seldom" (selten) etc. bejahende Kurzanhängsel.

Beispiel: You hardly sleep, do you?

Exercises
Übungen

Übungen

Add the correct question tag.
Füge das richtige Frageanhängsel hinzu!

1. Paul answered the phone, ...?
2. You work very hard, ...?
3. Simon is your best friend, ...?
4. Sheila isn't very old, ...?
5. You will come next week, ...?
6. Sally was always a good student, ...?
7. You like ice-cream, ...?
8. The Millers live in Bristol, ...?
9. She didn't write, ...?
10. You have got a car, ...?
11. She has never been in Paris, ...?
12. They never go to the theatre, ...?
13. Sam always knows the correct answer, ...?
14. He will earn a lot of money, ...?

15. She wasn't at home, . . .?
16. You don't remember me, . . .?
17. She wouldn't go, . . .?
18. The children mustn't eat chocolate, . . .?
19. They couldn't help you, . . .?
20. It might rain, . . .?
21. Your brother is older than you, . . .?
22. Your mother doesn't work, . . .?
23. You can go, . . .?
24. You can't speak French, . . .?
25. The workers went on strike, . . .?
26. Your German is very good, . . .?
27. Carlos comes from Spain, . . .?
28. The house was built in 1950, . . .?
29. Turn off the TV, . . .?
30. Your neighbour cuts the grass every week, . . .?

Short Answers

Kurzantworten

Da Antworten mit "yes" und "no" im normalen Sprachgebrauch ungewöhnlich sind, werden Kurzantworten verwendet um zu vermeiden, dass man bei Entscheidungsfragen (ja/nein) den Inhalt des ganzen Satzes noch einmal wiederholen muss.

Beispiel: Do you live in London? Yes, I do.

Die Bildung dieser Kurzantworten unterliegt zwei Regeln:

Bildung

Regel 1: Das *Hilfsverb* der Frage wird in der Kurzantwort wieder aufgegriffen.

Beispiel: Can you speak Italian?

Yes, I **can.**

Regel 2: Lautet die Antwort *"yes"*, ist die Kurzantwort bejaht.

Beispiel: Do you like football?

Yes, I do.

Lautet die Antwort *"no"*, ist die Kurzantwort verneint.

Beispiel: Do you like football?

No, I don't.

Beachte: Bei Kurzantworten mit "must" ist darauf zu achten, dass die Verneinung von "must" "needn't" heißt.

Beispiel: Must I make the beds now?

No, you **needn't.**

Exercises

Übungen

Answer the following questions.

Beantworte die folgenden Fragen!

1. Can you answer this question? – Yes, . . .
2. Is your mother better? – Yes, . . .
3. Have you got a house? – Yes, . . .
4. Didn't Carol tell you? – No, . . .
5. Are Maud and Sally coming? – No, . . .
6. Have you heard the news? – Yes, . . .
7. Will you go on holiday? – No, . . .
8. Wasn't she able to help you? – No, . . .
9. Must you work overtime? – No, . . .
10. Did you knit the pullover yourself? – No, . . .
11. Would you phone her? – Yes, . . .
12. Has your father told you? – Yes, . . .
13. May Billy climb the tree? – No, . . .
14. Had she lived in England before she got married? – No, . . .
15. Did Michael do the washing-up? – Yes, . . .
16. Was Sally doing her homework when you saw her? – No, . . .
17. Will you be in at 10 o'clock? – No, . . .
18. Are you an actor? – No, . . .
19. Has your mother got a job? – No, . . .
20. Did the guide explain everything to you? – Yes, . . .
21. May Tom leave the classroom? – Yes, . . .
22. Does your mother like housework? – No, . . .
23. Have you ever tried brandy? – No, . . .
24. Were you at the club yesterday? – No, . . .
25. Shall I open the window? – No, . . .
26. Have you seen Mrs Smith? – No, . . .
27. Can you tell me the way to the station? – Yes, . . .
28. Have you watered the plants? – Yes, . . .
29. Do you believe in UFOs? – No, . . .
30. Did your brother give you the book? – Yes, . . .

Final Test: Auxiliary Verbs

Abschlusstest: Hilfsverben

I. *Put the auxiliaries in brackets in the correct tense.*

   Setze die Hilfsverben in Klammern in die richtige Zeit!

1. Clare (can) play the piano when she was 5.
2. Stephen hopes that he (can) translate the English instruction manuals after the English course.
3. The Hulls (must) get up very early tomorrow.
4. Sally (may not) go out when she was 16.
5. Clara (never/to be) to England.
6. I (need not) go to the office yesterday.
7. When I was 17 I (cannot) afford such expensive hobbies.
8. He (never/can) write properly.
9. I (have not) a car.
10. We (must) move because my father got a new job.
11. If you go on learning, you (can) go to university next year.
12. Bill (may not) go to the party next weekend.
13. She (to be) a very pretty girl when she was young.
14. You spent 4 years in France, (do not) you?
15. Sam told me that he (must) to go to hospital the day before.
16. Restaurants (not to be allowed to) serve alcohol if they are not fully licensed.
17. I hope you (not to have to) go to work next Saturday.
18. In India some women (not to be allowed) to leave the house.
19. Yesterday we (must) call the doctor because Jean (to be) so ill.
20. I'm sorry, I (cannot) visit you next month.

II. *Translate the following sentences.*

   Übersetze die folgenden Sätze!

1. Könntest du mir bitte den Bleistift leihen?
2. Darf ich Ihnen Herrn Müller vorstellen?
3. Dürfen die Kinder im Garten spielen?
4. Er wird nicht ins Haus kommen können, weil er seine Schlüssel vergessen hat.
5. Kann deine Brille nicht auf dem Esstisch liegen?
6. Sie braucht Montag nicht zu arbeiten.
7. Können wir nicht ins Theater gehen?
8. Seit wann kannst du Französisch sprechen?
9. Peter mag keine klassische Musik, nicht wahr?
10. Kennst du George Orwell? – Ja.
11. Er hat gestern nicht vergessen das Auto abzuschließen.

12. Früher kosteten Lebensmittel viel weniger.
13. Maria hofft in 2 Jahren soviel Englisch sprechen zu können, dass sie mit den ausländischen Touristen in ihrem Souvenirladen sprechen kann.
14. Sie müssen seit 2 Wochen ihren Sohn jeden Tag zum Zahnarzt bringen.
15. Beim Betreten einer Moschee müssen die Schuhe ausgezogen werden.
16. Putzt deine Nachbarin wirklich jeden Tag die Fenster?
17. Ist deine Freundin letztes Jahr nach Spanien gezogen?
18. Dieser Pullover darf nicht gewaschen werden.
19. Die Baker-Kinder haben noch nie eine Party geben dürfen.
20. Könnte ich meinen Hut im Wagen gelassen haben?

Infinitive and Gerund

Infinitiv/Grundform und Gerundium/ substantiviertes Verb

Infinitiv und Gerundium sind **infinite (ungebeugte) Verbformen,** d. h. sie sind im Gegensatz zu den **finiten (gebeugten) Verbformen** nicht durch Person und Zeit bestimmt.

Infinitive
Infinitiv/Grundform

Zeit	Aktiv	Passiv
Present Tense Simple (Präsens)	(to) write	(to) be written
Present Tense Continuous (Präsens Verlaufsform)	(to) be writing	
Present Perfect Simple (Perfekt)	(to) have written	(to) have been written
Present Perfect Continuous (Perfekt Verlaufsform)	(to) have been writing	

Formen

Die Perfektformen drücken Vorzeitigkeit aus.
Der Infinitiv kann mit oder ohne "to" stehen.

The Infinitive without "to" – Der Infinitiv ohne "to"

Anwendung

Der Infinitiv ohne "to" steht:

▶ nach den modalen (unvollständigen) *Hilfsverben* (außer: ought, used), nach dem Hilfsverb "do", nach "dare" und "need".

Beispiel: I must go. – Ich muss gehen.

She doesn't work. – Sie arbeitet nicht.

▶ nach *Ausdrücken* wie: had better

would rather

would sooner

why not

why should we/you (not)

Beispiel: I would rather stay at home. – Ich würde lieber zu Hause bleiben.

▶ nach *Verben der Sinneswahrnehmung* + Objekt (z. B. to see, to hear, to feel, to watch), wenn ausgedrückt werden soll, dass die Handlung *beendet* ist.

Beispiel: I saw him enter the house. – Ich sah ihn das Haus betreten.

Soll der Ablauf einer Handlung betont werden, benutzt man nach Verben der Sinneswahrnehmung das Partizip Präsens (ing-Form).

Beispiel: I watched him entering the house. – Ich beobachtete ihn dabei,

wie er das Haus betrat.

▶ nach *"let"* + *Objekt* (erlauben, zulassen).

Beispiel: I let him go. – Ich ließ ihn gehen.

▶ nach *"let's"* (Vorschlag).

Beispiel: Let's go to the pub. – Lasst uns in den Pub gehen.

▶ nach *"make"* + *Objekt* (jemanden veranlassen).

Beispiel: He made me stay longer. – Er veranlasste mich länger zu bleiben.

The Infinitive with "to" – Der Infinitiv mit "to"

Anwendung

Der Infinitiv mit "to" kann stehen:

▶ in der Funktion eines *indirekten Fragesatzes* oder *Objektsatzes,* oft nach Fragewörtern oder nach "whether/if", nach Verben des Denkens, Sagens und Vermutens (z. B. to ask, to consider, to decide, to find out, to forget, to know, to learn, to remember, to see, to show, to teach, to wonder etc.).

Beispiel: He didn't know what to do. (He didn't know what he should do.) –

Er wusste nicht, was er tun sollte.

▶ als *adverbiale Bestimmung* in der Funktion eines Finalsatzes (Zwecksatzes) oder eines Konsekutivsatzes (Folgesatzes). Der Infinitiv mit "to" steht also verkürzend für Nebensätze, die mit "so that", "such that", "in order that" etc. eingeleitet werden.

Beispiel: Fresh air helps the flowers to grow. (Fresh air helps the flowers so

that they grow.) – Frische Luft hilft den Blumen zu wachsen.

▶ nach *Verben wie "to seem", "to appear",* die eine Ergänzung benötigen.

Beispiel: She seemed to be at home. – Sie schien zu Hause zu sein.

▶ nach *Verben des Befehlens, Veranlassens* (außer: to make) und des *Zulassens* (außer: to let) wie z. B. to allow, to ask, to cause, to expect, to order, to tell (befehlen), to want etc. + Objekt (von jemandem wollen, dass ...)

Beispiel: The teacher allowed him to go. – Der Lehrer erlaubte ihm zu gehen.

Beachte: Nach "to want" steht nie "that", sondern der Infinitiv mit "to".

Beispiel: I want to come. – Ich möchte, dass er kommt.

Beachte: Diese Konstruktion nennt man ACI (von lat. *accusations cum infinitivo*), also Akkusativ (der 4. Fall – Wen-Fall) mit Infinitiv. Da es im Englischen keinen eigentlichen Akkusativ gibt, wird auch die Bezeichnung "Objective Infinitive" benutzt. Bei diesen Infinitivkonstruktionen mit Objekt ist zu beachten, dass – falls das Objekt ein Pronomen ist – dieses natürlich im Objektfall (object case) stehen muss.

Beispiel: The teacher wants **me** to work harder.

> **you**
>
> **him, her, (it)**
>
> **us**
>
> **you**
>
> **them**

Im Deutschen sind solche Infinitivkonstruktionen nicht möglich. Stattdessen werden Nebensätze mit „dass" verwendet.

Beispiel: The teacher wants me to work harder. – Der Lehrer möchte von mir, dass ich ...

▶ nach *Ordnungszahlen* und *Superlativen,* wie z. B. the first, the second, the last, the next, the only etc.

Beispiel: Miss Gutter was the first to arrive. – Miss Gutter war die erste, die ankam.

▶ nach *"too"* + *Adjektiv.*

Beispiel: He is too young to go to the disco. – Er ist zu jung um in die Disco zu gehen.

▶ nach *Adjektiv* + *"enough".*

Beispiel: He is old enough to do it himself. – Er ist alt genug um es alleine zu machen.

▶ nach *"for"* + *Objekt.*

Beispiel: It's easy for him to do that. – Es ist leicht für ihn das zu tun.

▶ nach den meisten *Adjektiven* und ihren Steigerungsformen.

Beispiel: It's cheaper to go by train. – Es ist billiger mit dem Zug zu fahren.

▶ zum *Ausdruck eines Zwecks.*

Beispiel: He must learn hard (in order) to pass his exam. – Er muss hart arbeiten um sein Examen zu bestehen.

The Infinitive Passive Voice – Der Infinitiv Passiv

Bei passivischem Sinn steht in der Regel auch der Infinitiv Passiv. Anders als im Deutschen steht er aber auch nach den Verben "to be", "to remain" und "to leave". Es handelt sich hier um den Infinitiv mit "to".

Beispiel: The boys are to be pitied. – Die Jungen sind zu bemitleiden.

Trotz Passivsinn steht der Infinitiv Aktiv mit "to"

▶ oft nach "there" + Form von "to be".

Beispiel: There are some bills to pay. – Es sind einige Rechnungen zu bezahlen.

▶ nach Adjektiven wie "difficult", "easy", "hard", "pleasant", "nice" etc.

Beispiel: This question is easy to answer. – Diese Frage kann leicht beantwortet werden.

▶ bei den Verben "to blame" (tadeln) und "to let" (vermieten).

Beispiel: The house is to let. – Das Haus ist zu vermieten.

Exercises

Übungen

I. Decide whether to use the infinitive with or without "to".
Entscheide, ob man den Infinitiv mit oder ohne "to" benutzen muss!

1. The window was too dirty (to see) through.
2. He came (to help) the old lady.
3. Have you done this (to annoy) your parents?
4. He made her (to answer) the letter at once.
5. I've forgotten how (to spell) that word.
6. Mr Strict wouldn't (to let) his son (to drive).
7. You ought (to phone) her immediately.
8. The boss told me when (to repair) the engine.
9. Can you tell me how (to get) to the cinema?
10. Neil Armstrong was the first man (to land) on the moon.
11. The roof must (to be repaired) at once.
12. I don't consider it (to be) true.
13. After his A-level he wanted (to study) languages.
14. The fans waited for the pop star (to arrive).
15. He opened the door (to let) the dog in.

II. *Decide whether to use the infinitive active or passive voice with or without "to".*

Entscheide, ob der Infinitiv Aktiv oder Passiv mit oder ohne "to" benutzt werden muss!

1. It's not difficult for the students (to answer) the teacher's questions.
2. This boy shouldn't (to leave) alone.
3. The high prices caused many tourists (to stay) home.
4. The father wanted his son (to become) a lawyer.
5. The Bakers have arranged for the carpenter (to come) next week.
6. Leave the door open for father (to hear) the bell.
7. It's interesting (to listen) to other people.
8. She forgot (to lock) the door, so the burglar could easily (to get) in the house.
9. The boys were not sure whether (to elect) Paul chairman.
10. The walls ought (to paint).
11. The problem is (to discuss).
12. He seems (to be able to spend) a lot of money.
13. The glasses were (not to find).
14. It's very difficult (to get) a good job.
15. Who is (to blame)?

III. *Shorten the sentences by using infinitive constructions.*

Kürze die Sätze, indem du Infinitivkonstruktionen benutzt!

1. When Tom had lost his purse he didn't know where he should go to.
2. Sheila is the only student who deserves the prize.
3. She couldn't find a piece of paper which she could leave the note on.
4. We urgently need somebody who can look after our children.
5. He gave them land which they could live on.
6. The English runner was the second who reached the finishing line.
7. Mr Smithers was the only person who was hurt in the accident.
8. The old lady really needs somebody who she can talk to.
9. I want a pullover which goes with my red skirt.
10. They didn't know whether they should accept the invitation.
11. Sir Francis Drake was the first Englishman who sailed around the world.
12. The doctor told me how I should take this medicine.
13. Sue is always the first person who arrives and the last person who leaves.
14. Little Billy is the youngest boy who acts in this play.
15. Years ago she didn't even know how she could translate the letters.

IV. *Translate the following sentences. Use infinitive constructions.*
   Übersetze die folgenden Sätze! Benutze Infinitivkonstruktionen!
   1. Der Hausmeister möchte, dass alle Schüler die Schule um 13 Uhr verlassen.
   2. Herr Clumsy ist der Zweite, der heute vom Pferd fällt.
   3. Es ist nicht leicht die englische Grammatik zu lernen.
   4. John ist der einzige Junge, der den Nähkurs belegt hat.
   5. Herr Kurz ist viel zu alt um an dem Tanzwettbewerb teilzunehmen.
   6. Die Hausaufgaben sollten ordentlich erledigt werden.
   7. Der neue Chef möchte, dass ich am Freitag länger im Büro bleibe.
   8. Unser Nachbar hat gestern gesehen, dass ein Mann den Garten betrat.
   9. Könntest du bitte am nächsten Wochenende kommen um mir bei den Vorbereitungen für die Party zu helfen?
   10. Es ist an der Zeit für ihn sich einen neuen Arbeitsplatz zu suchen.
   11. Ich kann dir zeigen, wie man einen Reifen repariert.
   12. Die Polizei suchte überall, aber die Pistole wurde nicht gefunden.
   13. Bevor wir einziehen können, ist noch viel Arbeit zu erledigen.
   14. John muss jetzt gerade dabei sein, sein Abendessen einzunehmen.
   15. Es gibt keine Zeit zu verlieren.

Gerund
Gerundium/substantiviertes Verb

Das Gerundium ist ein substantiviertes Verb, d. h. ein ehemaliges Tätigkeitswort ist zum Hauptwort geworden. Im Deutschen geschieht dies durch Großschreibung des Infinitivs.
Beispiel: das Lesen
Im Englischen wird das Gerundium durch die ing-Form vertreten.
Beispiel: reading
(Zur Bildung der ing-Form und zu Rechtschreibbesonderheiten siehe S. 20 f.).

Die Formen des Gerundiums in den verschiedenen Zeiten:

Formen

Zeit	Aktiv	Passiv
Present Tense (Präsens)	writing	being written
Present Perfect (Perfekt)	having written	having been written

Die Aktivform Präsens kommt am häufigsten vor. Die Perfektform drückt Vorzeitigkeit aus.

Das Gerundium steht:

▶ *als Subjekt*

Beispiel: Writing books is hard work. – Das Bücherschreiben ist harte Arbeit.

▶ *nach Präpositionen*

after	– nach
in spite of	– trotz
before	– vor
instead of	– (an)statt
without	– ohne
by	– durch
because of	– wegen etc.

Beispiel: Instead of going to bed early, he went out. – Anstatt früh ins Bett zu gehen, ging er aus.

▶ *nach Ausdrücken mit Präpositionen*

a) *Verb + Präposition:*

to adjust to	– (sich) anpassen an
to agree with	– übereinstimmen mit
to apologize for	– sich entschuldigen für
to ask about	– fragen nach
to ask for	– bitten um
to be afraid of	– sich fürchten vor
to begin by	– beginnen mit
to be looking forward to	– sich freuen auf
to be for/against	– dafür/dagegen sein
to care for	– sich kümmern um
to complain about	– sich beschweren über
to concentrate on	– sich konzentrieren auf
to consist of	– bestehen aus
to cope with	– fertig werden mit (etwas bewältigen)
to decide for/against	– sich entscheiden für/gegen
to depend on	– abhängen von
to die of	– sterben an
to dream about/of	– träumen von
to escape from	– flüchten vor
to give up	– aufgeben
to go on	– weitermachen
to insist on	– bestehen auf
to keep on	– fortfahren mit
to pay for	– bezahlen für
to prevent (somebody) from	– jemanden hindern an
to put off	– aufschieben
to spend (money/time) on	– Geld ausgeben für, Zeit verbringen mit

to succeed in	– Erfolg haben mit
to take part in	– teilnehmen an
to talk about/of	– sprechen über etc.

Beispiel: I apologize for coming late. – Ich entschuldige mich für das Zuspätkommen.

b) Adjektiv + Präposition:

angry about/at	– ärgerlich über
clever at	– gut in
crazy about	– verrückt nach
disappointed about	– enttäuscht über
excited about	– aufgeregt über
famous for	– berühmt für
fond of	– begeistert von
glad about	– froh über
good at	– gut in
impressed by	– beeindruckt von
interested in	– interessiert an
keen on	– begeistert von
proud of	– stolz auf
tired of	– genug (haben) von
used to	– gewöhnt an
worried about	– besorgt über etc.

Beispiel: She is afraid of flying. – Sie fürchtet sich vor dem Fliegen.

c) Nomen + Präposition:

advantage of	– Vorteil (von)
alternative of	– Alternative zu
chance of	– Chance zu
choice between	– Wahl zwischen
difficulty in	– Schwierigkeit bei
doubt about	– Zweifel über/an
experience in	– Erfahrung mit
opportunity of	– Gelegenheit zu
place for	– Platz zum/für
possibility of	– Möglichkeit zu
reason for	– Grund für
trouble in	– Ärger mit
way of	– Art und Weise zu

Beispiel: She has a lot of experience in typing. – Sie hat eine Menge Erfahrung im Tippen.

▶ *nach bestimmten Ausdrücken wie:*

to be busy	– beschäftigt sein mit
to be like	– sein wie
to be near	– nahe daran sein
to be no good	– nicht gut sein
to be no use	– keinen Sinn haben
to be worth	– wert sein
can't help	– nicht anders können als
can't stand	– nicht ertragen können
to be no good at	– nicht gut sein in/bei

Beispiel: He is busy writing. – Er ist mit dem Schreiben beschäftigt.

▶ *nach bestimmten Verben als Objekt:*

to admit	– zugeben
to appreciate	– schätzen, begrüßen
to avoid	– vermeiden
to consider	– in Betracht ziehen
to delay	– aufschieben
to deny	– abstreiten
to dislike	– nicht mögen
to enjoy	– Freude haben an
to escape	– entkommen
to finish	– beenden
to imagine	– sich (etwas) vorstellen
to mention	– erwähnen
to mind	– etwas dagegen haben
to miss	– verpassen
to practise	– üben
to reject	– zurückweisen
to resist	– widerstehen
to risk	– riskieren
to suggest	– vorschlagen
to stop	– aufhören
to understand	– verstehen

Beispiel: I enjoyed sailing. – Ich hatte Freude am Segeln.

Infinitive or Gerund

Infinitiv/Grundform oder Gerundium/ Substantiviertes Verb

Manche Verben können einen Infinitiv oder ein Gerundium nach sich ziehen. In einigen Fällen hat dies keine Auswirkung auf die Bedeutung, in anderen Fällen ist ein Bedeutungsunterschied damit verbunden:

Anwendung

▶ Folgende Verben können *wahlweise mit Infinitiv oder Gerundium* stehen, ohne dass sich die Bedeutung ändert:

to begin	– beginnen
to continue	– weitermachen
to intend	– beabsichtigen
to start	– anfangen

Beispiel: The little girl started to cry.
The little girl started crying.

▶ Verben des Mögens oder Nichtmögens wie "to like", "to love", "to prefer", "to hate" stehen mit *Gerundium,* wenn eine *allgemeine Vorliebe oder Abneigung* ausgedrückt werden soll.

Beispiel: Children like eating chocolate. – Kinder mögen es Sch. zu essen.
Liegen jedoch *konkrete Einzelfälle* oder *eingeschränkte Aussagen* (besonders mit "would") vor, so stehen diese Verben mit *Infinitiv.*

Beispiel: The children usually don't like eating vegetables, but today they would love to eat some. – Normalerweise mögen die Kinder kein Gemüse, aber heute würden sie es gern essen.

▶ Bei folgenden Verben *ändert sich die Bedeutung,* je nachdem ob ein Gerundium oder ein Infinitiv folgt:

a) to remember + Gerundium	– sich erinnern etwas getan zu haben
to remember + Infinitiv	– daran denken etwas zu tun
b) to regret + Gerundium	– bereuen etwas getan zu haben
to regret + Infinitiv	– bereuen etwas tun zu müssen
c) to forget + Gerundium	– vergessen etwas getan zu haben
to forget + Infinitiv	– vergessen etwas zu tun
d) to stop + Gerundium	– aufhören etwas zu tun
to stop + Infinitiv	– aufhören um etwas anderes zu tun
e) to try + Gerundium	– etwas probieren
to try + Infinitiv	– sich bemühen etwas zu tun
f) to go on + Gerundium	– etwas weiterhin tun
to go on + Infinitiv	– etwas (Neues) als Nächstes tun

Beispiel: I remember meeting Jill for the first time. – Ich erinnere mich daran, als ich Jill das erste Mal traf.
I must remember to post the letters. – Ich muss daran denken die Briefe aufzugeben.

Exercises
Übungen

I. Form sentences using the expressions in brackets plus gerund.
   Bilde Sätze! Benutze die Ausdrücke in Klammern plus Gerundium!

1. Harry promised he wouldn't smoke any more. (to give up)
2. The guide said we could also visit the gallery. (opportunity of)
3. He is very proud. He has passed his exam. (proud of)
4. He is not very happy. He doesn't earn enough money. (to complain about)
5. The teacher said to the students, "If you don't learn your new words, you won't get a good mark." (choice between)
6. Sam has a dream. He wants to be a pop star. (to dream of)
7. Don't rely on Simon. (to be no use)
8. My mother is very busy. She's preparing dinner. (to be busy)
9. Peter is very tired in the evening because of the long work. (not to be used to)
10. I will be pleased to meet your sister next week. (to be looking forward to)
11. The workers painted the walls last week. I'll have to pay them. (to pay for)
12. You shouldn't read that book. (not to be worth)
13. It wasn't easy for us to find the way. (difficulties in)
14. I play tennis every weekend. (to be fond of)
15. My brother is not at home. You needn't phone him. (to be no use)
16. If I go to the concert, I'll meet her. (not to be able to avoid)
17. I didn't see the film, because I didn't know that it was on. (to miss)
18. He finally got his driving licence. (to succeed in)
19. We had dinner. Then we went for a walk. (after)
20. He is a very good dancer. (good at)

II. Translate the following sentences. Use gerunds.
   Übersetze die folgenden Sätze! Benutze Gerundien!

1. Er hatte immer große Angst vor dem Fliegen.
2. Ich riskiere meinen Job zu verlieren, wenn ich dir helfe.
3. Die Kinder sind nicht daran gewöhnt so lange aufzubleiben.
4. Er war sehr enttäuscht, dass du nicht zu seiner Geburtstagsparty gekommen bist.
5. Sie kamen nach England, weil sie hofften dort ein besseres Leben führen zu können.
6. Er wollte nicht zugeben, dass er einen Fehler gemacht hatte.
7. Was ist der Grund dafür, dass du schon wieder zu spät kommst?
8. Ich kann langes Warten nicht ertragen.
9. Der Kunde besteht darauf den Manager zu sprechen.
10. Der Pfarrer fuhr fort seine Rede zu halten.
11. Es hat keinen Zweck ihn im Krankenhaus zu besuchen.

12. Macht es Ihnen etwas aus, wenn ich das Fenster öffne?
13. Anstatt seine Arbeit zu beenden, fuhr er in Urlaub.
14. Ich hatte überhaupt keine Gelegenheit Fragen zu stellen.
15. Sie können verhindern, dass die Pflanzen absterben, wenn Sie sie regelmäßig gießen.
16. Du solltest einmal in Betracht ziehen mit Sally zusammenzuarbeiten.
17. Er war dagegen noch mehr Geld für den Urlaub auszugeben.
18. Anstatt mir endlich die Wahrheit zu sagen erfand er weitere Lügen.
19. Ihm hat das Reisen immer sehr viel Spaß gemacht.
20. Judith war sehr ärgerlich darüber, dass sie dich nicht getroffen hat.

Test

Final Test: Infinitive and Gerund

Abschlusstest: Infinitiv und Gerundium

Decide whether to use infinitive or gerund.
Entscheide, ob Infinitiv oder Gerundium benutzt werden muss!

1. Would you like (to have) dinner with me one evening next week?
2. I would rather (to go) by train than (to walk).
3. The teacher had no pen (to write) with.
4. He entered the room without (to see) me.
5. The dog was too fast (to be run) over.
6. This book is easy (to understand).
7. She couldn't help (to laugh).
8. My father is busy (to cut) the grass.
9. The teacher allowed the students (to go) half an hour earlier.
10. It's time for them (to go).
11. I wouldn't like (to swim) in that dirty water.
12. Lock the door before (to leave) the house.
13. It's possible (to get) the missing parts.
14. The student was very proud of (to win) the prize.
15. The radio needs (to repair).
16. I regret (to say) that he has made a mistake.
17. It's no use (to try) (to make) him change his mind.
18. We were asked (to finish) our test without (to look up) words.
19. I forgot (to tell) you that I don't like (to play) cards.
20. After (to practise) a lot the band started (to play).
21. The caretaker made the boys (to leave) the building.
22. I don't want him (to come) so often.
23. (to look at) these photos is almost like (to be) there.
24. The criminal was arrested for (to rob) the shop.

Conditional Clauses – If-Clauses

Konditionalsätze / Bedingungssätze / If-Sätze

Ein "Conditional Clause", ein Bedingungssatz, ist ein **Nebensatz, der mit "if"** **(wenn), "in case" (falls) oder "unless" (wenn nicht) beginnt.** Dieser Nebensatz bildet zusammen mit einem Hauptsatz ein Satzgefüge.

Beispiel: <u>**If it rains,**</u> <u>**I will not go out.**</u>

Nebensatz Hauptsatz
(subordinate clause) (main clause)

Im Englischen gibt es drei Typen von If-Sätzen. Jeder Typ hat eine bestimmte Regel für die Zeitenfolge. Die Wahl des Typs richtet sich nach der Art der Bedingung, die durch den If-Satz ausgedrückt werden soll.

Type I: Probable Condition

Typ I: wahrscheinliche Bedingung

Kurzregel	Steht im If-Satz **Präsens** (Present Tense), so steht im Hauptsatz **Futur I** (Future I).		*Grund-regel*
Beispiel	If it rains, Wenn es regnet,	I will stay at home. bleibe ich zu Hause.	
Zeit (tense)	Präsens (Present Tense)	Futur I (Future I)	
Bildungsweise	1. Verbform bei he, she, it + "-(e)s"	will + 1. Verbform	
Art der Bedingung	Die Bedingung (wenn es regnet) ist erfüllbar. Es ist wahrscheinlich (probable), dass es regnet.		

Diese Kurzregel zur Verwendung der Zeiten im If-Satz Typ I muss jedoch präzisiert werden, um alle denkbaren Fälle abzudecken.

Erweiterung der Kurzregel

In "Conditional Clauses" vom Typ I sind folgende Zeiten möglich:

Erweiterung

If-Satz	Hauptsatz
Present Tense Simple (einfaches Präsens)	→ Future I (Futur I)
Present Tense Continuous (Präsens Verlaufsform)	→ Imperative (Imperativ/Befehlsform)
Present Perfect (Perfekt)	→ Modal Auxiliary (unvollständiges Hilfsverb)
should + Infinitive	→ Present Tense Simple (einfaches Präsens)

Fall 1

If-Satz	Hauptsatz
Present Tense Simple	Future I *oder* Imperative *oder* Modal Auxiliary

Beispiel: If it rains, I will stay at home.

If it rains, stay at home!

If it rains, we can stay at home.

Present Tense Simple im If-Satz drückt aus, dass sich die Bedingung auf ein zukünftiges Geschehen bezieht.

Fall 2

If-Satz	Hauptsatz
Present Tense Continuous	Future I *oder* Imperative *oder* Modal Auxiliary

Beispiel: If he is working now, he'll phone me later.

If he is working now, tell him to phone me later!

If he is working now, he can phone me later.

Present Tense Continuous im If-Satz drückt aus, dass die Bedingung noch im Verlauf ist.

Fall 3

If-Satz	Hauptsatz
Present Perfect	Future I *oder* Imperative *oder* Modal Auxiliary

Beispiel: If he has already finished his work, he'll come soon.

If he has already finished his work, ask him to come soon!

If he has already finished his work, he can come soon.

Present Perfect im If-Satz drückt aus, dass sich die Bedingung auf schon Geschehenes bezieht.

Das Verb
If-Sätze

If-Satz	**Hauptsatz**
should + Infinitive	Future I *oder* Imperative *oder* Modal Auxiliary

Fall 4

Beispiel: If Bob should lose his job, he'll move.

If Bob should lose his job, don't worry!

If Bob should lose his job, he must move.

Should + Infinitive im If-Satz drückt aus, dass man es für wenig wahrscheinlich hält, dass die Bedingung verwirklicht wird.

If-Satz	**Hauptsatz**
Present Tense Simple	Present Tense Simple

Fall 5

Beispiel: If the battery is flat, the engine doesn't start.

Diese Kombination wird benutzt, wenn die Aussage allgemein gültig ist. "If" hat hier die Bedeutung "whenever" (immer wenn).

Exercises
Übungen

Übungen

I. Put the verb in brackets in the correct tense.

Setze das Verb in Klammern in die richtige Zeit!

1. If I get a dog for Christmas, I (to go) for a walk every day.
2. If Susan finds your book, she (to give) it back to you.
3. If you leave the window open, the cat (to jump) out.
4. If Tom hurries, he (to catch) the bus.
5. If she (to send) me an invitation, I (to go) to her party.
6. I will come around if I (to have) time.
7. If I find your ring, I (to telephone) you at once.
8. If the sun (to shine), he (to have) a barbecue.
9. If my uncle comes, he (to take) us to the cinema.
10. If my father (to find) a better job, we (to move).
11. We (to buy) a bigger house if we (to have) the money.
12. If the bus drivers go on strike, no buses (to run).
13. If the city hasn't got the money to pay the dustmen, there (to be) dirt everywhere.
14. If you (to send) the voucher, you (to get) a free record.
15. If you (to write) her a postcard, she (to be) pleased.
16. I (to call for) a doctor if she (not/to feel) better tomorrow.
17. If you (to go on) with your diet, you (to lose) weight soon.

18. If everybody (to come), there (to be) ten of us.

19. If we can afford it, we (to fly) to London.

20. If your brother (to lend) us his car, we (to be able to) go shopping.

II. *Translate the following sentences.*
   Übersetze die folgenden Sätze!

1. Wenn ich heute frei habe, gehe ich aus.

2. Falls sie kommen sollte, gebe ich dir Bescheid.

3. Wenn Sie Frau Bax treffen, sagen Sie ihr bitte, sie möge mich anrufen.

4. Wenn Conny gerade dabei ist ihr Fahrrad zu reparieren, wird sie gegen 5 Uhr fertig sein.

5. Wenn das Paket nicht bald ankommt, werde ich die Firma anrufen.

6. Wenn man Blumen am Tage gießt, wachsen sie besser.

7. Wenn Sam die Reise noch nicht gebucht hat, sollte er sich beeilen.

8. Wenn ich den Stadtplan finde, kann ich dir die Straße zeigen.

9. Wenn Carlo sich entschieden hat in London zu bleiben, sollte er sich eine Wohnung suchen.

10. Wenn Rick nach Deutschland kommt, wird er dich direkt anrufen.

Type II: Improbable Condition
Typ II: unwahrscheinliche Bedingung

<table>
<tr><td>Grund-regel</td><td>Kurzregel</td><td colspan="2">Steht im If-Satz Imperfekt (Past Tense), so steht im Hauptsatz Konditional I (Conditional I).</td></tr>
<tr><td></td><td>Beispiel</td><td>If   it rained,
Wenn es regnete,</td><td>I would stay at home.
bliebe ich zu Hause.</td></tr>
<tr><td></td><td>Zeit (tense)</td><td>Imperfekt
(Past Tense)</td><td>Konditional I
(Conditional I)</td></tr>
<tr><td></td><td>Bildungsweise</td><td>1. Verbform + "-ed" (oder
2. Verbform)</td><td>would + 1. Verbform</td></tr>
<tr><td></td><td>Art der Bedingung</td><td colspan="2">▶ Die Bedingung (wenn es regnete) wird für unwahrscheinlich gehalten.
▶ Die Bedingung ist nicht erfüllbar.
Beispiel: If I were you, I would go. – Wenn ich du wäre (was ich aber nicht sein kann), würde ich gehen.</td></tr>
</table>

Erweiterung der Kurzregel

In "Conditional Clauses" vom Typ II sind folgende Zeiten möglich:

Das Verb
If-Sätze

If-Satz	Hauptsatz
Past Tense (einfaches Imperfekt)	▶ Conditional I ▶ should/could/might/ought to + Infinitive ▶ Conditional II ▶ should/could/might/ought to + have + 3. Verbform (*oder* 1. Verbform + "-ed")

If-Satz	Hauptsatz
Past Tense	Conditional I *oder* should/could/might/ought to + Infinitive

Beispiel: If I had a lot of money, I would buy a house.

If I had a lot of money, I should buy a house.

If I had a lot of money, I could buy a house.

If I had a lot of money, I might buy a house.

If I had a lot of money, I ought to buy a house.

Sätze dieser Kombination drücken aus, dass die Bedingung – in Bezug auf die Gegenwart oder Zukunft gesehen – eine reine Annahme darstellt. Die verschiedenen benutzbaren Hilfsverben im Hauptsatz bringen lediglich Bedeutungsvarianten bezüglich der Folgerungen mit sich (würde, sollte, könnte,...).

If-Satz	Hauptsatz
Past Tense	Conditional II *oder* should/could/might/ought to + have + 3. Verbform (*oder* + 1. Verbform + "-ed")

Beispiel: If I had a lot of money, I would have bought a house.

If I had a lot of money, I should have bought a house.

If I had a lot of money, I could have bought a house.

If I had a lot of money, I might have bought a house.

If I had a lot of money, I ought to have bought a house.

Sätze dieser Kombination drücken aus, dass die Bedingung in Bezug auf die Gegenwart als Annahme gesehen wird, die sich aber bereits in der Vergangenheit ausgewirkt hätte. Die verschiedenen Hilfsverben bringen lediglich Bedeutungsvarianten für die Folgerung mit sich (würde ... haben/sein; sollte ... haben/sein; könnte ... haben/sein etc.).

"Was" oder "were" im If-Satz

Statt "was" in der 1. und 3. Person Singular (I, he, she, it) wird in If-Sätzen oft "were" benutzt, wenn etwas Irreales ausgedrückt werden soll.

Beispiel: If I were you,...

If I were a pop star,...

If I were at home,...

Exercises

Übungen

I. Put the verb in brackets in the correct tense.
   Setze das Verb in Klammern in die richtige Zeit!

1. If I had a car, I (to lend) it to you.
2. If a buglar tried to rob me, I (to call) the police.
3. If I (to be) you, I would write the letter immediately.
4. If Sam (to live) in London, he would go to the theatre every month.
5. If I had a house in that area, I (to be) very glad.
6. If Sally (to wear) a mini-skirt, everybody (to laugh).
7. If you (to leave) the bike outside, it (to be stolen).
8. She (to phone) you if she (to know) your number.
9. If there (to be) a bridge across the Channel, travelling to England (to become) much easier.
10. If I (to believe) in UFOs, I (to become) a member of the UFO Club.
11. If I (to know) him better, I (can / to tell) you more about him.
12. If Mrs Calm (to be) not so slow, she (to get) the job.
13. What (to say) your father if you (not to pass) the exam?
14. If I (to have) your hair, I (not to have) it cut.
15. He (to be) very angry if he (to see) you now.
16. If the Meyers (to have) a garden, the children (can / to play) outside.
17. Sue (can / to apply) for the job if she (to pass) the exam.
18. If our neighbours (to have) a baby-sitter, they (can / to go out) more often.
19. If I (to win) the pools, I (to buy) a villa in Italy.
20. If you (to read) the newspaper regulary, you (to be) better informed.

II. Translate the following sentences.
   Übersetze die folgenden Sätze!

1. Wenn ich genug Geld hätte, hätte ich den Recorder bereits gekauft.
2. Er bekäme den Zug noch, wenn er rennen würde.
3. Wenn das Wetter besser wäre, könnten wir schwimmen gehen.
4. Wenn Carmen ein bißchen höflicher wäre, bekäme sie nicht so oft Ärger.
5. Wenn weniger Schüler in einer Klasse wären, könnten die Schüler mehr lernen.
6. Wenn du die £ 1000 bekämst, solltest du wirklich ein Sparbuch eröffnen.
7. Ich hätte keine freie Minute mehr, wenn ich so oft wie du auf den Tennisplatz ginge.
8. Wenn meine Partei an der Regierung wäre, wäre alles besser.
9. Wenn ich gesund wäre, könnte ich mit euch wandern gehen.
10. Wenn wir ein neues Auto kaufen müßten, würden wir ein schnelleres aussuchen.

Type III: Impossible Condition

Typ III: unmögliche Bedingung

Kurzregel	Steht im If-Satz Plusquamperfekt (Past Perfect), so steht im Hauptsatz Konditional II (Conditional II).
Beispiel	If it had rained, / Wenn es geregnet hätte, — I would have stayed at home. / wäre ich zu Hause geblieben.
Zeit (tense)	Plusquamperfekt (Past Perfect) — Konditional II (Conditional II)
Bildungsweise	had + 1. Verbform + "-ed" (*oder* had + 3. Verbform) — would have + 1. Verbform + "-ed" (*oder* would have + 3. Verbform)
Art der Bedingung	Die Bedingung (wenn es geregnet hätte, was aber nicht der Fall war) ist unmöglich (impossible), da sie in der Vergangenheit nicht gegeben war.

Grund-regel

Erweiterung der Kurzregel

In "Conditional Clauses" vom Typ III sind folgende Zeiten möglich:

If-Satz	Hauptsatz
Past Perfect (einfaches Plusquamperfekt)	▶ Conditional II ▶ should/could/might/ought to + have + 3. Verbform (*oder* 1. Verbform + "-ed") ▶ Conditional I ▶ should/could/might/ought to + Infinitive

Erweiterung

If-Satz	Hauptsatz
Past Perfect	Conditional II *oder* should/could/might/ought to + have + 3. Verbform (*oder* 1. Verbform + "-ed")

Fall 1

Beispiel: If I had seen, I would have gone.

If I had ..., I should have ...

If I had ..., I could have ...

If I had ..., I might have ...

If I had ..., I ought to have ...

Sätze dieser Kombination drücken aus, dass die Bedingungen nicht erfüllt werden können, da sie sich auf die Vergangenheit beziehen. Die unterschiedlichen benutzbaren Hilfsverben bringen lediglich Bedeutungsvarianten bezüglich der Folgerungen mit sich (würde, sollte, könnte ... haben/sein). Die Folgerungen beziehen sich auf die Vergangenheit.

If-Satz	Hauptsatz
Past Perfect	Conditional I *oder* should/could/might/ought to + Infinitive

Beispiel: If she had seen, she would go.

If she had ..., she could ...

If she had ..., she should ...

If she had ..., she might ...

If she had ..., she ought to ...

Für Sätze dieser Kombination gilt das gleiche wie bei Fall 1 mit dem Unterschied, dass sich die Folgerungen auf die Gegenwart beziehen.

Exercises

Übungen

I. *Put the verbs in brackets in the correct tense.*

Setze die Verben in Klammern in die richtige Zeit!

1. If you had tried, you (to be) successful.
2. If we had gone to the party, we (to meet) him.
3. If she had hurried, she (to catch) the train.
4. If I (to know) this before, I would have helped you.
5. If your brother (to leave) in time, he wouldn't have been late for the meeting.
6. If the rescue team (to find) him earlier, they (can/to save) his life.
7. If the driver (not/to wear) a seat belt, he (to be) seriously injured.
8. If I (to know) that Sheila was coming, I (to pick) her up at the station.
9. If we (to be) back before midnight, the warden (not/to lock) us out.
10. If you (to do) as you were told, this (not/to happen).
11. If you (to phone) earlier, we (to be able to/to reserve) you a room.
12. If we (to go) to France, we (to stay) with my sister.
13. If the students (to go) to bed earlier, they (not/to be) so tired yesterday.
14. I (to leave) school last year if my father (not/to tell) me to finish the 10th form.
15. If his parents (to spend) more time on his education, he (not/to become) such a person.
16. If Sam (not/to drink) so much alcohol, he (not/to lose) his driving licence.
17. If you (to ask) Mr Carter, he (to get) you a cheaper ticket.
18. If the wages (to be raised), the workers (not/to go) on strike last month.
19. If Sally (to apply), she (to get) the job.
20. If I (to have) enough money with me, I (to buy) the dress.

II. *Translate the following sentences.*
   Übersetze die folgenden Sätze!

1. Wir hätten Ihnen gerne beim Umzug geholfen, wenn wir nicht in Urlaub gewesen wären.
2. Wenn Carl seine Schwester nicht dabei gehabt hätte, wäre es ein langweiliger Abend geworden.
3. Wenn du nicht so schnell gefahren wärst, hättest du die Ampel gesehen.
4. Ich hätte es auch nicht geglaubt, wenn ich nicht das Foto gesehen hätte.
5. Meine Mutter würde gerne mit ins Theater gehen, wenn sie nicht so krank gewesen wäre.
6. Ich hätte dir das Buch geliehen, wenn ich es nicht selbst gebraucht hätte.
7. Wenn Sheila nicht von ihren Eltern so verwöhnt worden wäre, wäre sie nicht so egoistisch.
8. Ich hätte das Auto selbst reparieren können, wenn ich die richtigen Werkzeuge gehabt hätte.
9. Wenn Leo nicht immer so faul gewesen wäre, hätte er die Prüfung bestehen können.
10. Es wäre besser gewesen, wenn du den Arzt gefragt hättest.

Final Test: Conditional Clauses (If-Clauses)
Abschlusstest: Bedingungssätze (If-Sätze)

Test

I. *Put the verbs in brackets in the correct tense.*
   Setze die Verben in Klammern in die richtige Zeit!

1. If the weather is fine, we (to go) out.
2. If he had watched the football match on TV, he (to know) the result now.
3. He (to be) here now if the train hadn't been late.
4. We (to go) to Spain in our next holidays if we can afford it.
5. If we went to Spain, we (to stay) at a first-class hotel.
6. If Peter passes his exam next week, he (to go) to university.
7. If you (to like), I'll get the ticket for you.
8. If he wants to see the new film, he (to have to/to go) to the cinema.
9. If he had read the instructions, he (not/to break) the machine.
10. If he takes another English course, he (to be) perfect by next year.
11. If I (to be) you, I (not/to visit) him this week.
12. If he hadn't been ill, he (can/to take part) in the game.
13. If he had been willing to spend another £ 5, he (to be able to/to get) a better pullover.
14. If you (not/to go) home so early, you wouldn't have missed the best part.
15. If there is no petrol in the tank, the car (not/to run).

16. If I (to be) a teacher, I wouldn't be so strict.
17. If he (to obey) the order, this wouldn't have happened.
18. If he (not/to rob) the bank, he wouldn't be in prison now.
19. If he (to marry) that horrible woman next month, he (to be) a prisoner for the rest of his life.
20. He would never be what he is now, if he (not/to work) very hard all his life.

II. Translate the sentences. Mind the type of if-clause.
   Übersetze die Sätze. Achte auf den Typ des If-Satzes!
1. Wenn er nicht so ein Dummkopf wäre, hätte er das niemals getan.
2. Wenn ich spreche, mag ich es nicht, unterbrochen zu werden.
3. Er wäre nicht entlassen worden, wenn er den Fehler gleich zugegeben hätte.
4. Wenn Sally sich im Moment nicht wohlfühlt, sollte sie zum Arzt gehen.
5. Wenn Pat das Auto verkauft, wird er wieder mit dem Bus fahren müssen.
6. Wenn Ron rechtzeitig ankommt, können wir noch in den Zoo gehen.
7. Wenn wir die Papiere früher gefunden hätten, hätte uns das eine Menge Arbeit erspart.
8. Die beiden Mädchen wären ertrunken, wenn nicht ein Boot in der Nähe gewesen wäre.

The German Verb „lassen" and its English Equivalents

Das deutsche Verb „lassen" und seine englischen Entsprechungen

Das deutsche Verb „lassen" führt bei der Übertragung ins Englische häufig zu Fehlern, da es verschiedene englische Entsprechungen gibt.

Etwas erlauben/zulassen – to allow/to permit/to let
Beispiel: Der Lehrer erlaubte dem Schüler früher zu gehen. -
The teacher allowed the student to go earlier.
The teacher permitted the student to go earlier.
The teacher let the student go earlier.
Beachte: Nach "allow" und "permit" steht der Infinitiv mit "to"; nach "let" jedoch der Infinitiv ohne "to".

Etwas vorschlagen – let's . . .

Beispiel: Lass uns ins Kino gehen. – Let's go to the cinema.

Jemanden zu etwas veranlassen – to make somebody do something

Beispiel: Der Lehrer veranlasste die Schüler (ließ die Schüler) den Text noch einmal ab(zu)schreiben. – The teacher made the students copy the text again.

Beachte: Die Person(en) nach "make" steht (stehen) im Objektfall. Mögliche Pronomen sind also: me, you, him, her, it, us, you, them.

Beispiel: The teacher made them copy the text again.

Veranlassen, dass etwas von jemand anderem getan wird – to have/get something done

Beispiel: Ich lasse meine Wohnung gerade streichen. – I am having/getting my flat painted.

Beachte: Das Objekt wird zwischen have/get und die 3. Verbform gestellt.

Beispiel: I have/get <u>my car</u> repaired.

Objekt

Nicht zu verwechseln mit:

I have repaired my car. – Ich habe mein Auto repariert. (selbst repariert/Present Perfect)

Einen Zustand lassen, wie er ist; etwas zurück-, hinter-, belassen – to leave something/somebody; to keep somebody doing something

Beispiel: Ich ließ mein Auto in der Garage (zurück). – I left my car in the garage.

Ich ließ den Motor laufen. – I left the engine running.

Lass ihn nicht warten! – Don't keep him waiting!

Einige Redewendungen mit „lassen"

Lass das!	Stop it!
Lass den Arzt kommen!	Send for the doctor!
Lass dir Zeit!	Take your time!
Lass mir Zeit!	Give me time!
Lass mich in Ruhe!	Leave me alone!

Exercises

Übungen

Translate the following sentences.
Übersetze die folgenden Sätze!

1. Lass deinen Bruder in Ruhe!
2. Ich werde die Kinder in den Garten gehen lassen.
3. Mutter ließ die Waschmaschine reparieren.
4. Der Chef ließ mich nach Hause gehen.
5. Verlassen Sie bitte sofort das Gebäude!
6. Ich werde den Brief schreiben lassen.
7. Lasst uns zusammen ein Geschenk für ihn kaufen.
8. Der Nachbar ließ die Kinder im Garten spielen.
9. Meine Mutter ließ mich den Spätfilm sehen.
10. Lass den Unfug!
11. Lass mir eine Stunde Zeit!
12. Lasst uns in eine Jugendherberge fahren.
13. Herr S. ließ mich eine halbe Stunde warten.
14. Der Arzt ließ den Patienten nicht aufstehen.
15. Lass das Buch dort liegen!
16. Er ließ seinen Rasen mähen.
17. Die Polizei ließ ihn seine Taschen leeren.
18. Er ließ seine Haare schneiden.
19. Ich lasse meine Pullover reinigen.
20. Meine Eltern lassen das Haus tapezieren (to wallpaper).
21. Der Trainer ließ die Sportler eine Stunde extra trainieren.
22. Sue ließ ihren kleinen Bruder nicht in Ruhe.
23. Er ließ seinen Koffer am Flughafen.
24. Der Pilot ließ das Flugzeug überprüfen.
25. Der Direktor lässt die Schüler den Hof aufräumen.

The Noun

Das Nomen/das Substantiv/das Hauptwort

Ein Nomen besitzt gewöhnlich eine **Einzahlform (Singular)** und eine **Mehrzahlform (Plural).**

Beispiel: Singular: book – Buch

Plural: books – Bücher

Ein Nomen kann in vier **Fällen,** auch **Kasus (cases)** genannt, stehen:

1. Fall: Werfall = Nominativ (subject case)
2. Fall: Wesfall = Genitiv (genitive)
3. Fall: Wemfall = Dativ (objekt case)
4. Fall: Wenfall = Akkusativ (object case)

Setzt man ein Nomen in die verschiedenen Fälle, so **dekliniert** man es:

	Singular	Plural
1. Fall	the girl (das Mädchen)	the girls (die Mädchen)
2. Fall	the girl's (des Mädchens)	the girls' (der Mädchen)
3. Fall	the girl (dem Mädchen)	the girls (den Mädchen)
4. Fall	the girl (das Mädchen)	the girls (die Mädchen)

Wie dieses Beispiel zeigt, gibt es im Englischen eigentlich nur drei Fälle, Dativ und Akkusativ fallen zum **Object Case** zusammen. Anders als im Deutschen werden die verschiedenen Fälle nicht durch Artikeländerung (das, des, dem etc.) gekennzeichnet. Im Englischen gibt es lediglich Endungen für den Genitiv und den Plural. Ansonsten ist aus der Satzstellung zu erkennen, ob ein Nomen Subjekt oder Objekt ist.

Im Bereich der Nomen gibt es also eigentlich nur zwei Bereiche, die Schwierigkeiten machen können.

▶ Plural
▶ Genitiv

The Plural

Der Plural/die Mehrzahl

Grund-regel

Ausnahmen

Gebildet wird der Plural wie folgt:

▶ Normalerweise wird ein -s an den Singular angehängt.

Beispiel: book – books

▶ Nach Zischlaut wird "-es" angehängt.

Beispiel: dress – dresses
Kleid – Kleider

▶ Nach Konsonant + y wird der Plural mit "-ies" gebildet.

Beispiel: city – cities
Stadt – Städte

▶ Einige Nomen auf "-o" bilden den Plural mit "-oes".

Beispiel: hero – heroes
Held – Helden

Dazu gehören: potato, tomato, negro, echo.

Beachte: Bei Fremdwörtern gilt diese Regel nicht.

Beispiel: kilos, pianos, studios, tobaccos, radios, photos etc.

▶ Nomen auf "-fe" oder "-f" bilden den Plural meist auf "-ves".

Beispiel: life – lives
(das) Leben – (die) Leben

Dazu gehören: knife, wife, leaf, loaf, thief, calf, half, shelf, wolf.
Ausnahmen: beliefs, briefs, chiefs, handkerchiefs, proofs, reefs, roofs.

▶ Fremdwörter behalten meist ihre ursprüngliche Pluralform.

Dazu gehören:

Singular	Plural	Singular	Plural
analysis	– analyses	minimum	– minima
bacillus	– bacilli	phenomenon	– phenomena
bacterium	– bacteria	stimulus	– stimuli
basis	– bases	thesis	– theses
crisis	– crises		

▶ Manche Nomen bilden unregelmäßige Pluralformen.

Dazu gehören:

Singular	Plural	Singular	Plural
child	– children	mouse	– mice
foot	– feet	ox	– oxen
goose	– geese	tooth	– teeth
louse	– lice	woman	– women
man	– men		

▶ Bei manchen Nomen ist die Pluralform gleich der Singularform.
Beispiel: fish – fish   Fisch – Fische
Dazu gehören: a) sheep, salmon, trout, deer, grouse
               b) Nationalitäten auf "-ese"
                 Beispiel: Japanese
               c) technische Geräte auf "-craft"
                 Beispiel: aircraft
               d) French, Swiss

The Plural of Compound Nouns

Die Pluralbildung bei zusammengesetzten Nomen

Bei zusammengesetzten Nomen gilt:
Ist ein übergeordnetes Nomen vorhanden, so tritt das Plural-"s" an dieses Nomen.

*Grund-
regel*

Beispiel: daughters-in-law – Schwiegertöchter
        Das "s" tritt an "daughter", da das zusammengesetzte Nomen die Hauptbedeutung „Tochter", nicht „Schwieger" hat.

▶ Ist kein übergeordnetes Nomen vorhanden, so tritt das Plural-"s" ans Ende.

Ausnahmen

Beispiel: grown-ups – Erwachsene
▶ Bei Zusammensetzungen aus "man/woman" + Nomen treten beide Bestandteile in den Plural, wenn eine Geschlechtszugehörigkeit gemeint ist.
Beispiel: women clerks – weibliche Angestellte

Exercises

Übungen

Übungen

I. **Put the nouns into the plural.**
   Setze die Nomen in den Plural!

1. shop	8. photo	15. bush
2. child	9. tomato	16. boy
3. hovercraft	10. car	17. gentleman
4. bookshelf	11. bus	18. American
5. family	12. friend	19. Japanese
6. day	13. company	20. foot
7. wife	14. boat	21. cigarette

22. glass	32. body	42. brother
23. pen	33. chief	43. key
24. clock	34. apple	44. purse
25. piece	35. street	45. radio
26. ticket	36. manager	46. picture
27. house	37. teacher	47. tree
28. ferry	38. basis	48. box
29. window	39. letter	49. flower
30. nose	40. parrot	50. bag
31. toy	41. donkey	

II. Put the compound nouns into the plural.
Setze die zusammengesetzten Nomen in den Plural!

1. chairman	11. horseman	21. bus-driver
2. handbag	12. passer-by	22. ticket-collector
3. record-shop	13. sit-in	23. have-not
4. bathing-costume	14. schoolboy	24. snowman
5. son-in-law	15. armchair	25. fellow
6. air traffic controller	16. bookcase	26. schoolmaster
7. teach-in	17. man student	27. onlooker
8. mouse-trap	18. forget-me-not	28. bedroom
9. manservant	19. roundabout	29. good-for-nothing
10. woman-hater	20. broadcasting-station	30. dining-table

Plural or Singular
Plural oder Singular

Besonder-
heiten

Es gibt Nomen, die nur eine Singularform oder eine Pluralform haben, deren Bedeutung sich aber nicht unbedingt mit der Form deckt. Folgende Gruppen sind zu unterscheiden:

▶ Nomen, die *Singularform* haben und bei denen das dazugehörige *Verb im Singular* steht.
Dazu gehören:
a) Materialbezeichnungen, wie z. B.
butter, coal, wood, water, iron, salt, oil etc.
Beispiel: Butter is on special offer. – Butter ist im Sonderangebot.
b) einige Sammelbegriffe (viele davon auf "-ry"), wie z. B.
jewellery, machinery, crockery, garbage, luggage, hair, furniture etc.
Beispiel: My luggage is still in the car. – Mein Gepäck ist noch im Auto.

c) viele abstrakte Begriffe, wie z. B.

advice, information, knowledge, damage, progress, strength, confusion, work, evidence, homework etc.

Beispiel: His advice was very good. – Sein Rat war sehr gut.

Beachte: Einige der Wörter aus Gruppe a) können durch "a piece of . . ." eindeutige Singularbedeutung erhalten.

Beispiel: a piece of information – eine Information

a piece of furniture – ein Möbelstück

▶ Nomen, die *Singularform, aber Pluralbedeutung* haben und bei denen das zugehörige *Verb im Plural* steht.

Dazu gehören Gruppenbezeichnungen (collective nouns), wenn Tätigkeit oder Zustand der einzelnen Gruppenmitglieder gemeint sind, wie z. B.

police, family, staff, crew, band, choir, orchestra, government, company, firm, class, club, audience, cattle, group, party, jury, people etc.

Beispiel: The band are taking their instruments. – Die Band nimmt gerade ihre Instrumente.

Beachte: Wenn die Gesamtheit der Gruppe gemeint ist, steht das Verb im Singular.

Beispiel: The band is playing my favourite song. – Die Band spielt gerade mein Lieblingslied.

▶ Nomen, die *Pluralform, aber Singularbedeutung* haben, bei denen das zugehörige *Verb* aber dennoch *im Plural* steht.

Dazu gehören:

a) Paarwörter, d. h. Bezeichnungen für Gegenstände, die aus zwei gleichartigen Teilen bestehen, wie z. B.

scales, trousers, shorts, binoculars, glasses, scissors, jeans, tights, earphones, pyjamas etc.

Beispiel: Your trousers are on the bed. – Deine Hose ist auf dem Bett.

Beachte: Soll betont werden, dass es sich um einen einzigen Gegenstand handelt, so setzt man die Bezeichnung "a pair of . . ." hinzu.

Beispiel: a pair of glasses – eine Brille

b) folgende Wörter: stairs, goods, clothes, belongings, wages, outskirts.

▶ Nomen, die *Pluralform, aber Singularbedeutung* haben und bei denen das zugehörige *Verb im Singular* steht.

Dazu gehören:

a) Lehrfächer auf "-cs", wie z. B.

mathematics, physics, politics, linguistics, economics etc.

Beispiel: Mathematics is my favourite subject. – Mathematik ist mein Lieblingsfach.

b) einige Krankheiten, wie z. B.
mumps, measles etc.
Beispiel: Measles is a children's disease. – Masern ist eine Kinderkrankheit.
c) "news" und "the United States"
Beispiel: The news comes next. – Als Nächstes kommen die Nachrichten.
d) einige Spiele, wie z. B.
billiards, dominoes, darts etc.
Beispiel: Billiards is played in pubs. – Billard wird in Pubs gespielt.

Exercises

Übungen

Übungen

I. *Put the verbs in brackets into the correct Present Tense form.*
Setze die Verben in Klammern in die richtige Präsensform!

 1. The scissors (to be) in the drawer.
 2. These goods (to be) very expensive.
 3. This (to be) the news.
 4. The United States (to support) many other countries.
 5. Darts (to be played) by people of all ages.
 6. Electronics (to be) a very interesting subject.
 7. His wages (to be) very high.
 8. The police (to be) trying to catch the man.
 9. The stairs (to lead) to the cellar.
10. Some people (to be) very angry with you.
11. His knowledge of English (not/to be) very good.
12. I think your glasses (to lie) on the table.
13. This information (to be given) to me by the office.
14. My family (to have to) stay at home.
15. The government (to have) a major interest in solving the problem.
16. The outskirts of the city (not/to be) very nice.
17. His hair (to turn) grey.
18. Coal (to be found) in some parts of England.
19. Class 8b (just/to have) a party.
20. The party (to consist) of 25 students.
21. The scales (to be) in the kitchen.
22. Your trousers (to be) very dirty.
23. The cattle (to be) in the meadow.

146

24. My friend's family (to be) very nice persons.
25. The clergy (to be) at the meeting.

II. *Translate the following sentences.*
   Übersetze die folgenden Sätze!
1. Das Personal hat Urlaub.
2. Das Publikum wird gebeten ruhig zu sein.
3. Die Klasse schreibt gerade einen Test.
4. Die Hausaufgaben sind ziemlich schwierig.
5. Diese Informationen standen nicht in der Zeitung.
6. Große Fortschritte sind gemacht worden.
7. Deine Jeans ist zerrissen.
8. Die Leute waren sehr aufgeregt.
9. Mumps ist eine unangenehme Krankheit.
10. Das Fernglas gehört meinem Großvater.
11. Die Geschworenen ziehen sich zur Beratung zurück.
12. Der Chor singt gerade mein Lieblingslied.
13. Die kurze Hose ist schon im Koffer.
14. Die Gruppe besteht aus 10 Mitgliedern.
15. Die Firma benötigt neue Büroräume.

The Genitive: s-Genitive and of-Genitive

Der Genitiv/der „Wesfall": s-Genitiv und of-Genitiv

Im Englischen gibt es zwei Möglichkeiten den Genitiv oder „Wesfall" auszudrücken:

▶ den s-Genitiv
▶ den of-Genitiv

The s-Genitive

Der s-Genitiv

Der s-Genitiv wird verwendet um deutlich zu machen, dass Personen oder Tieren etwas gehört oder dass eine Zugehörigkeit vorliegt.
Beispiel: father's car – Vaters Auto (das Auto, das Vater gehört)

Die Bildung des s-Genitivs:

Bildung

Singular: Singularform des Nomens + 's
Plural: Pluralform des Nomens + ' (wenn der Plural auf -s endet)
Beispiel: Mary's book – Marys Buch
the boys' book – das Buch der Jungen
Beachte: Der Genitiv Singular bedeutet, dass der Besitzer *eine* Person (*ein* Tier) ist.
Der Genitiv Plural bedeutet, dass *mehrere* Personen (*mehrere* Tiere) Besitzer sind.
Beispiel: Genitiv Singular: Mary's book – Marys Buch
Genitiv Plural: the boys' book – das Buch der Jungen
Wie viele Gegenstände etc. (z. B. Buch, Bücher) besessen werden, hat keine Auswirkung auf die Genitivbildung.
Beispiel: Tom's book (Toms Buch)
Tom's books (Toms Bücher)

Zu beachten ist:

Besonder-heiten

▶ Hat ein Nomen *kein Plural-"s"*, so bildet man den Genitiv Plural wie bei einem Singularwort.
Beispiel: the women's dresses – die Kleider der Frauen
▶ Hat ein Nomen *bereits im Singular ein "-s"*, so bildet man den Genitiv Singular wie bei einem Pluralwort.
Beispiel: Mrs Evans' house – das Haus von Frau Evans

Der s-Genitiv wird verwendet:

Anwendung

▶ bei *Personen* und *Tieren*.
Beispiel: the boy's pullover – der Pullover des Jungen
the dog's bone – der Knochen des Hundes
▶ zur Angabe eines *Zeitmaßes*.
Beispiel: an hour's walk – ein einstündiger Spaziergang
2 years' experience – zweijährige Erfahrung
Beachte: Wenn die Zeitangabe einen Plural enthält, wird der Genitiv Plural verwendet.
▶ zur Bezeichnung von *Örtlichkeiten* bei Geschäften, Wohnungen etc. ohne Bezugswort.

Beispiel: at the butcher's – beim Metzger
at the doctor's – beim Arzt
at the Miller's – bei den Millers
Beachte: Auch hier steht der Genitiv Plural, wenn die Besitzer im Plural gemeint sind.

▶ oft bei *Staaten.*
Beispiel: Britain's problems – die Probleme Großbritanniens

The of-Genitive
Der of-Genitiv

Die Bildung des of-Genitivs:
Singular: "Of" + Artikel/Pronomen + Nomen im Singular
Beispiel: the colour of the car – die Farbe des Autos
Plural: "Of" + Artikel/Pronomen + Nomen im Plural
Beispiel: the colour of the cars – die Farbe der Autos

Bildung

Der of-Genitiv wird verwendet:
▶ bei *Sachbezeichnungen.*
Beispiel: the end of the road – das Ende der Straße
▶ bei Personen, wenn ein *langes Attribut* (Beifügung) nachgestellt ist.
Beispiel: the house of our reporter stationed in London – das Haus unseres in London stationierten Reporters.

Anwendung

Double Genitive
Doppelter Genitiv

Der doppelte Genitiv ist eine Kombination aus of- und s-Genitiv.
Beispiel: a play of Shakespeare's – eines von Shakespeares Stücken

Der doppelte Genitiv steht:
▶ bei *Personen,* wenn ein *Teilverhältnis* ausgedrückt werden soll.
Beispiel: a friend of Peter's – ein Freund Peters (einer von Peters Freunden; er hat also noch andere Freunde)
▶ nach *a, some, any, serveral* oder *Zahlwort* + Nomen.
Beispiel: some of Peter's books – einige von Peters Büchern

Anwendung

149

The s-Genitive without a Referent
Der s-Genitiv ohne Bezugswort

Der s-Genitiv kann ohne ein ihm folgendes Bezugswort stehen, wenn

▶ ein bereits genanntes Nomen nicht wiederholt werden soll.
   Beispiel: If you haven't got a bag, you can have my mother's (bag).
   Wenn du keine Tasche hast, kannst du die (Tasche) meiner Mutter haben.
▶ bei Geschäften, Wohnungen etc., wenn Nomen wie "house", "flat" etc. als selbstverständlich gelten.
   Beispiel: at the Bakers' [house] – bei den Bakers

Exercises

Übungen

I. Write the s-genitive.
   Schreibe den s-Genitiv!

1. (my cat) toys
2. (mother) purse
3. (the ladies) hairdresser
4. (Fred) room
5. (women) magazines
6. (my sister) birthday
7. (father) lighter
8. (the girls) handbags
9. (James) uniform
10. (a five minutes) walk
11. (grandfather) armchair
12. (today) newspaper
13. (the greengrocer)
14. (America) government
15. (the chemist)
16. (your aunt) invitation
17. (the Smiths) house
18. (our neighbours) garden
19. (the dog) collar
20. (the secretaries) typewriters
21. (my little brother) bike
22. (the boss) desk
23. (my brother) keys
24. (Anne) camera
25. (my friends) children
26. (tomorrow) date
27. (Mr Carter) argument
28. (the morning) post
29. (my parents) decision
30. (the students) room

II. Write the genitive. Use either s- or of-genitive.
   Schreibe den Genitiv! Benutze entweder s- oder of-Genitiv!

1. (the garden) wall
2. (tea) cup
3. (the book) page
4. (3 minutes) discussion
5. (the bird) cage
6. (my employer) office
7. (the picture) frame
8. (the briefcase) loss
9. (Shakespeare) work
10. (Madame Tussaud)

11. (London) University
12. (last month) business
13. (Mr Red) secretary
14. (the article) headline
15. at the (Porters)
16. (the letter) length
17. (the teachers) room
18. (the old man) coat
19. (the Beatles) records
20. (the manager) salary

21. (the door) lock
22. (the waiter) purse
23. (the book) size
24. (the guests) order
25. (the men) suitcases
26. (the painting) colour
27. (my sister) CD-player
28. (my friend) party
29. (Paul) birthday
30. (the flowers) growth

Final Test: The Noun
Abschlusstest: das Nomen

Translate the following sentences.
Übersetze die folgenden Sätze!

1. Die gestrigen Nachrichten waren schockierend.
2. Einer von Herrn Grants Kollegen ist krank geworden.
3. Die Menge stand herum, als ich kam, und alle warteten darauf beim Bäcker ein Autogramm des Sportlers zu bekommen.
4. Nach der zweistündigen Sitzung waren alle Mitglieder des Clubs ziemlich müde.
5. Die Besatzung des Flugzeugs streikt gerade. Wir werden also mit einer der Privatmaschinen meines Chefs fliegen müssen.
6. Die zweite von Karls Ideen scheint die beste zu sein.
7. Der Schlafanzug von Davis ist schon wieder verschwunden. Er wird einen von Tom nehmen müssen.
8. Das Hab und Gut des Bettlers bestand aus einem Koffer und einer alten Uniformhose.
9. Die Gruppe arbeitet noch an ihrem Projekt, aber die finanzielle Situation der Firma wird dem Projekt bald ein Ende setzen.
10. Durch die Explosion des Gasherds wurde großer Schaden verursacht.

The Article

Der Artikel/
das Geschlechtswort

Im Englischen gibt es wie in der deutschen Sprache **bestimmte (definite)** und **unbestimmte (indefinite) Artikel (articles).** Allerdings gibt es im Englischen keine verschiedenen Formen für männlich, weiblich oder sächlich.

Bestimmte Artikel	Unbestimmte Artikel
der die } the das	ein eine } a(n) ein

The Definite Article
Der bestimmte Artikel

Vor gesprochenem Vokal (Selbstlaut: a, e, i, o, u) spricht man den bestimmten Artikel "the" [ði:] statt [ðə] aus.
Beispiel: the book [ðə] ; the orange[ði:]
    aber: the university [ðə], weil nicht [u], sondern [j] als erster Laut gesprochen wird.

Use of the Definitive Article
Der Gebrauch des bestimmten Artikels

Omission of the Definite Article
Das Fehlen des bestimmten Artikels

Anders als im Deutschen steht **kein** bestimmter Artikel:
▶ a) bei *abstrakten Begriffen,* wie z. B.
    life, time, peace, nature, work, history, society etc.
  b) bei *Stoffbezeichnungen,* wie z. B.
    bread, coal, water etc.

c) bei *Gattungsbezeichnungen im Plural,* wie z.B.
children, pupils, animals etc.
Voraussetzung ist, dass sie *im allgemeinen Sinn gebraucht werden.*

▶ bei *Eigennamen* und *geographischen Bezeichnungen* im Singular (z.B. Länder, Berge, Seen etc.)

Beispiel: Buckingham Palace is near Trafalgar Square. – Der Buckinghampalast ist in der Nähe des Trafalgarplatzes.

häufige Ausnahmen: the Tower of London
the High Street
the City
the Golden Gate Bridge
the British Museum
the World Trade Center
the White House
und Flüsse, z.B. the Rhine

▶ bei *Monaten, Wochentagen, Tages-, Mahl- und Jahreszeiten.*

Beispiel: December was very cold. – Der Dezember war sehr kalt.

Ausnahmen: in the morning/evening/night/ . . .
during the afternoon/night/ . . .
throughout the day/afternoon/ . . .

Außerdem steht der bestimmte Artikel, wenn die Begriffe näher bestimmt werden.

Beispiel: The dinner I had with Sue was great.

▶ bei *Institutionen* wie z.B. church, college, hospital, prison, school, university, wenn nicht das Gebäude, sondern die Funktion gemeint ist.

Beispiel: Every Sunday I go to church. – Ich gehe jeden Sonntag in die Kirche.

aber: There is a school near the church. – Es gibt eine Schule in der Nähe der Kirche (in der Nähe des Gebäudes).

▶ bei *"by"* + *Verkehrsmittel.*

Beispiel: I go by train. – Ich fahre mit dem Zug.

▶ a) vor *"most of".*

Beispiel: Most of the students were in time. – Die meisten der Schüler waren pünktlich.

b) vor *"most"* (die Mehrheit, der größte Teil).

Beispiel: Most students were in time. – Die meisten Schüler waren pünktlich.

aber: "most" als Mengenbezeichnung kann mit oder ohne Artikel stehen.

Beispiel: He made (the) most mistakes. – Er machte die meisten Fehler.

▶ in folgenden *Ausdrücken:*

to be in office	– im Amt sein
to be in opposition	– in der Opposition sein
to be at hand	– zur Hand sein
to be in power	– an der Macht sein
to keep in mind	– im Gedächtnis behalten
to come to light	– ans Licht kommen
to take in hand	– in die Hand nehmen
to get out of hand	– aus der Hand gleiten
to lose courage	– den Mut verlieren
to lose sight of s. th.	– etwas aus den Augen verlieren
to put to flight	– in die Flucht schlagen
to take (to) flight	– die Flucht ergreifen
to shake hands	– die Hand schütteln
at first sight	– auf den ersten Blick
out of sight, out of mind	– aus den Augen, aus dem Sinn
in practice	– in der Praxis

Inclusion of the Definite Article
Das Setzen des bestimmten Artikels

Besonderheiten

Anders als im Deutschen steht der bestimmte Artikel:

▶ bei *Musikinstrumenten.*

   Beispiel: He plays the guitar. – Er spielt Gitarre.

▶ nach *all, both, half, double, twice etc.*

   Beispiel: He drove at double the speed. – Er fuhr mit doppelter Geschwindigkeit.

▶ bei folgenden *Ausdrücken:*

in the absence of	– in Abwesenheit von
by the help of	– mit Hilfe von
in the presence of	– in Gegenwart von
to be out of the question	– nicht infrage kommen

Anders als im Deutschen kann der bestimmte Artikel nicht alleine stehen. Er nimmt dann stellvertretend für das fehlende Nomen das Stützwort "one" oder stellvertretend für ein Nomen im Plural "ones" zu sich.

Beispiel: Which picture do you like best?   – The one in the window.
Welches Bild gefällt dir am besten?   – Das (Bild) im Fenster.
Which cars do you like best?   – The ones over there.
Welche Autos gefallen dir am besten?   – Die (Autos) da drüben.

The Indefinite Article

Der unbestimmte Artikel

Vor gesprochenem Vokal (Selbstlaut: a, e, i, o, u) wird statt "a" "an" benutzt.
Beispiel: a book
            an orange
    aber: an hour, weil nicht [h], sondern [a] als erster Laut gesprochen wird.

Use of the Indefinite Article

Der Gebrauch des unbestimmten Artikels

Inclusion of the Indefinite Article
Das Setzen des unbestimmten Artikels

Anders als im Deutschen steht der unbestimmte Artikel

▶ bei *Berufen,* Angehörigen von *Volksgruppen, Nationalitäten, religiösen Gruppen oder politischen Parteien,* wenn die Person als Vertreter einer solchen Gruppe charakterisiert wird.
  Beispiel: I am a mechanic. – Ich bin Mechaniker.
  Ausnahmen: a) Ohne "a/an" stehen Titel- oder Rangbezeichnungen mit "of".
                  Beispiel: the rank of captain – der Kapitänsrang
            b) Nach "turn" (werden) steht kein "a/an".
                  Beispiel: He turned Democrat. – Er wurde Demokrat.

▶ zwischen *"as" und (Attribut +) Nomen.*
  Beispiel: I got the book as a present. – Ich bekam das Buch als Geschenk.
            He is known as a good friend. – Er ist als guter Freund bekannt.

▶ bei folgenden *Ausdrücken:*

to be at an end	– am Ende sein
to come to an end	– zum Ende kommen
to be in a hurry	– in Eile sein
to be in a good temper/mood	– in guter Stimmung sein
it's a pity	– es ist schade
to have a good appetite	– guten Appetit haben
to have a fancy for s. th.	– Gefallen an etwas finden
to have a headache/temperature	– Kopfschmerzen/Fieber haben
to make a noise	– Lärm machen
to make it a condition	– es zur Bedingung machen
to make it a rule	– es sich zur Regel machen

to seek a quarrel	– Streit suchen
to take a great interest in	– großes Interesse haben an
as a rule	– in der Regel
as a whole	– als Ganzes
at a distance	– aus der Ferne
for a change	– zur Abwechslung
in a friendly manner	– auf freundliche Art
in a great measure	– in hohem Maße
without a break	– ohne Unterbrechung
without a ticket	– ohne Fahrkarte etc.

▶ vor *Mengen-, Maß- und Zeitangaben* in der Bedeutung „pro/je".

Beispiel: Sugar costs 60 p a kilo. – Zucker kostet 60 p je Kilo.

▶ nach *such, half, quite, rather, what, so + Adjektiv* und nach *too + Adjektiv;* aber nur bei zählbaren Begriffen, d. h. nur bei solchen, die „viele/wenige" vor sich haben können.

Beispiel: such a nice house – so ein nettes Haus

too difficult a question – eine zu schwierige Frage

aber: such nonsense – so ein Unsinn ("nonsense" ist nicht zählbar)

▶ bei Zahlen in der Bedeutung von "one".

Beispiel: a hundred (one hundred) – (ein)hundert

Exercises

Übungen

I. *Put "a" or "an" in front of the words.*
   Setze "a" oder "an" vor die Wörter!

1. cup of tea	**11.** order	**21.** ideal solution
2. old lady	**12.** room	**22.** apple
3. end	**13.** bike	**23.** tree
4. pencil	**14.** roadmap	**24.** error
5. action	**15.** van	**25.** clock
6. dress	**16.** umbrella	**26.** old house
7. sign	**17.** honour	**27.** wall
8. American businessman	**18.** telephone	**28.** desk
9. window	**19.** English book	**29.** building
10. radio	**20.** table	**30.** street

Der Artikel
Bestimmter und unbestimmter Artikel

II. Put in "a" or "an", but only where necessary.
Setze "a" oder "an" ein, aber nur, wenn notwendig!

1. Pam has ... nice sister.
2. He went out without ... umbrella.
3. I was in ... hurry, so I forgot to buy ... ticket.
4. He was treated as ... good friend.
5. Susan's father is ... artist.
6. I have ... terrible headache.
7. Mary Stuart was ... Catholic.
8. The shop sells about ... hundred fridges ... year.
9. What ... wonderful castle!
10. This student visited London in ... June.
11. His car does 90 miles ... hour.
12. Our neighbour is rather ... nice man.
13. They live in ... bungalow at the seaside.
14. ... certain Mr Smith wants to speak to you.
15. We usually watch ... film at 7 o'clock.
16. As ... coach he was ... great success.
17. I want to become ... engineer.
18. He is not in ... good temper today.
19. We haven't had such ... good weekend for years.
20. Sally was ... stewardess before she became ... actress.

III. Put in "the" where necessary.
Setze "the" ein, wenn notwendig!

1. ... life is short.
2. ... life of Charlie Chaplin was very interesting.
3. They charged us double ... price, because we were tourists.
4. Don't be late for ... dinner.
5. When does ... school begin?
6. He works at ... hospital in ... Main Street.
7. ... gold is more expensive than ... silver.
8. ... lady over there is ... waitress.
9. The workers are painting ... walls of ... prison.
10. ... bread is made from ... flour.
11. I can't keep ... name in ... mind.
12. ... students are often lazy. (allgemeine Aussage)
13. On ... Sunday before our holidays we went to see ... Grandma.
14. Many people spend their lunchtime at ... Hyde Park.
15. ... Museum of London shows ... history of ... town.
16. In ... absence of ... Mr Bat ... decision was made.
17. Listen! Sue is playing ... piano.

18. . . . most children like sweets.

19. Every morning my father goes to . . . work by . . . tube.

20. During . . . afternoon it got colder.

IV. Put the missing articles (definite or indefinite) in the right place.
Setze die fehlenden bestimmten oder unbestimmten Artikel an die richtige Stelle!

1. I have never seen such beautiful pullover.

2. He had already drunk half bottle of wine when I came home.

3. It's too absurd story to believe.

4. Tom is quite nice boy.

5. Both parents were ill.

6. He is regarded as good lawyer.

7. This sherry is £ 5.50 bottle.

8. What good view!

9. Half sum could be raised.

10. Don't be in such hurry.

Final Test: The Article

Abschlusstest: der Artikel

I. Put in "a", "an" or "the" where necessary.
Setze "a", "an" oder "the" ein, wenn notwendig!

1. Hans had to stay in . . . hospital for 2 weeks.

2. In this photo you can see . . . Tower of London.

3. Last week I saw rather . . . nice dress in the shop-window.

4. . . . Turkey is . . . very interesting country.

5. How quickly . . . time passes.

6. . . . most people in this town are steelworkers.

7. . . . eagles can fly very high.

8. . . . Mont Blanc is . . . highest mountain in Europe.

9. Many employees think that . . . Monday is . . . worst day of . . . week.

10. You have to take . . . medicine three times . . . day.

11. We can talk about it at . . . lunch.

12. . . . school begins at 8 o'clock.

13. We can go by . . . bus for . . . change.

14. He goes on holidays twice . . . year.

15. Mr Moore turned . . . Socialist.

II. Translate the following sentences.
Übersetze die folgenden Sätze!

1. Die Natur ist manchmal grausam.
2. Die Arbeit, die ich momentan mache, ist langweilig.
3. Nach seinem Abitur wird mein Sohn die Universität besuchen.
4. Der Hausmeister befestigte einen Lautsprecher auf dem Dach der Schule.
5. Als Simon den Hund sah, ergriff er die Flucht.
6. In der Regel ist unsere Sekretärin immer sehr zuverlässig.
7. Er ist so ein schwieriger Junge.
8. Als guter Freund kann ich dir folgenden Rat geben.
9. Gestern war ein ziemlich kalter Tag.
10. Peter ist ein ziemlich kräftiger Junge. Er hat immer guten Appetit.
11. Er arbeitete 5 Stunden ohne Unterbrechung.
12. Es ist wirklich schade, dass du nicht kommen kannst.
13. Die meisten Schüler mögen Grammatik nicht.
14. Mein Onkel arbeitet als Psychiater im Gefängnis.
15. Einer seiner Patienten ist „Big Sam", der seit fünf Jahren im Gefängnis ist.

The Adjective

Das Adjektiv/
das Eigenschaftswort

Ein Adjektiv dient zur Bezeichnung von Eigenschaften eines Nomens. Ein Adjektiv ist im Englischen in seiner Form *nicht* veränderlich nach **Numerus (Einzahl oder Mehrzahl), Genus (männlich, weiblich, sächlich)** und **Kasus (Fall).**
Beispiel: the blue car – the blue cars / das blaue Auto – die blauen Autos

Die Funktionen des Adjektivs:

Funktionen

▶ Steht ein Adjektiv vor dem Nomen, so ist es Attribut (Beifügung) zum Nomen. Man spricht von *attributivem Gebrauch.*
Beispiel: The **little** boy plays outside. – Der kleine Junge spielt draußen.
"Little" ist Attribut zu "boy".

▶ Ist ein Adjektiv Teil des Prädikats (Satzaussage), so spricht man von *prädikativem Gebrauch.*
Beispiel: The car is new. – Der Wagen ist neu.
Prädikat

▶ Adjektive können als Nomen benutzt werden (d.h. als *Gerundiv).*
Beispiel: the poor – die Armen
a) Ein Adjektiv kann als Nomen benutzt werden, wenn ein Artikel vorausgeht und eine Gruppe bezeichnet werden soll. Das Adjektiv hat dann kein Plural-"s", wird aber mit Pluralverb konstruiert.
Beispiel: The blind have a special reading system. – Blinde haben ein spezielles Leseverfahren.
Sind Einzelpersonen gemeint (nicht die Gesamtheit der Personen), so muss dem Adjektiv ein Nomen folgen oder das Stützwort "one" bzw. "ones".
Beispiel: the blind man ...
b) Ein Adjektiv kann als Nomen benutzt werden, wenn etwas Abstraktes gemeint ist. In diesem Fall liegt Singularbedeutung vor und das Verb steht im Singular.
Beispiel: The good doesn't always win. – Das Gute siegt nicht immer.
Ist etwas Konkretes gemeint, muss jedoch "thing" oder Ähnliches dem Adjektiv folgen.
Beispiel: The good thing about the story was ... – Das Gute an der Geschichte war ...

The Comparison of the Adjective
Die Steigerung des Adjektivs

Die meisten Adjektive können gesteigert werden, d. h. man kann zu der **Grundstufe (Positiv)** eine **Steigerungsstufe (Komparativ)** und eine **Höchststufe (Superlativ)** bilden.

Beispiel: Positiv (Positive)   : neu   – new
Komparativ (Comparative) : neuer   – newer
Superlativ (Superlative)   : (am) neuesten – (the) newest

The Regular Comparison with "-er"/"-est"
Die regelmäßige Steigerung mit "-er"/"-est"

Mit "-er" (Komparativ) und "-est" (Superlativ) werden folgende Adjektive gesteigert:

*Grund-
regel*

▶ *einsilbige Adjektive.*
    Beispiel: low – lower – lowest
                niedrig – niedriger – am niedrigsten
                high – higher – highest
                hoch – höher – am höchsten
▶ *zweisilbige Adjektive auf "-er", "-le", "-ow", "-y".*
    Beispiel: clever – cleverer – cleverest
                schlau – schlauer – am schlausten
                simple – simpler – simplest
                einfach – einfacher – am einfachsten

Rechtschreibbesonderheiten:
▶ y wird zu i.
    Beispiel: easy – easier – easiest
▶ Wegfall von stummem End -"e".
    Beispiel: large – larger – largest
▶ Verdoppelung des Endkonsonanten nach kurzem, betontem Vokal (a, e, i, o, u).
    Beispiel: thin – thinner – thinnest

*Recht-
schreibung*

The Regular Comparison with "more"/"most"
Die regelmäßige Steigerung mit "more"/"most"

*Grund-
regel*

Mit "more" (Komparativ) und "most" (Superlativ) werden folgende Adjektive gesteigert:

▶ *zweisilbige Adjektive,* die nicht auf "-er", "-le", "-ow", "-y" enden.
   Beispiel: useful   – more useful   – most useful
              nützlich   – nützlicher   – am nützlichsten
▶ *drei- und mehrsilbige Adjektive.*
   Beispiel: interesting – more interesting – most interesting
              interessant – interessanter – am interessantesten

The Irregular Comparison
Die unregelmäßige Steigerung

Ausnahmen

Einige Adjektive werden unregelmäßig gesteigert:

good	– better	– best
well	– better	– best
bad	– worse	– worst
ill	– worse	– worst
little (klein)	– smaller	– smallest
little (wenig)	– less	– least
much	– more	– most
many	– more	– most

Adjectives with Different Comparison Forms
Adjektive mit verschiedenen Steigerungsformen

*Besonder-
heiten*

Einige Adjektive haben zwei Komparativ- oder Superlativformen mit unterschiedlichen Anwendungsweisen:

▶ late – later – latest (zeitlich)
  late – latter – latter (Reihenfolge)
▶ far – further/farther – furthest/farthest (räumliche Entfernung)
  far – further – ––– („weiter" im Sinne von „zusätzlich", im übertragenen Sinne benutzt)

▶ near	– nearer	– nearest	(örtlich)
near	– –––	– next	(Reihenfolge)
▶ old	– older	– oldest	(allgemein)
old	– elder	– eldest	(bei Familienmitgliedern)

Sentences with Comparisons
Der Vergleich im Satz

▶ Zum Ausdruck der *Gleichheit:*
as + (Positiv) + as
Beispiel: Linda is as clever as Bill. – Linda ist so schlau wie Bill.

▶ zum Ausdruck der *Ungleichheit:*
not as + (Positiv) + as
Beispiel: Linda is not as tall as Bill. – Linda ist nicht so groß wie Bill.
oder:
less + (Positiv) + than
Beispiel: Linda is less tall than Bill. – Linda ist weniger groß als Bill.
Beachte: Steht nach "than" ein Personalpronomen, so steht dieses im "object case" (z. B. me, him, her etc.).

▶ zum Ausdruck eines *höheren Grades:*
(Komparativ) + than
Beispiel: Susan is taller than Mary. – Susan ist größer als Mary.

▶ zum Ausdruck des *höchsten Grades:*
the + (Superlativ)
Beispiel: The tower is the highest in the world. – Der Turm ist der höchste der Welt.

▶ zum Ausdruck einer *allmählichen Steigerung:*
(Komparativ) + and + (Komparativ)
Beispiel: The situation is getting worse and worse. – Die Situation wird immer schlechter.
Beachte: Bei Adjektiven, die mit "more"/"most" gesteigert werden, drückt man die allmähliche Steigerung mit "more and more" aus.
Beispiel: The discussion got more and more interesting. – Die Diskussion wurde immer interessanter.

▶ zum Ausdruck von „je ... desto ...":
the + (Komparativ) (...) the + (Komparativ) (...)
Beispiel: The angrier the teacher got, the louder the children became.
Je wütender der Lehrer wurde, desto lauter wurden die Kinder.

Exercises

Übungen

I. Write down the comparatives and superlatives of the following adjectives.
Steigere die folgenden Adjektive!

1. clean	11. great	21. efficient
2. hot	12. narrow	22. nervous
3. radical	13. small	23. cheap
4. thirsty	14. young	24. dirty
5. nice	15. quick	25. characteristic
6. soft	16. polite	26. sunny
7. happy	17. large	27. pretty
8. democratic	18. difficult	28. lucky
9. thick	19. cool	29. ugly
10. fat	20. simple	30. competent

II. Translate the following expressions.
Übersetze die folgenden Ausdrücke!

1. leichter als (easy)
2. so teuer wie (expensive)
3. je eher, desto besser (soon/good)
4. am kleinsten (small)
5. so schön wie (nice)
6. nicht so alt wie (old)
7. weniger groß als (big)
8. immer teurer (expensive)
9. am besten (good)
10. fauler als (lazy)
11. so billig wie (cheap)
12. länger als (long)
13. immer besser (good)
14. am schwierigsten (difficult)
15. weniger hübsch als (nice)
16. am interessantesten (interesting)
17. neuer als (new)
18. so dick wie (thick)
19. weniger höflich als (polite)
20. je mehr Kinder, desto lebhafter (many/lively)
21. so müde wie (tired)
22. am reichsten (rich)
23. nicht so lang wie (long)
24. durstiger als (thirsty)

Final Test: The Adjective

Abschlusstest: das Adjektiv

Translate the following sentences.

Übersetze die folgenden Sätze!

1. Die Reichen können sich Dienstpersonal (servants) leisten.
2. Diese Übung ist schwieriger als die letzte.
3. Das Auto meines Vaters ist fast so schnell wie ein Sportwagen.
4. Mr Pit ist der älteste Einwohner dieser Stadt.
5. Lebensmittel werden immer teurer.
6. Manchmal verstehen die Jungen die Alten nicht.
7. Mein älterer Bruder arbeitet bei einer Bank.
8. Die Polizei macht weitere Ermittlungen (investigations).
9. Wo ist die nächste Bushaltestelle?
10. Die Schüler werden immer kindischer.
11. Weniger Leute als erwartet kamen zum Konzert.
12. Mein Freund ist zwei Jahre älter als ich.
13. Je mehr er hat, desto mehr will er.
14. Er ist weniger dumm, als ich dachte.
15. Mein Freund ist der intelligenteste Junge der Klasse.
16. In der letzten Hälfte des Jahrhunderts kam es zu wirtschaftlichen Schwierigkeiten.
17. Sam ist nicht so gut wie Kelly in der Schule.
18. Je mehr er spricht, desto besser wird sein Englisch.
19. Immer weniger Leute besuchen den Gottesdienst.
20. Weitere Einzelheiten teile ich Ihnen später mit.

The Adverb
Das Adverb/
das Umstandswort

Im Englischen gibt es zwei Arten von Adverbien:

► **ursprüngliche Adverbien** (z. B. here, there, now etc.), die vor allem Orts- und Zeitangaben darstellen.
► **von Adjektiven abgeleitete Adverbien** (z. B. nicely).

Von **„adverbialer Bestimmung" (adverbial phrase)** spricht man, wenn das Adverb als nähere Bestimmung zum Verb zum selbstständigen Satzglied wird. Ähnlich wie im Deutschen zählen zu adverbialen Bestimmungen auch Zusammensetzungen aus Präpositionen und Nomen.
Beispiel: at home

The Formation of Adverbs
Die Bildungsweise von Adverbien

Bildung

Die Bildung der Adverbien:
Viele abgeleitete Adverbien werden gebildet, indem man an das Adjektiv "-ly" anhängt.
Beispiel: nice (Adjektiv) – nicely (Adverb)

Ausnahmen

Bei einigen Adjektiven gelten jedoch Sonderregeln:
► Bei mehrsilbigen Adjektiven wird y zu i.
   Beispiel: easy – easily
► Nach Konsonant (Mitlaut) entfällt "-le".
   Beispiel: simple – simply
► Stummes End-"e" entfällt bei "due", "true", "whole".
   Beispiel: whole – wholly
            true – truly

► Endet ein Adjektiv bereits auf "-ly", so bildet man das Adverb mit "in a . . . way".

Beispiel: friendly – in a friendly way

► Das Adverb zu "difficult" heißt "with difficulty".

► Das Adverb zu "good" heißt "well".

► Endet ein Adjektiv auf "-ic", so bildet man das Adverb mit "-ally".

Beispiel: systematic   – systematically

Ausnahme: public   – publicly

► Adjektive auf "-ll" bilden das Adverb nur mit "-y"

Beispiel: dull – dully

► Adjektiv und Adverb haben manchmal gleiche Form und gleiche Bedeutung.

Dazu gehören: daily, hourly, weekly, monthly, quarterly, yearly etc.

Außerdem: early, likely, fast, long, far, straight, low

► Adjektiv und Adverb haben manchmal gleiche Form, aber unterschiedliche Bedeutungen. Dazu gehören:

Begriff	Als Adjektiv	Als Adverb
well	gesund	gut
ill	krank	schlecht
still	still	noch
only	einzig	erst, nur

► Manche Adjektive haben zwei Adverbformen, die gleiche oder unterschiedliche Bedeutungen haben können. Dazu gehören:

Adjektiv	1. Adverb	2. Adverb
right (richtig)	right (richtig)	rightly (zurecht)
slow (langsam)	slow (langsam)	slowly (langsam)
hard (hart)	hard (hart)	hardly (kaum)
fair (fair)	fair (fair)	fairly (ziemlich)
deep (tief)	deep (tief)	deeply (zutiefst)
pretty (hübsch)	pretty (ziemlich)	prettily (hübsch)
high (hoch)	high (hoch)	highly (höchst)
late (spät)	late (spät)	lately (in letzter Zeit)
most (am meisten)	most (am meisten)	mostly (meistens)
just (gerecht)	just (nur)	justly (gerecht)
ready (fertig)	ready (fertig)	readily (bereitwillig)
short (kurz)	short (kurz)	shortly (in Kürze)
express (ausdrücklich)	express (per Eilpost)	expressly (ausdrücklich)

Ausnahmen

The Comparison of Adverbs

Die Steigerung von Adverbien

Grund-regel

▶ Ursprüngliche Adverbien und mit Adjektiven formgleiche Adverbien werden mit *"-er"/"-est"* gesteigert.

Beispiel: soon – sooner – soonest

fast – faster – fastest

early – earlier – earliest

▶ Abgeleitete Adverbien auf *"-ly"* werden mit *"more"/"most"* gesteigert.

Beispiel: easily – more easily – most easily

▶ Manche Adverbien haben *unregelmäßige Steigerungsformen.*

Ausnahmen

Dazu gehören:

well	– better	– best
much	– more	– most
little	– less	– least
badly/ill	– worse	– worst
near	– nearer	– nearest
---	---	– next
far	– further/farther	– furthest/farthest
---	– further	---
late	– later	– latest
---	----	– last

Wie bei den Adjektiven, von denen diese Adverbien abgeleitet sind, ist mit Doppelformen oft Doppelbedeutung verbunden. Siehe deshalb S. 162 f.

The Position of Adverbs and Adverbial Phrases

Die Stellung von Adverbien und adverbialen Bestimmungen

Adverbien und adverbiale Bestimmungen haben bestimmte, festgelegte Positionen im Satz. Wo ein Adverb oder eine adverbiale Bestimmung stehen kann, hängt von seiner Bedeutung ab. Unterschieden werden allgemein folgende Klassen von Adverbien:

Adverbs of Manner
Adverbien der Art und Weise

Sie beschreiben die Art und Weise, die Methode, wie eine Handlung ausgeführt wird (z. B. quickly, easily, in a friendly way etc.). In diese Gruppe gehören vor allem Adverbien auf "-ly". Adverbien der Art und Weise können an drei verschiedenen Stellen im Satz stehen:

▶ *am Satzende.*

Position

 Beispiel: He repaired the car **easily.**
▶ *vor dem Vollverb* oder *nach dem ersten Hilfsverb,* wenn der Betonungsschwerpunkt auf dem Verb liegen soll.
 Beispiel: He **easily** repaired the car.
 He has **quickly** eaten his lunch.
 Beachte: Sie stehen nach dem Vollverb, wenn kein Objekt folgt.
 Beispiel: He spoke **slowly.**
▶ *am Satzanfang,* wenn sie einen Rahmen für den folgenden Satz bilden sollen. Das Adverb wird dann durch Komma abgetrennt.
 Beispiel: **Silently,** he left the house.

Adverbs of Frequency
Adverbien der Häufigkeit

Sie geben an, wie oft eine Handlung getan wird (z. B. often, seldom, always, once, monthly, generally etc.). Adverbien der Häufigkeit können an drei verschiedenen Stellen im Satz stehen:

▶ *am Satzende,* wenn es sich um Adverbien der bestimmten Häufigkeit handelt (z. B. once, daily, weekly etc.).

Position

 Beispiel: She goes shopping **weekly.**
 Beachte: Stehen diese Adverbien am Satzende zusammen mit anderen Adverbien, so wird folgende Reihenfolge eingehalten: Ortsadverb – Adverb der Häufigkeit – Zeitadverb.
 Beispiel: She went shopping <u>in London</u> <u>twice</u> <u>last week.</u>

 Ort Häufig- Zeit
 keit

▶ *vor dem Vollverb* bzw. *nach dem ersten Hilfsverb,* wenn es sich um Adverbien der unbestimmten Häufigkeit handelt (z. B. usually, always, sometimes etc.).

Beispiel: She **always** goes shopping on Friday.

She has **always** done her shopping on Friday.

Beachte: Wird "to be" als Vollverb benutzt, so steht das Adverb dahinter.

Beispiel: She is **usually** late.

▶ *am Satzanfang* um einen zeitlichen Rahmen für die folgende Aussage zu setzen (diese Position geht nicht bei "just").

Beispiel: Usually, there aren't many tourists in this area.

Adverbs of Place and Time
Adverbien des Ortes und der Zeit

Adverbien des Ortes und der Zeit können *am Satzanfang oder am Satzende* stehen, wobei die Satzanfangsposition meist nur benutzt wird, wenn ein Kontrast ausgedrückt werden soll. Treffen beide Adverbien aufeinander, so gilt die Regel „Ort vor Zeit".

Beispiel:	Ort:	(in London)	I met Paul **in London.**
	Zeit:	(yesterday)	I met Paul **yesterday.**
	Ort vor Zeit:	(in London yesterday)	I met Paul **in London yesterday.**

Adverbs of Degree
Gradadverbien

Gradadverbien drücken eine Verstärkung, eine Abschwächung oder eine Einschränkung aus (z. B. completely, almost, hardly etc.). Sie können drei verschiedene Positionen im Satz einnehmen.

▶ a) Sie stehen *vor dem Vollverb* bzw. *nach dem ersten Hilfsverb,* wenn sie eine Einschränkung ausdrücken.

Beispiel: He **hardly** answered me.

He has **hardly** answered me.

▶ b) Sie stehen *vor dem Vollverb* oder *nach dem letzten Hilfsverb,* wenn sie eine Verstärkung ausdrücken.

Beispiel: He **greatly** admired her.

He would have **greatly** admired her.

Ausnahme: "almost" und "nearly" stehen nach dem ersten Hilfsverb.

Beispiel: He would **almost** have helped her.

▶ *Am Satzende* können folgende Gradadverbien stehen:
a bit, a little, a great deal, a lot, by far, for sure, for certain
Beispiel: He didn't like it **a bit.**

▶ Gradadverbien, die ein Adjektiv oder Adverb näher bestimmen, stehen *vor diesem Wort.*
Beispiel: He is **very** nice.

Adverbs Modifying a Whole Sentence
Adverbien, die sich auf einen ganzen Satz beziehen

Adverbien, die sich auf einen ganzen Satz beziehen, stehen am *Satzanfang.* Dazu gehören:

Position

in fact, maybe, naturally, obviously, perhaps, possibly, really, surely, (un)fortunately, (un)luckily.
Beispiel: Unfortunately, he couldn't come.

Several Adverbs at the End of a Sentence
Mehrere Adverbien am Satzende

Stehen zwei oder mehr Adverbien am Satzende, so gelten folgende Regeln:

Position

▶ Adverbien der Art und Weise vor Orts- und Zeitadverbien
(Merkregel: A – O – Z; wie im Alphabet).
Beispiel: He went slowly to the door.

▶ Richtungsangabe vor Ortsangabe.
Beispiel: He went to the shop at the corner.

▶ Ort vor Zeit (Merkregel: O – Z; wie im Alphabet).
Beispiel: He went to Spain last summer.

▶ genauere Zeitangabe vor allgemeinerer Zeitangabe.
Beispiel: He arrived at 7 o'clock in the morning.

Exercises

Übungen

I. *Write down the suitable adverbs.*

Schreibe die passenden Adverbien auf!

1. direct	10. silly	19. good	28. hopeful
2. fast	11. cheap	20. sad	29. basic
3. full	12. probable	21. far	30. wise
4. fantastic	13. busy	22. powerful	31. angry
5. correct	14. pretty	23. sweet	32. whole
6. careful	15. fair	24. loud	33. polite
7. happy	16. rare	25. sensible	34. weekly
8. true	17. recent	26. brave	35. fluent
9. extreme	18. intelligent	27. slow	36. regular

II. *Write down the comparative and superlative of the following adverbs.*

Steigere die folgenden Adverbien!

1. well	9. extremely	17. gladly
2. slowly	10. quickly	18. loudly
3. long	11. ill	19. soon
4. quietly	12. fluently	20. early
5. deeply	13. softly	21. high
6. nervously	14. nicely	22. angrily
7. little	15. prettily	23. fast
8. much	16. sweetly	24. badly

III. *Put the adverbs or adverbial phrases in suitable positions.*

Setze die Adverbien oder adverbialen Bestimmungen an passende Stellen!

1. The student went. (at 7 o'clock/to the bus stop)
2. My sister Maud was studying. (in her room/very hard/yesterday/all day)
3. He has been. (to London/in his life/never)
4. Let's go. (this evening/to the cinema)
5. Sue sang. (at the competition/very well/in Oxford/2 days ago)
6. The visitors had to wait. (in front of the door/a little while)
7. Come! (soon/again)
8. He had seen a musical. (never/on stage/before)
9. He has been. (twice/in the park/today)
10. She walked. (once/before supper)
11. He had to stay. (unfortunately/in hospital/for 3 days)
12. Our friend helps me. (usually/in the garden/at the weekend)
13. The cat was lying. (on the sofa/quietly)
14. I go shopping. (seldom/in Paris)

Adverb or Adjective

Adverb oder Adjektiv

Ob Adverb oder Adjektiv benutzt werden muss, hängt vom Bezugswort ab. Ein **Adjektiv** bezieht sich auf ein *Nomen oder ein Pronomen.*

Beispiel: She is a **nice** girl.

   She is **nice.**

Ein **Adverb** kann sich beziehen:

▶ auf ein *Verb.*

   Beispiel: She sings **nicely.**

▶ auf ein *Adjektiv.*

   Beispiel: She is **seriously** ill.

▶ auf ein anderes *Adverb.*

   Beispiel: She sings **extremely well.**

▶ auf einen *ganzen Satz.*

   Beispiel: **Suddenly,** they left the house.

Hierbei gelten folgende Ausnahmen:

▶ Bei Verben, die einen *Zustand* ausdrücken, steht *kein Adverb.*
   Dazu gehören: to be (sein),

   to become, to get, to grow, to turn (werden),

   to remain, to stay, to keep (bleiben),

   to seem (scheinen)

   Beispiel: He remained silent.

▶ Bei Verben der *Sinneswahrnehmung* steht *kein Adverb,* es sei denn, die Sinnesorgane tun wirklich etwas. Dazu gehören:

Verb	Bedeutung ohne Adverb	Bedeutung mit Adverb
to look	aussehen	schauen
to feel	sich (an)fühlen	fühlen (im Sinne von tasten)
to smell	riechen (z. B. Fisch)	riechen (mit der Nase)
to sound	klingen, sich anhören	---
to taste	schmecken (Mahlzeit)	schmecken (mit dem Mund)

Exercises

Übungen

Decide whether to use adverbs or adjectives.

Entscheide, ob Adverbien oder Adjektive benutzt werden müssen!

1. The driver was (serious) hurt in the accident.
2. The damage to the building was very (serious).
3. My grandfather always talks (serious).
4. The dog (usual) barks (loud).
5. The new clerk didn't stick to the (usual) order.
6. The (loud) music from the neighbours sounds (terrible).
7. She was smiling (happy).
8. There is a restaurant called "The (Happy) Eater".
9. The couple have been (happy) married for 20 years.
10. The mountain is very (high).
11. She speaks with a very (high) voice.
12. She is always (high) (elegant).
13. He told me (surprising) news.
14. (Surprising), he (real) came to the party.
15. He was (surprising) (polite).
16. Mary speaks French very (good).
17. She is a very (good) secretary.
18. I have some (good) news for you.
19. The fire destroyed the house (complete).
20. She won a (complete) dinner set.
21. The house was (complete) empty.
22. The buses run (regular).
23. He should attend class (regular).
24. English is (easy) to learn.
25. English can be learned (easy).
26. You can (easy) wash this pullover yourself.
27. Simon is a (careless) driver.
28. (Especial) when he has had a few drinks, he drives (careless).
29. He shouldn't (real) have a driving-licence.
30. He is a (real) danger to the other people.
31. Both teams seemed to be very (nervous).
32. Your idea sounds (great).
33. When Paul heard the news, he became very (sad).
34. The doctor (careful) examined the patient.
35. The patient felt very (weak).
36. He didn't look very (good) today.
37. He looked (angry) at the children who had broken the vase.

Final Test: The Adverb

Abschlusstest: das Adverb

Translate the following sentences.
Übersetze die folgenden Sätze!

1. Sally sieht sehr hübsch in ihrem extrem langen Mantel aus.
2. Zuerst klangen seine Erklärungen seltsam, aber dann stellten sie sich als wahr heraus.
3. Wenn der Kuchen noch länger im Ofen bleibt, wird er nicht mehr so gut schmecken.
4. Vom Flugzeug aus sahen die Berge nicht so hoch aus.
5. Die Katze lag vor dem Kamin. Ihr Fell fühlte sich weich und warm an.
6. Er arbeitete sehr hart, hatte aber kaum Erfolg.
7. Hast du die gute Marmelade schon probiert?
8. Kevin ist sehr krank. Gestern fühlte er sich schlechter als je zuvor.
9. Als er plötzlich ein Geräusch hörte, schaute er aufgeregt hinter sich.
10. Warum muss Sam sich immer so dumm benehmen? Er ist doch ziemlich intelligent.
11. Sie fühlte sich immer so müde, dass sie kaum die Augen offen halten konnte.
12. Jede Regel wird so einfach wie möglich erklärt werden.
13. Der Patient wartete ungeduldig auf den Arzt.
14. Glücklicherweise war er nicht ernsthaft verletzt.
15. Da er sein Studium nicht sehr ernst nimmt, wird er voraussichtlich kein gutes Examen machen.
16. Der Braten sieht köstlich aus und riecht sehr gut.
17. Wie gewöhnlich saß mein Großvater auf der behaglich warmen Veranda (porch).
18. Als er im Keller ein merkwürdiges Geräusch hörte, tastete er vorsichtig seine Pistole.
19. Mary sieht nicht sehr gut, aber sie ist dennoch eine gute Schülerin.
20. Sam klang sehr fröhlich, als er die gute Nachricht hörte.

The Pronoun

Das Pronomen/
das Fürwort

The Personal Pronoun

Das Personalpronomen/das persönliche Fürwort

*Grund-
regel*
Personalpronomen stehen stellvertretend für **Personen, Tiere, Dinge** etc. Personalpronomen können wie die Nomen, deren Stellvertreter sie sind, Subjekt oder Objekt eines Satzes sein.

Beispiel: Peter is at home. – (Peter – Subjekt)

      He is at home. (he = Peter – Subjekt)

      I saw Peter. (Peter – Objekt) I saw **him**. (him = Peter – Objekt)

Personalpronomen haben dementsprechend eine **Subjektform** und eine **Objektform.** Da es im Englischen keine Unterscheidung zwischen Dativ und Akkusativ gibt, liegt nur *eine* Objektform vor.

Formen

Person		Subjektform (auf die Frage „Wer oder was?")	Objektform (auf die Frage „Wem, wen oder was?")
1. Person	Singular	I	me
2. Person		you	you
3. Person		he, she, it	him, her, it
1. Person	Plural	we	us
2. Person		you	you
3. Person		they	them

Ausnahmen
Statt der Subjektform steht die Objektform

▶ im *Vergleich* nach "as" und "than".

    Beispiel: Paul is taller than me. – Paul ist größer als ich.

▶ in *Kurzantworten* auf "who"-Fragen.

    Beispiel: Who is it? – Wer ist es?

            It's us. – Wir sind es.

▶ in *verkürzten Sätzen,* in denen das Pronomen ohne Prädikat steht.
    Beispiel: My brother wanted to come, not me. – Mein Bruder wollte
        kommen, nicht ich.

Das deutsche „man"

"You" und "they" (people) können für das deutsche unpersönliche „man"
stehen.
Beispiel: You can't say that. – Man kann das nicht sagen.
            They say he has been in prison. – Man sagt, er sei im Gefängnis ge-
            wesen.

Im formellen Englisch wird "one" für das deutsche „man" benutzt.
Beispiel: One can never tell. – Man kann nie wissen.

Exercises
Übungen

Übungen

I.   *Replace the underlined words by personal pronouns.*
    Ersetze die unterstrichenen Wörter durch Personalpronomen.

1. Mary can't find her handbag.
2. I met the Millers last week.
3. The book is on the table.
4. Did you see the photos?
5. Father's pipe is in the kitchen.
6. I like the house very much.
7. He got his new car yesterday.
8. The telephone is out of order.
9. Did you see Simon and his brother?
10. My mother baked the cake yesterday.
11. I've lost my pen.
12. The dog is in the garden. His name is Henry.
13. Don't forget to water the plants.
14. Our suitcases are still in the car.
15. We've forgotten the records.
16. Leave the TV on, please.
17. The worker repaired the house.
18. I got a present from my father.
19. Where are my cigarettes?
20. My father and I repaired the bike ourselves.
21. Can you do the washing-up for me?
22. The church was built in the 18th century.

23. Please, shut <u>the door</u>.
24. I couldn't find <u>your trousers</u>.
25. <u>The boys</u> are doing their homework.
26. <u>The lady</u> has just left the house.
27. <u>The butler</u> opened <u>the door</u>.

II. *Translate the following sentences.*
   Übersetze die folgenden Sätze!
   1. Ich finde, du bist hübscher als sie alle.
   2. Wer klopft da? – Ich bin es.
   3. Kannst du ihn mir vorstellen?
   4. Ich habe euch doch gestern erst gesehen.
   5. Ich habe sie (die Mädchen) noch nie hier gesehen.
   6. Er ist so alt wie ich.
   7. Wer kommt mit ins Kino? – Ich!
   8. Kannst du ihnen die Briefe bitte geben?
   9. Man muss immer seine Pflicht tun.
   10. Man sagt, der Winter wird sehr kalt.

The Possessive Pronoun

Das Possessivpronomen/ das besitzanzeigende Fürwort

Grund-regel

Possessivpronomen drücken ein Besitz- oder Zugehörigkeitsverhältnis aus. Sie können entweder **attributiv (vor dem Nomen stehend)** oder **substantivisch (allein stehend, mit Bezug auf ein vorangehendes Nomen)** gebraucht werden.
Beispiel: attributiv: This is **my** pullover.
   substantivisch: This is not your pullover. It's **mine**.

Person		Attributiv	Substantivisch
1. Person		my	mine
2. Person	Singular	your	yours
3. Person		his, her, its	his, hers, (its)
1. Person		our	ours
2. Person	Plural	your	yours
3. Person		their	theirs

Zu beachten ist:

▶ Anders als im Deutschen müssen Possessivpronomen *bei Kleidungsstücken und Körperteilen* benutzt werden.

Beispiel: He had his hands in his pockets. – Er hatte die Hände in den Taschen.

She shook her head. – Sie schüttelte den Kopf.

▶ Possessivpronomen stehen auch bei *abstrakten Begriffen* wie "life", "death", "mind" etc., wenn die Zugehörigkeit zu bestimmten Einzelwesen gemeint ist.

Beispiel: They lost their lives. – Sie verloren das Leben.

Die Nomen stehen dabei gewöhnlich im Plural (z. B. lives), wenn sie sich auf mehrere Personen beziehen.

Besonder-heiten

Verstärkung des Possessivpronomens durch "own"

"Own" („eigen", „selbst") darf nur in Verbindung mit attributivem Possessivpronomen verwendet werden. Dabei gelten folgende Regeln:

▶ *Possessivpronomen + "own"* steht vor dem Nomen.

Beispiel: He did it with his own hands. – Er machte es mit seinen eigenen Händen.

▶ *"Of" + Possessivpronomen + "own"* stehen hinter dem Nomen.

Beispiel: He has a house of his own. – Er hat ein eigenes Haus.

▶ Soll die Wiederholung eines genannten Nomens verhindert werden, so steht *Possessivpronomen + "own" alleine.*

Beispiel: It's my brother's house, not my own (house). – Es ist das Haus meines Bruders, nicht mein eigenes.

"Of" + Possessivpronomen

"Of" + Possessivpronomen steht hinter einem Nomen, das mit "a", einem Zahlwort oder einem Demonstrativpronomen verbunden ist.

▶ "Of" + attributives Possessivpronomen + "own" (eigenes, selbst)

Beispiel: Have you got a car of your own? – Hast du ein eigenes Auto?

▶ "Of" + substantivisches Possessivpronomen (einer, zwei, keiner etc. von...)

Beispiel: He is a friend of mine. – Er ist ein Freund von mir (einer meiner Freunde).

Exercises

Übungen

I. Replace the underlined words by a possessive pronoun or add the missing possessive pronouns.

Ersetze die unterstrichenen Wörter durch ein Possessivpronomen oder ergänze die fehlenden Possessivpronomen!

1. My brother's car is in the garage.
2. Sally's dress is very nice.
3. Have you already met my brother's wife?
4. He is a colleague of my father's.
5. Is this Tom's book?
6. Carol's bike is in front of the house.
7. The ticket collector's uniform is blue.
8. Whose are those records? They must be Sally's.
9. Have the Millers got a garden of . . . own?
10. Are those your handkerchiefs? – No, they aren't . . .
11. This room is my mother's.
12. Sheila has always been a friend of my sister's.
13. This isn't my pullover. It must be Mary's.
14. The boy has got a room of . . . own.
15. My father hurt . . . leg.
16. We knew that . . . lives were in danger.
17. Carol's and Pat's records are very good.
18. I can't get it out of . . . mind.
19. The waitresses' uniforms are usually black.
20. The Duke's house is visited by hundreds of tourists.
21. The boys painted . . . faces red.
22. I've got a room of . . . own.
23. Sally's report wasn't very good last year.
24. The boys want to spend . . . holidays in a camp.
25. Sam hadn't got any money in . . . pocket.
26. The students forgot . . . bags in the classroom.
27. Mr Meekins is going to meet . . . wife at 6 o'clock.
28. The lady never leaves the house without . . . hat.
29. The boy scouts' meeting place is in Church Road.
30. I seldom forget . . . homework.

II. *Translate the following sentences.*

Übersetze die folgenden Sätze!

1. Hast du meine Tasche gesehen?
2. Der Umschlag meines Buches fehlt.
3. Er ist ein Kollege von ihm.
4. Peter hat immer ein eigenes Zimmer gehabt.
5. Sie besuchten ihren dreimonatigen Französischkurs.
6. Das ist nicht Ihr Koffer. Es ist meiner.
7. Die Idee geht mir nicht aus dem Sinn.
8. Ich habe seine Schwester schon getroffen.
9. Euer Haus ist sehr hübsch.
10. Hast du ein eigenes Zimmer?

The Interrogative Pronoun

Das Interrogativpronomen/ das Fragefürwort

Interrogativpronomen **leiten Fragen ein.** Die Wahl des Interrogativpronomens hängt von folgenden Faktoren ab:

▶ ob nach einer *Person* oder nach einem *Ding* gefragt wird.
▶ nach welchem *Satzglied* (Subjekt, Objekt etc.) gefragt wird.
▶ ob nach Personen oder Dingen aus einer bestimmten oder uneingeschränkten *Anzahl* gefragt wird.

Formen

Satzglied	Frage nach Personen	Frage nach Dingen
Subjekt	→ who (wer?) Who phoned me?	→ what (was)? What was the result?
	→ what (was für …?) What man phoned me?	→ what (was für …?) What colours do you like?
	→ which (welche/r/s?) Which of my friends phoned me?	→ which (welche/r/s?) Which of the books is missing?

Satzglied	Frage nach Personen	Frage nach Dingen
Genitiv-objekt	whose (wessen?) Whose car is this?	---
Objekt	→ who (whom im förm-lichen Stil) (wem, wen?)* Who(m) did you give the book to? Who(m) do you mean?	→ what (was?)* What do you want to buy?
	→ what (was für ...?) What people do you know?	→ what (was für ...?) What subjects do you learn?
	→ which (welche/r/s?) Which of the boys did you meet?	→ which (welche/r/s?) Which subject do you like better – English or French?

"What" oder "which"?

"What" (was für ...?) fragt nach Personen oder Dingen aus einer uneinge-schränkten Anzahl.

Beispiel: What (kind of) people were in the pub?
What (kind of) books do you like?

"Which" (welcher, welche, welches?) fragt nach Personen oder Dingen aus ei-ner bestimmten eingeschränkten Anzahl.

Beispiel: Which of the girls is your sister?
Which city do you prefer, London or Paris?

Beachte: Da "of" + Nomen/Pronomen immer eine Einschränkung ausdrückt, kann nur "which" bei einer "of"-Gruppe stehen.

Beispiel: Which of the pullovers do you like best?

---

* Bei Fragen mit "who" oder "what" werden Präpositionen nach-, bei Fragen mit "whom" vorgestellt.
Beispiel: Who are you looking for? For whom are you looking? What are you interested in?

Exercises

Übungen

I. *Put in "what" or "which".*

Setze "what" oder "which" ein!

1. ... handbag is yours, the black or the brown one?
2. ... kind of records do you usually buy?
3. ... of these flowers would you take?
4. ... river is longer, the Thames or the Rhine?
5. ... is your telephone number?
6. ... kind of sports do you like best?
7. ... of the books on the table are yours?
8. ... house is yours, number 45 or 46?
9. ... comes next?
10. ... of you can give me the answer?
11. ... people were at the party?
12. ... of your friends shall we invite?
13. ... way shall we go, this one or that one?
14. ... of your brothers works in London?
15. ... city has more inhabitants, New York or Munich?
16. ... cities have you been to?
17. ... car is your father's, the VW or the BMW?
18. ... of the two pictures would you take?
19. ... size is this dress?
20. ... sort of meat do I need for this recipe?

II. *Put in the correct interrogative pronoun.*

Setze das richtige Interrogativpronomen ein!

1. ... shall we do?
2. ... are they talking about?
3. ... did you help yesterday?
4. ... did you do on Sunday?
5. Can you see ... is in the living-room?
6. ... room is that – Sally's or Maud's?
7. ... do you need the tools for?
8. I don't know ... keys they are. Maybe they are Pam's.
9. ... unit did we get up to last lesson?
10. ... of the poems did you like best?
11. ... kind of girl is she?
12. ... can tell me the way to the station?
13. ... did you find under the sofa?
14. ... would you like to drink?

15. ...did you lend the book to?
16. ...spoke to you in front of the house?
17. ...is your favourite pudding, apple pie or trifle?
18. ...of you hasn't finished the exercise?
19. ...brother is Tom, Maggy's or Eileen's?
20. ...was taken to hospital?

III. *Ask for the underlined words.*
   Frage nach den unterstrichenen Wörtern!
1. I would like to spend my holidays with <u>my aunt</u>.
2. My father is looking at an <u>English</u> magazine.
3. My favourite pop-group are <u>the Rolling Stones</u>.
4. I was introduced to <u>many interesting people</u>.
5. My brother sold his car to <u>our neighbour</u>.
6. <u>Mr Mud</u> called you half an hour ago.
7. I have to send <u>Patrick</u> the photos at once.
8. <u>The tennis racket</u> is in the wardrobe.
9. The boys are laughing at <u>the new student</u>.
10. There are three cars in front of the hotel. <u>The green one</u> is mine.
11. I have seen <u>this man</u> before.
12. <u>My friend</u> knows Mr Baker.
13. I like <u>science fiction</u> films best.
14. <u>The Guinness Book of Records</u> is published by a brewery.
15. My mother would like to talk to <u>the headmistress</u>.

The Reflexive Pronoun

Das Reflexivpronomen/ das rückbezügliche Fürwort

Reflexivpronomen können zwei Funktionen erfüllen:
► Sie können als eigentliche Reflexivpronomen *rückbezüglich* gebraucht werden und eine Übereinstimmung von Subjekt (S) und Objekt (O) kennzeichnen (deutsch: mich, mir, dich, dir etc).
Beispiel: <u>I</u> bought <u>**myself**</u> a new dress. – Ich kaufte mir ein neues Kleid.
   (S)   (O)

► Sie können ein Subjekt oder Objekt besonders stark *hervorheben* (deutsch: selbst).

Beachte: Verstärkende Reflexivpronomen können hinter dem Nomen/ Pronomen, das sie hervorheben sollen, stehen. Ist dieses Nomen/ Pronomen jedoch Subjekt, so treten sie meist ans Satzende.

Beispiel: <u>The Duke</u> [himself] opened the door himself. – Der Herzog öffnet
(S)   die Tür selbst.

I met **the Mayor** himself at the meeting. – Ich traf den Bürger-
(O)   meister selbst bei der
                                                Tagung.

Person		Reflexivpronomen
1. Person		myself
2. Person	Singular	yourself
3. Person		himself, herself, itself
1. Person		ourselves
2. Person	Plural	yourselves
3. Person		themselves

Reflexivpronomen mit "by" stehen in der Bedeutung „alleine".

Beispiel: He did it all by himself. – Er hat es ganz alleine gemacht.

Beachte: ► Nach Ortspräpositionen wie "above", "in front of", "behind", "with" etc. stehen im Englischen statt Reflexivpronomen nur Personalpronomen.

Beispiel: He had his sister with him. – Er hatte seine Schwester bei sich.

► Einige Verben haben im Gegensatz zur deutschen Bedeutung kein Reflexivpronomen (auch kein Personalpronomen) bei sich. Dazu gehören:

to approach	– sich nähern
to behave	– sich benehmen
to change	– sich verändern
to complain	– sich beschweren
to dress	– sich anziehen
to happen	– sich ereignen
to hide	– sich verstecken
to hurry	– sich beeilen
to imagine	– sich vorstellen (geistig)
to lie down	– sich hinlegen
to look forward to	– sich freuen auf

to meet	– sich treffen
to move	– sich bewegen
to recover	– sich erholen
to relax	– sich entspannen
to rely on	– sich verlassen auf
to remember	– sich erinnern
to sit down	– sich setzen
to turn to	– sich wenden an
to wonder	– sich wundern

Beispiel: I recover.

▶ Folgende Verben stehen mit einem Reflexivpronomen:

to absent oneself	– fehlen
to betake oneself	– sich begeben
to make oneself at home	– es sich bequem machen
to pride oneself	– stolz sein auf sich
to seat oneself	– sich setzen

▶ Wenn mit „sich" eine wechselseitige Beziehung („sich" im Sinne von „einander") ausgedrückt werden soll, steht kein Reflexivpronomen, sondern "each other" oder "one another".

Beispiel: They looked at each other and smiled. – Sie schauten sich (einander) an und lächelten.

Exercises

Übungen

I. *Put in the correct reflexive pronoun.*
   Setze das richtige Reflexivpronomen ein!

1. I introduced ... to our new neighbour.
2. She made ... a pullover.
3. The father decided to repair the car ...
4. You'll have to finish your homework ...
5. In the youth hostel we had to make the beds ...
6. I would like to speak to the doctor ..., not his secretary.
7. Grandpa was sitting in the living-room all by ...
8. He helped ... to a second piece of cake.
9. She knew him better than he knew ...
10. The Millers like talking about ...
11. The boss decided to answer the phone call ...
12. Mother made ... a cup of tea.

13. You pride . . . very much on your cleverness, don't you, Tom?
14. Good bye, Mary! Enjoy . . . !
15. It's really true, I saw it . . .
16. I cut . . . with a knife.
17. I don't think they'll be able to manage by . . .
18. You must look after . . . on the journey.
19. She has made . . . very popular.
20. Do it . . . !

II. *Decide whether to use a reflexive or a personal pronoun.*
Entscheide, ob ein Reflexiv- oder ein Personalpronomen benutzt werden muss!

1. Shut the door behind . . . !
2. Have we got to do this all by . . . ?
3. We enjoyed . . . very much at the theatre.
4. The boss brought a lot of work with . . .
5. When I saw her she had a dog beside . . .
6. The model looked at . . . in the mirror.
7. Sally is too young to go out by . . .
8. My brother . . . saw the accident.
9. The elephant washed . . .
10. The boys are old enough to look after . . .
11. Has your brother got any matches on . . . ?
12. Suddenly we saw a car in front of . . .
13. You really have to solve that problem . . .
14. Did your mother paint the picture . . . ?
15. As the cleaning lady was ill she had to clean the house . . .

III. *Put in the correct reflexive or personal pronoun if possible.*
Setze, wenn möglich, das richtige Reflexiv- oder Personalpronomen ein!

1. I can't remember . . . what his name was.
2. It's raining. You should take your raincoat with . . .
3. I would like to see the castle . . . , not just a picture.
4. The Queen . . . gave him the medal.
5. She liked the ring . . . but not the ruby.
6. Take care of . . .
7. The accident happened . . . at the corner of Church Road.
8. He sat . . . down on the armchair.
9. My mother makes most of her dresses . . .
10. Little Billy doesn't want to go to the dentist by . . .
11. Carol only thinks of . . . , never of the rest of the family.
12. Would you please lock the garage door behind . . . ?

13. They have changed . . . a lot since I last met them.
14. Since the workers were on strike, Mr Carter had to do the work . . .
15. He told me that it was really true. He had seen it . . .
16. People in the Third World must be encouraged to help . . .
17. Since she didn't feel well, she lay . . . down for a while.
18. What happened . . . last week?
19. They met . . . in front of the hotel.
20. When I was in London, I saw the Queen . . ., not only her guards.
21. What does your father . . . think of it?
22. She is a woman who always feels sorry for . . .
23. I can't imagine . . . living in a big city.
24. The old lady often talks to . . .
25. Do you live in this huge house all by . . .?

IV. *Put in the correct reflexive or personal pronoun or "each other"/*
"one another", if possible.
Setze, wo möglich, das richtige Reflexiv- oder Personalpronomen oder
"each other"/"one another" ein!
1. Tom and Sue lost . . . in the crowd in front of the cinema.
2. We could see . . . in the surface of the water.
3. Sally could see . . . in the surface of the water.
4. My father and his colleague have known . . . for 10 years.
5. Did you cook that delicious meal . . .?
6. The Millers and the Coopers are good friends. They always help . . .
7. The landlady told me to help . . . to another glass of beer.
8. This book is mine. I wrote my name in it . . .
9. They didn't say a word. They only looked at . . . as if they understood . . .
   without saying anything.
10. When we built our house we had to do a lot of things . . .

The Demonstrative Pronoun

Das Demonstrativpronomen/ das hinweisende Fürwort

Die Demonstrativpronomen weisen ganz besonders auf **eine Person oder ein Ding** hin, das entweder schon bekannt oder noch näher zu beschreiben ist.

Singular	Plural
this – dies hier	these – diese hier
that – das da, jenes	those – diese da, jene

Formen

▶ "This" und "these" bezeichnen das räumlich/zeitlich Nähere (in Bezug auf die Gegenwart).

▶ "That" und "those" bezeichnen das räumlich/zeitlich Entferntere (in Bezug auf die Vergangenheit). "That" und "those" können auch verwendet werden um eine Abneigung oder Geringschätzung auszudrücken.

Beispiel: This pullover is nice, but that one over there is much nicer.
 Dieser Pullover ist hübsch, aber jener dort drüben ist hübscher.
 These keys are mine, those keys on the table are yours.
 Diese Schlüssel (hier) gehören mir, jene Schlüssel auf dem Tisch sind deine.
 Whose are those dirty jeans?
 Wem gehören denn diese schmutzigen Jeans? (Abneigung)

Demonstrativpronomen können

▶ *attributiv* vor Nomen gebraucht werden.

Anwendung

 Beispiel: Do you know this boy. – Kennst du diesen Jungen?
▶ *allein stehend* (wie ein Nomen) gebraucht werden:
 a) im Plural in Bezug auf ein vorangehendes oder folgendes Nomen
 Beispiel: Whose are these keys? – Wessen Schlüssel sind das hier?
 These are mine. – Diese hier sind meine.
 b) im Singular in der Bedeutung „dies/das" wie ein Neutrum
 Beispiel: This is Peter. – Das ist Peter.
 Beachte: Bei den Singularformen in Bezug auf vorangehende Personen muss das Stützwort "one" verwendet werden.
 Beispiel: This girl is smaller than **that one**. – Dieses Mädchen ist kleiner als jenes.
▶ *adverbial* (as, so) besonders im American English; im British English nur umgangssprachlich gebraucht werden.
 Beispiel: I can't climb that (so) high. – Ich kann nicht so hoch klettern.

Exercises

Übungen

I. *Put "this"/"that" and "these"/"those" in front of the nouns.*
   Setze "this"/"that" und "these"/"those" vor die Nomen!

 1. . . . pen   – . . . pen over there
 2. . . . books   – . . . books over there
 3. . . . cake   – . . . cakes over there
 4. . . . pictures   – . . . pictures over there
 5. . . . student   – . . . student over there
 6. . . . car   – . . . car over there
 7. . . . boy   – . . . boy over there
 8. . . . bike   – . . . bike over there
 9. . . . raincoat   – . . . raincoat over there
10. . . . shirt   – . . . shirts over there
11. . . . suitcase   – . . . suitcase over there
12. . . . umbrella   – . . . umbrella over there
13. . . . sign   – . . . signs over there
14. . . . lady   – . . . lady over there
15. . . . house   – . . . houses over there

II. *Put in the correct demonstrative pronoun.*
   Setze das richtige Demonstrativpronomen ein!
 1. . . . were the days.
 2. . . . building over there is Charing Cross Station.
 3. . . . tins are empty, but . . . tins over there are full.
 4. Look! Can you see the bridge in the distance? . . . is Westminster Bridge and
    . . . bridge right in front of us is Tower Bridge.
 5. . . . week I haven't been able to write a single letter, but . . . week when
    Patrick was here I finished ten letters.
 6. Is . . . your handbag here? – No, . . . handbag over there is mine.
 7. . . . painting here is much nicer than . . . other one.
 8. I don't like . . . sort of material.
 9. Last year we were in Italy in our holidays. . . . were very enjoyable days.
10. "I've missed you so much." . . . were his first words when he came home.

III. *Translate the following sentences.*
   Übersetze die folgenden Sätze!
 1. Unser Haus ist viel kleiner als das von unserem Nachbarn.
 2. Sind das Ihre Koffer dort drüben?
 3. Dies hier sind meine Freunde, Pit und Herbert.
 4. Welches von den Mädchen ist Sue? – Dieses hier.

5. Ich finde, diese Stühle sind viel bequemer als jene.
6. Welchen Anzug findest du hübscher? Diesen oder jenen?
7. Ich kann nicht so weit laufen.
8. Ist das nicht der berühmte Sänger dort drüben?
9. Du kannst entweder diesen oder jenen Weg nehmen.
10. Diese Dame dort drüben habe ich noch nie gesehen.

The Relative Pronoun

Das Relativpronomen/das bezügliche Fürwort

Relativpronomen leiten Nebensätze ein (**Relativsätze/relative clauses**). Entsprechend ihrer Bezüglichkeit lassen sich Relativpronomen in drei Gruppen unterteilen.

▶ a) Relativpronomen, die sich auf ein *Wort* beziehen und einen *notwendigen Relativsatz* einleiten.

   b) Relativpronomen, die sich auf ein *Wort* beziehen und einen *nicht notwendigen Relativsatz* einleiten.

▶ Relativpronomen, die sich auf einen vorausgehenden oder folgenden *Satz* beziehen.

▶ Relativpronomen, die *ohne Beziehungswort oder -satz* stehen.

Relative Pronouns in the Defining Relative Clause
Relativpronomen im notwendigen Relativsatz

Notwendige Relativsätze geben Informationen, die für das Verständnis des Hauptsatzes unentbehrlich sind. Sie werden im Englischen nicht durch Komma(ta) abgetrennt.

Beispiel: This is the boy who(m) I saw yesterday. – Das ist der Junge, den ich gestern sah.

Satzteil	Für Personen	Für Dinge
Subjekt	who/that	that/which
Besitzanzeige	whose	whose/of which
Objekt	who(m)/that	that/which

Beispiel: *Person/Subjekt:*

This is the man **who (that)** works as a mechanic. – Das ist der Mann, der als Mechaniker arbeitet.

Person/besitzanzeigend:

This is the man **whose** car was stolen. – Das ist der Mann, dessen Auto gestohlen wurde.

Person/Objekt:

This is the man **who(m) (that)** I mean. – Das ist der Mann, den ich meine.

Ding/Subjekt:

This is the book **which (that)** was published in 1996. – Das ist das Buch, welches 1996 erschien.

Ding/besitzanzeigend:

This is the factory **whose** owner (the owner **of which**) died.

– Das ist die Fabrik, deren Besitzer starb.

Ding/Objekt:

This is the book **which (that)** I like best. – Das ist das Buch, welches im am liebsten mag.

Wegfall des Relativpronomens

In notwendigen Relativsätzen können die Relativpronomen wegfallen, wenn sie *Objekt* sind, d. h., wenn im Relativsatz ein Subjekt (Nomen/Pronomen) steht.

Beispiel: This is the girl (whom) **I** remember well. – Das ist das Mädchen, an das ich mich gut erinnere. (I – ich – Subjekt des Relativsatzes)

Relativpronomen mit Präposition

In notwendigen Relativsätzen stehen Präpositionen gewöhnlich *hinter* dem Verb.

Beispiel: The boy who you were talking **to** is my brother. – Der Junge, mit dem du sprachst, ist mein Bruder.

Im *förmlichen Stil* steht die Präposition *vor* dem Relativpronomen. "Who" und "that" dürfen jedoch nicht hinter einer Präposition stehen.

Beispiel: Here are the results **of** which Mr Cooper is very proud. (Here are the results that Mr Cooper is very proud **of**.) – Hier sind die Ergebnisse, auf die Mr Cooper sehr stolz ist.

Relative Pronouns in the Non-Defining Relative Clause

Relativpronomen im nicht notwendigen Relativsatz

Nicht notwendige Relativsätze geben Zusatzinformationen, die für das Verständnis des Hauptsatzes entbehrlich sind. Sie werden durch Komma(ta) abgetrennt. Relativpronomen können nicht wegfallen.

Beispiel: The boys, who are quite young, can already read and write.

Die Jungen, die noch ziemlich jung sind, können schon lesen und schreiben.

Satzteil	Für Personen	Für Dinge
Subjekt	who	which
Besitzanzeige	whose	whose/of which
Objekt	whom	which

Formen

Beispiel: *Person/Subjekt:*

Mr Baker, **who** lives in London, hates the provinces. – Mr Baker, der in London lebt, hasst die Provinz.

Person/besitzanzeigend:

Mr Baker, **whose** father is a millionaire, lives in London. – Mr Baker, dessen Vater Millionär ist, wohnt in London.

Person/Objekt:

Mr Baker, **whom** I met the other day, told me the story. – Mr Baker, den ich neulich traf, erzählte mit die Geschichte.

Ding/Subjekt:

The shop, **which** sells the books, is closed today. – Der Laden, der die Bücher verkauft, ist heute geschlossen.

Ding/besitzanzeigend:

My favourite shop, **whose** windows (the windows of which) are painted red, is closed today. – Mein Lieblingsladen, dessen Fenster rot gestrichen sind, ist heute geschlossen.

Ding/Objekt:

Mr Green's shop, **which** I like best, is closed today. – Mr Greens Laden, den ich am liebsten mag, ist heute geschlossen.

Relativpronomen mit Präposition

In nicht notwendigen Relativsätzen stehen Präpositionen gewöhnlich *vor* dem Relativpronomen.

Beispiel: The country, about which she knew so little, was a great experience for her. – Das Land, über das sie so wenig wusste, bedeutete eine große Erfahrung für sie.

Relative Pronouns Referring to a Sentence
Relativpronomen, die sich auf einen Satz beziehen

▶ "Which" (was) kann sich auf einen *vorangehenden* Satz beziehen.
Beispiel: He said he had seen her, **which** I can't believe. – Er sagte, er hätte sie gesehen, was ich nicht glauben kann.
▶ "What" (was) kann sich auf einen *folgenden* Satz beziehen.
Beispiel: He is a nice person and, **what** is even more important, you can trust him. – Er ist ein netter Mensch und, was noch viel wichtiger ist, man kann ihm vertrauen.

In beiden Fällen wird der Relativsatz durch Komma(ta) abgetrennt.

Relative Pronouns without a Referent
Relativpronomen ohne Bezugswort/-satz

Die verallgemeinernden Relativpronomen "whatever" (was auch immer/alles, was), "whoever" (wer/wen auch immer/jeder, der) und "whichever" (welches auch immer/das, was) haben kein Bezugswort/keinen Bezugssatz. Sie entsprechen einer Verbindung von Demonstrativpronomen (z. B. that/those) oder unbestimmtem Zahlwort (z. B. anyone) + Relativpronomen.

Beispiel: Choose whoever you like. (Choose anybody who you like.) – Wähle, wen immer du magst.

Exercises

Übungen

I. *Put in "who(m)" or "which".*
   Setze "who(m)" oder "which" ein!

1. Our secretary, ... might have been able to help you, is on holiday.
2. We spent our last holidays in Amalfi, ... is really an interesting town.
3. There's somebody ... wants you on the phone.
4. The book ... is lying on the table is mine.
5. The man ... wrote this letter phoned half an hour ago.
6. The letter, ... I posted 2 days ago, hasn't arrived yet.
7. The student ... you want has just left.
8. The sweets ... I bought yesterday are very good.
9. The record ... you lent me 2 weeks ago is very interesting.
10. The postcard ... we received yesterday came from Spain.
11. The garden ... is behind the bungalow has a swimming-pool.
12. The coat ... you are wearing is marvellous.
13. The ring ... I got for Christmas has three rubies.
14. The bush ... stands in front of the house has wonderful flowers.
15. The French course ... I attended was very interesting.
16. The boy ... lives next door is very clever.
17. Can you remember the person ... gave it to you?
18. The noise ... you can hear comes from upstairs.
19. The restaurant ... I went to yesterday is very expensive.
20. Students ... work hard will always be successful.

II. *Put in the correct relative pronoun.*
   Setze das richtige Relativpronomen ein!

1. The boy ... mother had had the accident also had to go to hospital.
2. The building ... belongs to my grandfather is very old.
3. Susan, ... usually talks a lot, is not coming to the party.
4. Harrod's, ... is a famous department store in London, sells nearly everything.
5. The pop star, ... she had once seen on stage, was staying in the hotel opposite.
6. Everybody was fond of the presents ... she had bought in Paris.
7. Brighton, ... is a famous English seaside resort, has a lot of nice shops.
8. The artist ... painted this picture is very famous.
9. The house ... roof was damaged by the storm is very old.
10. Sam is the person ... my father is so angry about.
11. The lady ... car was stolen went to the police at once.
12. This is the boy ... has stolen my handbag.

13. Carol, ... father is a rich man, lives in an expensive apartment.
14. The man ... wrote "War and Peace" is Tolstoi.
15. The Tower, ... used to be a prison, is now a museum.
16. He has failed the exam, ... is a pity.
17. Simon was the only one ... remembered the correct date.
18. My brother didn't help me, ... annoyed me a lot.
19. Covent Garden, ... used to be the old London fruit market, is a tourist attraction now.
20. Shakespeare, ... father was a common man, became the most famous English dramatist.

III. *Put in the correct relative pronoun, but only where necessary.*
    Setze das richtige Relativpronomen ein, aber nur wo notwendig!
 1. Is there a place ... does teas at that time of the day?
 2. There are a lot of things ... she has to arrange.
 3. There is one problem ... must be discussed.
 4. Where are the papers ... I put on the table?
 5. The house ... they are going to buy has five bedrooms.
 6. The bill ... we got today must be paid within 8 days.
 7. Is this the book ... you wanted to read?
 8. This is not the hotel-room ... we've booked.
 9. The pretty girl ... you are speaking to is my girl-friend.
10. Grammar, ... most students dislike, is very important.
11. Smoking, ... is a bad habit, is dangerous to your health.
12. Eton, ... has a famous college, is a very nice little town.
13. My uncle, ... is on holiday in Australia, has just written me a postcard.
14. The family next door, ... name I can't remember, are going to move.
15. Chess, ... is a very old game, is hard to learn.
16. My son, ... studies mathematics, is 27 years old.
17. Where are the chairs ... you want to sell?
18. She doesn't like champagne, ... is rather a pity.
19. The letter to the editor ... was published yesterday expresses exactly my opinion.
20. The train to Cambridge ... you wanted to take is late.

Final Test: The Pronoun

Abschlusstest: das Pronomen

Translate the following sentences.

Übersetze die folgenden Sätze!

1. Er lässt immer die Tür hinter sich offen.
2. Das große Feuer von London, das 1666 in einer Bäckerei in der Pudding Lane ausbrach, zerstörte große Teile Londons.
3. Das "Museum of London", das die Stadtgeschichte zeigt, ist montags geschlossen.
4. Wessen Mantel hast du da an? Ist das nicht meiner?
5. Ist das hier meine Tasche? – Nein, die dort drüben ist deine.
6. Er hat sich gestern in den Finger geschnitten.
7. Diese Rosen dort drüben sind wirklich schön. Denkst du, deine Tante würde mir welche geben?
8. Wem hast du dein neues Fahrrad geliehen?
9. Können Sie mir bitte Ihre Telefonnummer aufschreiben?
10. An wen schreibst du gerade?
11. Ich kann mich nicht erinnern, deine Schwester schon mal gesehen zu haben.
12. Meine Freundin, deren Mutter Köchin ist, kann überhaupt nicht kochen.
13. Wer wohnt (denn) in diesem großen Haus dort drüben?
14. Der Mann, den die Polizei gerade sucht, ist aus jenem Gefängnis ausgebrochen.
15. Er hat drei Töchter, die alle bei der gleichen Firma arbeiten.
16. Er hat ihr das Buch noch nicht zurückgegeben.
17. Sie sprachen wie gute Freunde miteinander, obwohl sie sich gar nicht kannten.
18. Darf ich mich setzen oder ist dieser Platz besetzt?
19. Welchen Mantel soll ich mitnehmen, den dicken blauen oder den dünnen schwarzen?
20. Ich brauche das Buch als Geschenk für ihn, nicht für mich selbst.
21. Das Glas, aus dem du trinkst, ist noch schmutzig.
22. Das Paket, das sie mir schickte, war beschädigt.
23. Ich mag diese Leute nicht.
24. Peter bot sofort seine Hilfe an, was sehr überraschend war.
25. Welche Farbe hat dein Haar?
26. Er wohnt mit seiner Schwester in diesem kleinen Haus dort drüben.
27. Simon ging ganz alleine Weihnachtsgeschenke kaufen.
28. Er kam mit dem Hut in der Hand.
29. Ich habe ihn persönlich noch nicht kennen gelernt.
30. An wen denkst du gerade?

The Preposition

Die Präposition/
das Verhältniswort

Function and Position

Funktion und Stellung

Präpositionen sind **Verhältniswörter,** d. h. sie bezeichnen das Verhältnis zweier Gegenstände, zweier Wörter oder Satzglieder zueinander.

Beispiel: "I – London" gibt noch keinen Sinn. Auch wenn ein Verb hinzutritt, ist der Sinn noch nicht ausreichend: "I – go – London."
Erst die Präposition bezeichnet das Verhältnis von "I" und "London" genau: "I go to London".

Präpositionen lassen sich der Form nach in zwei Gruppen unterteilen:
► **einfache Präpositionen,** wie z. B.
   at, by, in etc.
► **zusammengesetzte Präpositionen,** wie z. B.
   into, instead of, next to etc.

Bezüglich ihrer Benutzung lassen sich Präpositionen in fünf Hauptgruppen unterteilen:

Anwendung

► Raum (z. B. on, in front of).
► Zeit (z. B. during, before).
► Art und Weise, Mittel (z. B. with, by means of).
► Zweck, Absicht (z. B. for, in order to).
► Ursache, Grund (z. B. due to, because of).

Die Ursprungsbedeutungen der Präpositionen können jedoch verblasst sein oder auch im übertragenen Sinn verwendet werden.

Beispiel: I am in the house. (Raum)
I am in the computer business. (verblasste Bedeutung)
I am in tears. (übertragene Bedeutung)

Die Stellung von Präpositionen

▶ Präpositionen stehen, wie der Name (von lat. *praepositio* – das Voransetzen) bereits sagt, gewöhnlich *vor dem Objekt* (O).

Beispiel: She looked at **him.**

(O)

She is interested in **music.**

(O)

▶ Präpositionen treten an das *Satzende* bei
a) Fragen nach dem Objekt.
   Beispiel: What is he interested in? (Siehe auch Kapitel „The Interrogative Pronoun – Das Interrogativpronomen", S. 181 ff.)
b) notwendigen Relativsätzen.
   Beispiel: This is the person (who) I was introduced to. (Siehe auch Kapitel „The Relative Pronoun – Das Relativpronomen", S. 191 ff.)
c) Infinitivkonstruktionen.
   Beispiel: He had no pen to write with.

Das präpositionale Objekt

Das Objekt nach einer Präposition kann z. B. ein Nomen oder ein Pronomen sein. Da es Nomencharakter haben muss, kommt als Verbform nur ein Gerundium (ing-Form) als Objekt in Frage. (Siehe auch Kapitel „Gerund – Gerundium", S. 117 ff.)

Beispiel: He is interested in **music.**

Objekt (Nomen)

He is interested in **it.**

Objekt (Pronomen)

He is interested in **reading.**

Objekt (Gerundium)

Beachte: Auch bei der Präposition "to" folgt ein Gerundium, kein Infinitiv!
Beispiel: He is looking forward to **meeting** Sam.

The Most Common Prepositions and their Uses

Die gebräuchlichsten Präpositionen und ihre Verwendung

Manche Präpositionen sind sich bezüglich ihrer Bedeutung sehr ähnlich und werden daher oft verwechselt. Im Folgenden werden die gebräuchlichsten Präpositionen, die vor Substantiven stehen und bei denen die Gefahr der Verwechslung besteht, erläutert.

"At", "in", "on" in räumlicher Bedeutung

At – an einem Punkt

Beispiele:

at the table	– am Tisch
at the party	– auf der Party
at the station	– am Bahnhof
at home	– zu Hause
at the beginning	– am Anfang

Beachte:

▶ at + Kleinstadt, Dorf	– in ...
(at Epsom	– in Epsom)
▶ at + bestimmter Arbeitsplatz	– bei ...
(at Sainsbury's	– bei Sainsbury's)
▶ at + bestimmte Adresse	– in ...
(at 2 Station Road	– in der Bahnhofstr. 2)
▶ at + church, school etc.	– beim Gottesdienst, Unterricht
▶ at + Genitiv	– im Haus von ...
(at the Millers'	– im Haus der Millers)
▶ at court	– bei Hofe
aber: in court	– vor Gericht

In – in einem Raum

Beispiele:

in the kitchen	– in der Küche
in the picture	– auf dem Bild
in the world	– auf der Welt
in the sky	– am Himmel

Die Präposition
Verwendung

Beachte: ▶ in + Großstadt — in . . .
(in Paris — in Paris)
▶ in + Art des Arbeitsplatzes
oder der Wohnung — in . . .
(in an office — in einem Büro)
(in a flat — in einer Wohnung)
▶ in + church, school etc. — in der Kirche,
im Schulgebäude

▶ in the street — auf der Straße (in der Stadt)
aber: on the road — auf der Straße (Landstraße)
▶ in court — vor Gericht
aber: at court — bei Hofe

On – auf einer Oberfläche
Beispiele: on the table — auf dem Tisch
on the wall — an der Wand
on the 2nd floor — im zweiten Stock
on the way — auf dem Weg
on the left (side) — auf der linken Seite

Beachte: ▶ on the road — auf der Straße (Landstraße)
aber: in the street — auf der Straße (in der Stadt)
▶ on the sea/lake — am (auf dem) Meer/See
aber: at sea — auf See

"At", "in", "on" in zeitlicher Bedeutung

At – zu einem genauen Zeitpunkt
Beispiele: at 10 o'clock — um 10 Uhr
at sunrise/sunset — bei Sonnenauf-/untergang
at midnight — um Mitternacht
at the moment — im Augenblick
at Christmas — an Weihnachten

Beachte: ▶ on + bestimmte Tage — am . . .
(on Easter Monday — am Ostermontag)
▶ at the beginning — zu Beginn (Zeitpunkt)
aber: in the beginning — anfangs (Zeitraum)
▶ at night — nachts
▶ at times — gelegentlich

▶ at that time	– zu jener Zeit
▶ at what time	– um welche Uhrzeit
▶ at the same time	– zur gleichen Zeit (Zeitpunkt)
aber: in the same time	– in der gleichen Zeit (Zeitraum)

In – in einem Zeitraum

Beispiele: in the afternoon   – am Nachmittag, nachmittags

in winter	– im Winter
in the 19th century	– im 19. Jahrhundert
in 1987	– 1987
in a short time	– in kurzer Zeit

Beachte:	▶ in the beginning	– anfangs (Zeitraum)
	aber: at the beginning	– zu Beginn (Zeitpunkt)
	▶ in the end	– am Ende, schließlich (zeitlich)
	aber: at the end	– am Ende (örtlich)
	at the end of the week	– am Ende der Woche (Zeitpunkt)
	▶ in the same time	– in der gleichen Zeit (Zeitraum)
	aber: at the same time	– zur gleichen Zeit (Zeitpunkt)
	▶ in these (those) days	– an diesen Tagen (damals)
	▶ in the night	– in der Nacht
	aber: at night	– nachts
	▶ in time	– rechtzeitig
	aber: on time	– pünktlich

On – an bestimmten Tagen

Beispiele: on Monday   – am Montag

on Mondays	– montags
on the 2nd of April	– am 2. April
on Christmas Eve	– am Heiligabend
on my birthday	– an meinem Geburtstag

Beachte:	▶ on + Tagesabschnitt	– am ...
	(on the morning of April 2nd	– am Morgen des 2. April)
	▶ in + Tagesabschnitt	– morgens, abends etc.
	(in the morning	– morgens)
	▶ on end	– ununterbrochen
	▶ on this occasion	– bei dieser Gelegenheit
	▶ on time	– pünktlich
	aber: in time	– rechtzeitig

"Above", "over", "across", "via" – über

Above – oberhalb
(ohne Berührung mit der Grundfläche)
Beispiel: The plane is above the clouds. – Das Flugzeug ist über (oberhalb) den (der) Wolken.

Over – genau über
(in Ruhe)
Beispiel: The lamp hangs over the table. – Die Lampe hängt über dem Tisch.

Over – über ... hinweg
Beispiel: He jumps over the wall. – Er springt über die Mauer.
Beachte: ▶ over there   – dort drüben
        ▶ all over the world   – auf der ganzen Welt

Across – quer über
Beispiel: There is a bridge across the river. – Es gibt eine Brücke über den Fluss.

Via – über
(Wegangabe)
Beispiel: He drove to Vienna via Salzburg. – Er fuhr über Salzburg nach Wien.

"Under", "below" – unter

Under – senkrecht oder unmittelbar unter
Beispiel: The cat is under the table. – Die Katze ist unter dem Tisch.

Below – unterhalb
(ohne Berührung mit der Grundfläche)
Beispiel: The plane is below the clouds. – Das Flugzeug ist unter den Wolken.

"Between", "among" – zwischen

Between - zwischen zweien
Beispiel: I am standing between Pam and Sue. – Ich stehe zwischen Pam und Sue.

Among – zwischen vielen, unter mehreren

Beispiel: I am standing among many people. – Ich stehe zwischen vielen Leuten.

aber: "Between" steht statt "among", wenn die Beziehung zu jedem Einzelnen der Gruppe ausgedrückt werden soll.

Beispiel: She divided the money between her three sisters. – Sie teilte das Geld unter ihren drei Schwestern auf.

"To", "towards" – zu(m)

To – zu(m)
(Endziel)
Beispiel: I went to the building. – Ich ging zu dem Gebäude.

Towards – zu, in Richtung auf
(ob das Endziel erreicht wird, bleibt offen)
Beispiel: I went towards the building. – Ich ging auf das Gebäude zu.

"To", "as far as" – bis

To – bis
(Endziel)
Beispiel: I walked to the house. – Ich ging bis zu dem Haus.

As far as – bis
(Teilziel)
Beispiel: On Monday we travelled as far as the French border, the next day we reached Paris. – Am Montag reisten wir bis zur französischen Grenze, am nächsten Tag erreichten wir Paris.

"After", "behind", "beyond", "past" – hinter

After – hinter ... her
Beispiel: The police ran after the thief. – Die Polizei rannte hinter dem Dieb her.

Behind – hinter
Beispiel: The garden is behind the house. – Der Garten ist hinter dem Haus.

Beyond – hinter, jenseits
Beispiel: The village is beyond the hill. – Das Dorf ist hinter dem (jenseits des) Hügel(s).

Past – hinter, an ... vorbei
Beispiel: The building is 300 metres past the church. – Das Gebäude ist 300 Meter hinter der Kirche (an der Kirche vorbei).

"In front of", "before" – vor

In front of – vor
(räumlich)
Beispiel: The tree is in front of the house. – Der Baum ist vor dem Haus.

Before – vor
(zeitlich, Reihenfolge)
Beispiel: "A" comes before "B" in the alphabet. – „A" kommt im Alphabet vor „B".

"Ago", "before" (beide nachgestellt) – vor

Ago – vor
(von der Gegenwart aus gerechnet)
Beispiel: 2 years ago I spent my holidays in Spain. – Vor 2 Jahren (von heute aus gesehen) verbrachte ich meinen Urlaub in Spanien.

Before – vor (vorher)
(von einem Zeitpunkt der Vergangenheit aus gerechnet)
Beispiel: 2 years before his mother had had the accident. (Past Perfect) – 2 Jahre vorher (von damals aus gesehen) hatte seine Mutter den Unfall gehabt.

"Since", "for" – seit

Since – seit (einem Zeitpunkt)
(seit wann?)
Beispiel: I haven't seen him since May. – Ich habe ihn seit Mai nicht gesehen.

For – seit (für einen Zeitraum)
(wie lange?)
Beispiel: I haven't seen him for 2 months. – Ich habe ihn seit 2 Monaten nicht gesehen.

"By", "with" – mit

By – mit
(Verkehrsmittel)
Beispiel: by train   – mit dem Zug

By – mit
(Mittel)
Beispiel: by hand   – mit der Hand

With – mit
(Werkzeug)
Beispiel: with a knife – mit einem Messer

Exercises

Übungen

I.   *Choose the correct prepositions.*
     Wähle die richtigen Präpositionen!
"At", "in" or "on"?
1. Last week there was a terrible storm ... England.
2. The people had to stay ... their houses because of the rain.
3. ... school I'm always very tired.
4. My uncle lives ... New York.
5. Paul is not ... home ... the moment.
6. ... the morning I usually do the housework.
7. ... July 15th we'll have an important meeting.

8. There is a drink for you ... the fridge.
9. My birthday is ... the 11th of December.
10. I was born ... August 2nd, 1968.
11. Please, don't put your feet ... the sofa.
12. I work ... a bookstore.
13. The ladies' department is ... the third floor.
14. I met him ... the bus stop.
15. ... what time will he come?
16. She lives ... a nice apartment.
17. Go straight on, the building is ... your right.
18. Do you have to work ... Saturdays?
19. She lives ... 34 River Way.
20. The plane is going to leave ... time.

"Above", "over", "across" or "via"?
1. The shirt costs ... £ 10.
2. The sky ... was grey.
3. The thief climbed ... the wall and tried to escape.
4. The plane was flying 200 feet ... the sea.
5. We are going to Dover ... Canterbury.
6. Mother put the blanket ... the bed.
7. The neighbour looked ... the fence at us.
8. The temperature was ... zero.
9. England lies ... the Channel.
10. We go to England ... Ostende.
11. They came to a river with no bridges ... it.
12. You can see the tower ... the trees.
13. I helped the old lady ... the street.
14. We walked ... the bridge.
15. She lives just ... the street.

"Under" or "below"?
1. When you are on top of the hill, you can see the village down ...
2. The dog is lying ... the table.
3. It's 5 degrees ... zero.
4. She put the English Grammar ... her pillow.
5. The cottage is ... the top of the mountain.
6. The people who live ... us are always very noisy.
7. He always hides things ... the bed.
8. They were sitting ... the branches of an oak tree.
9. Some animals live in holes ... the ground.
10. The wreck lies some hundred feet ... sea level.

"Between" or "among"?

1. Our house is . . . the school and the factory.
2. We tied a rope . . . the two trees.
3. Peter is somewhere . . . the children.
4. He is . . . 20 and 25 years old.
5. He lost his wife . . . the crowd.
6. I discovered him . . . the people in the queue.
7. You can choose . . . these books.
8. There has never been a fence . . . the two houses.
9. The leader sat . . . the boy scouts.
10. She divided the presents . . . us.

"To" or "towards"?

1. I go . . . school every morning.
2. A person came . . . us, but after 10 metres he stopped.
3. He looked . . . the sky.
4. Yesterday my father flew . . . Rome.
5. I wrote a letter . . . my pen-friend.
6. He has a strange attitude . . . foreigners.
7. The apple fell . . . the ground.
8. We walked . . . the castle.
9. Can you tell me the way . . . the post office?
10. When I saw them they were walking . . . the river, but I'm not sure where they wanted to go to.

"To" or "as far as"?

1. The last train . . . London is at 12 o'clock at night.
2. I haven't been . . . the cinema for 2 months.
3. We wanted to walk . . . the youth hostel, but we only got . . . Maidstone.
4. They finally came . . . the house.
5. On the first day we drove . . . Munich, on the second day we reached our hotel.
6. When are you returning . . . London?
7. They wanted to walk . . . the top of the mountain.
8. They only came . . . the cottage.
9. He went . . . the shop.
10. How do I get . . . the theatre?

"After", "behind", "beyond" or "past"?

1. If you go . . . the house you can see the sea.
2. John is hiding . . . the tree.
3. The butler stood . . . the chair.
4. The children are playing . . . the house.

5. All the people were queuing. One person was standing . . . the other.
6. You'll find his house . . . the church.
7. The teacher walked in front and the students came . . .
8. The dog ran . . . the cat.
9. I ran . . . him because he had forgotten his keys.
10. John arrived . . . me.
11. Look . . . you! Someone is following us.
12. I sent . . . him, but he had already left.
13. The place you are looking for is . . . the river.
14. The boys are . . . her, because she's so pretty.
15. I left my book . . .

"In front of" or "before"?
1. The car is standing . . . the house.
2. Sue sits . . . me at school.
3. His name should come . . . mine on the list.
4. The lady . . . me came . . . me.
5. I can't come . . . 8 o'clock.
6. There is a nice garden . . . the house.
7. Finish your homework . . . dinner.
8. I have never seen her . . .
9. They were standing . . . the hotel.
10. I don't know this record. That was . . . my time.

"Ago" or "before"?
1. He had lost his purse 2 weeks . . .
2. Some days . . . I met him in front of the cinema.
3. I was in England 2 months . . .
4. I had been in France the week . . . you arrived.
5. His father died a year . . .
6. I had never seen him . . .
7. My brother had visited my uncle one year . . .
8. Three years . . . he went to Australia.
9. The year . . . he had been to America.
10. A week . . . I got my new car.

"Since" or "for"?
1. . . . he was a young boy
2. . . . 1st of March
3. . . . my birthday
4. . . . I came to Germany
5. . . . 4 years

6. ... last Saturday

7. ... 2 days

8. ... a few weeks

9. ... Christmas day

10. ... last week

11. ... last weekend

12. ... a few months

13. ... then

14. ... I remember

15. ... some weeks

"By" or "with"?

1. I went to London ... plane.

2. You cannot open this parcel ... a pair of scissors.

3. I sent the letter ... airmail.

4. I seldom go to work ... car.

5. He didn't go ... bus.

6. He made the desk ... saw and hammer,

7. The letter wasn't written ... hand.

8. He opened the letter ... a knife.

9. He came to school ... bike.

10. Can't you repair it ... those tools?

Prepositions Which are Dependent on Verbs

Präpositionen, die von Verben abhängig sind

Präpositionen sind oft von Verben abhängig. Manche Verben können verschiedene Präpositionen bei sich haben, was jedoch **Bedeutungsveränderungen** mit sich bringt. Im Folgenden werden die wichtigsten Verben mit den möglichen Präpositionen alphabetisch mit deutscher Bedeutung aufgeführt.

to agree in	– übereinstimmen in
~ on/upon	– über eine Sache einig werden
~ to	– einer Sache zustimmen

to agree with	– übereinstimmen mit, gut bekommen
to apply for	– sich bewerben um
~ to	– sich wenden an
to ask about	– sich nach einer Sache erkundigen
~ after	– sich nach dem Befinden einer Person erkundigen
~ for	– bitten um
to call at/on	– vorsprechen bei (kurzen Besuch machen)
~ for	– verlangen nach, erfordern
~ up	– jemanden anrufen (Telefon)
to care about/for	– Interesse haben an
~ for	– gerne mögen
~ for	– sorgen für, sich kümmern um
to change for	– vertauschen gegen, umsteigen nach
~ into	– (sich) verwandeln in
to charge for	– verlangen, fordern (Preis)
~ with	– beauftragen mit, eines Verbrechens beschuldigen
to come about	– geschehen
~ across	– zufällig stoßen auf
~ for	– kommen wegen
to compare to	– gleichstellen mit
~ with	– vergleichen mit
to complain about/of	– sich beschweren über
~ to	– sich beschweren bei (jemandem)
to condemn for	– verurteilen wegen
~ to	– verurteilen zu
to consist of	– bestehen aus
to deal in	– handeln mit (einer Ware)
~ with	– handeln von (z. B. Buch), umgehen mit (jemandem), Handel treiben mit (jemandem)
to die by	– sterben durch (z. B. Feuer)
~ for	– sterben für
~ from/of	– sterben an (z. B. Hunger)
to distinguish between	– unterscheiden zwischen zweien
~ oneself by	– sich auszeichnen durch
~ from	– unterscheiden von
to divide among/ between	– teilen unter/zwischen zweien
~ something by	– etwas teilen/dividieren durch
~ something into	– etwas einteilen (in)
to give in (to)	– nachgeben
~ up	– aufgeben
to hope for	– hoffen auf

the hope of	– die Hoffnung auf
to inquire about	– sich erkundigen nach
~ after	– sich nach jemandes Befinden erkundigen
~ of	– sich bei jemandem erkundigen
to introduce into	– etwas/jemanden einführen in (bekannt machen)
~ to	– jemanden vorstellen
to judge about/of	– urteilen über
~ by/from	– urteilen nach
to lean against	– lehnen an/gegen
~ on	– sich stützen auf
to live by	– seinen Lebensunterhalt verdienen durch
~ on	– leben von (z. B. Brot)
~ with	– leben (wohnen) bei
to look about	– sich umsehen
~ after	– sich kümmern um
~ at	– ansehen, blicken auf
~ down upon somebody	– herabsehen auf jemanden
~ for	– suchen nach
~ forward to	– sich freuen auf
~ in	– einen kurzen Besuch machen
~ into	– hineinsehen in, untersuchen
~ like (Adverb)	– aussehen wie
~ on	– zuschauen
~ on/upon as	– betrachten als
~ out	– aufpassen, sich in Acht nehmen
~ over	– durchsehen (prüfen)
~ through	– sorgfältig durchlesen
~ up	– nachschlagen (z. B. im Lexikon)
~ up to somebody	– zu jemandem aufblicken
to point at	– zeigen auf, richten auf
~ out	– aufzeigen
~ to	– hinweisen auf
to speak about	– sprechen über/von
~ of	– erwähnen
~ on	– eine Rede halten über
~ to	– sprechen mit (jemandem)
~ up	– lauter sprechen
~ with	– sich unterhalten mit (jemandem)
to stay away	– wegbleiben
~ in (out)	– im Haus (außerhalb des Hauses) bleiben
~ up	– aufbleiben
~ with	– bei jemandem bleiben (zu Besuch sein)

to take by	– anfassen an, packen bei
~ for	– (jemanden) fälschlich halten für
~ off	– ausziehen (Kleidung), abheben (Flugzeug)
to think about	– nachdenken über
~ of	– denken an
to turn against	– sich feindlich wenden gegen
~ away (from)	– sich abwenden (von)
~ back	– umkehren
~ down	– (jemandem) etwas abschlagen (Nein sagen)
~ inside out	– etwas umdrehen (z. B. Taschen)
~ into	– verwandeln in
~ off	– etwas abdrehen (z. B. Heizung)
~ on	– etwas andrehen (z. B. Heizung)
~ out	– sich herausstellen (als)
~ to	– sich wenden an
~ up	– erscheinen
to wait behind	– zurückbleiben
~ for	– warten auf
~ on	– (jemanden) bedienen
~ up	– wachbleiben und warten
to weep for	– weinen um (jemanden)
~ over	– weinen über
~ with/for	– weinen vor
to write about	– über etwas schreiben
~ back	– zurückschreiben (Brief beantworten)
~ down	– (etwas) aufschreiben
~ in	– schreiben mit (z. B. Tinte)
~ off	– etwas abschreiben (als verloren ansehen)
~ out	– etwas ausfüllen (z. B. Scheck)
~ to	– jemandem schreiben
~ with	– schreiben mit (z. B. Füller)

Exercises

Übungen

Put in the correct preposition.
Setze die richtige Präposition ein!

 1. Please turn the radiator..., it's too warm.
 2. I can't find my glasses, I've been looking...them all day.
 3. The lady inquired...the buses to Canterbury.
 4. I'm looking forward...seeing you next month.
 5. Divide 50...10!
 6. We all hope...the best.
 7. The story turned...to be not true.
 8. The policeman took the thief...the collar.
 9. I'm sorry, we are late. We had to wait...the bus.
10. The plane took...at 10 a.m.
11. The teacher complained...the student's bad marks.
12. The soldiers died...hunger.
13. May I introduce you...my father.
14. When I was in England I stayed...a host family.
15. The old man leaned...his walking stick.
16. Because I was ill, I had to stay...last week.
17. The answers have to be written...
18. When she heard the news, she wept...joy.
19. The man next door lives...selling cars.
20. You can look...the unknown words in the appendix.
21. Don't write...pencil, but...ink!
22. The children wrote postcards...their parents.
23. The students applied...a holiday job.
24. My mother came...the letter in my desk.
25. The book deals...social problems.
26. The magician changed the parrot...a rabbit.
27. The prisoner was condemned...murder.
28. How much did he charge...the spare parts?
29. He is similar to his father. He looks...his father.
30. Could you please look...my cat while I'm on holiday?
31. The actress looked...the mirror.
32. The doctor told me to give...smoking.
33. On Saturday the children stayed...till 10 o'clock.
34. He is looked...an expert.
35. The speaker pointed....that the work had to be continued.
36. They provided two servants to wait...us.
37. Please write to me...your next job.

Final Test: The Preposition

Abschlusstest: die Präpositionen

I. Put in the correct prepositions.

   Setze die richtigen Präpositionen ein!

   1. We arrived . . . the station . . . midnight.

   2. I don't care . . . sport.

   3. You must learn to distinguish . . . good and bad.

   4. The students complained . . . the homework.

   5. I haven't been in town . . . 3 weeks.

   6. Simon is sitting . . . . the other children.

   7. We are going . . . Paris . . . Straßbourg.

   8. 3 weeks . . . we talked about this problem.

   9. I didn't come . . . train, I came . . . bus.

  10. My father works . . . Harrods.

  11. He hasn't written . . . me . . . last month.

  12. My mother is preparing dinner . . . the kitchen.

  13. The accident happened . . . the road to Sevenoaks.

  14. 2 years . . . I had already been . . . Germany.

  15. The robber was condemned . . . 5 years imprisonment.

  16. Can you distinguish a horse . . . a donkey?

  17. He wanted to pick up his record. He came . . . his record.

  18. Our firm has never dealt . . . Simsons Ltd.

  19. The man was charged . . . blackmailing.

  20. The text consists . . . five chapters.

  21. The meal didn't agree . . . me.

  22. Don't put your bike in front of the house, put it . . . the house.

  23. Why are you always so obstinate? You never give . . . !

  24. Be careful! Look . . . !

  25. Could you please write . . . a cheque?

II. Translate the following sentences.

   Übersetze die folgenden Sätze!

   1. Wir wohnen seit 1995 in der Kirchstr. 25.

   2. Er bestand darauf den Safe zu öffnen.

   3. Kinder unter 16 Jahren dürfen nicht in einen Pub gehen.

   4. Ich warte schon seit 1 Stunde auf Tom.

   5. Er starb vor 2 Tagen an Herzversagen.

   6. Ich habe schon so viel von ihr gehört, dass ich mich darauf freue sie zu sehen.

   7. Bitte sei pünktlich morgen!

   8. Wir haben einen kleinen Garten hinter dem Haus.

9. Er hat gestern seine Brieftasche in der U-Bahn verloren.
10. Sie hat sich vor einer Woche um die Stelle einer Sekretärin bei der Firma Cup Ltd. beworben.
11. Auf der rechten Seite kannst du unser Haus auf dem Bild sehen.
12. Ich bin abends gewöhnlich um 18 Uhr zu Hause.
13. Du kannst mich zwischen 13 und 14 Uhr im Büro erreichen.
14. Er schrieb einen Brief an seine Tante und schickte ihn per Luftpost.
15. Er wurde auf einem Felsen unterhalb des Gipfels gefunden.
16. Meine Mutter arbeitet schon seit 3 Jahren im Supermarkt.
17. Er lebte 5 Jahre lang unter den Indianern.
18. Er verstand die Warnung zwischen den Zeilen.
19. Unter den Bewerbern waren drei geeignete Kandidaten.
20. Wir kamen rechtzeitig zum Abendessen im Hotel an.
21. Als er über die Brücke ging, sah er ein Flugzeug über sich.
22. Am Abend des 13. Oktobers passierte der Unfall.
23. Er lebte gerne bei den Indianern im Urwald.
24. Sieh deinen Aufsatz noch einmal durch. In Zeile 2 ist ein Fehler.
25. Sie sprechen schon seit einer halben Stunde über seine Probleme.

The Conjunction

Die Konjunktion/
das Bindewort

Wörter, die Sätze oder Satzteile miteinander verbinden, nennt man Konjunktionen. Wir unterscheiden:

▶ **nebenordnende Konjunktionen (co-ordinating conjunctions),** die gleichartige Satzglieder, Hauptsatz (HS) mit Hauptsatz oder Nebensatz (NS) mit Nebensatz verbinden.

Anwendung

Beispiel: He was expecting a prize, but he was disappointed.

Er erwartete einen Preis, aber er wurde enttäuscht.

       HS   nebenordnende   HS
            Konjunktion

Dazu gehören: also, and, besides, but, either ... or, for, however, neither ... nor, nevertheless, nor, or, so, still, therefore, thus, too, yet etc.

▶ **unterordnende Konjunktionen (subordinating conjunctions),**
die bei einem Satzgefüge (Hauptsatz und Nebensatz) den Nebensatz einleiten.

Beispiel: If it rains, I'll stay in.

          NS

Wenn es regnet, **werde ich drinnen bleiben.**

unter-   HS
ordnende
Konjunktion

Dazu gehören: after, as, because, before, if, now, since, so that, that, unless, until, when, where, whereas, while etc.

Im Folgenden werden die Konjunktionen behandelt, die entweder leicht mit anderen Konjunktionen oder aber mit Wörtern anderer Wortarten (z. B. Präpositionen) verwechselt werden.

Das deutsche „wenn":
"if" oder "when"?

If – wenn/falls
leitet einen *Bedingungssatz* – Conditional Clause, (siehe auch Kapitel "Conditional Clauses", S. 129 ff. ein.

Beispiel: If it rains, we can't have our picnic. – Wenn (falls) es regnet, können wir kein Picknick machen.

When – wenn, sobald als
leitet einen *Zeitsatz* (Temporal Clause) ein.

Beispiel: When he comes, we can leave. Wenn (sobald) er kommt, können wir gehen.

Das deutsche „während":
"during", "while" oder "whereas"?

During – während
steht als Präposition vor einem *Nomen (bzw. Artikel / Pronomen + Nomen)*.

Beispiel: During the holidays he wrote many letters. – Während der Ferien schrieb er viele Briefe.

While – während
als Konjunktion leitet einen *Nebensatz der Zeit* (Temporal Clause) ein.

Beispiel: While he was on holiday he wrote many letters. – Während er in Ferien war, schrieb er viele Briefe.

Whereas – während, wohingegen
leitet als Konjunktion einen *Nebensatz des Gegensatzes* (Adversative Clause) ein.

Beispiel: He went on holiday, whereas I stayed at home. – Er fuhr in Urlaub, während (wohingegen) ich zu Hause blieb.

Das deutsche „weil"/„da":
"because", "since", "as" oder "for"?

Because – weil, da

steht, wenn ein Hauptsatz vorangeht, d. h. *nicht am Satzanfang.*

Beispiel: He was late because he had missed the bus. – Er war zu spät, weil (da) er den Bus verpasst hatte.

Beachte: because of – wegen (Präposition vor Nomen)

Beispiel: Because of his illness, he couldn't come. – Wegen seiner Krankheit konnte er nicht kommen.

Since – weil, da

steht, wenn ein *Hauptsatz folgt* und der Grund des Geschehens dem Hörer *bekannt* ist.

Beispiel: Since he had missed the bus, he was late. – Da er den Bus verpasst hatte, war er zu spät.

As – weil, da

steht, wenn ein *Hauptsatz folgt* und der Grund des Geschehens nur *beiläufig erwähnt* wird.

Beispiel: As he had missed the bus, he was late. – Da er den Bus verpasst hatte, war er zu spät.

For – denn

leitet einen *Hauptsatz* ein und steht *nie am Satzanfang.*

Beispiel: He was late, for he had missed the bus. – Er kam zu spät, denn er hatte den Bus verpasst.

Das deutsche „auch (nicht)":
"too", "also", "as well", "so", "neither" oder "nor", "not either"?

Too – auch

steht meist am *Satzende* und wird durch Komma abgetrennt.

Beispiel: My friends go to school, too.

    oder: My friends, too, go to school. – Meine Freunde gehen auch zur Schule.

Also – auch

steht in der Regel *nicht am Satzanfang*, sondern hinter dem hervorzuhebenden Wort.

Beispiel: My friends also go to school. – Meine Freunde gehen auch zur Schule.

As well – auch

steht am *Satzende*.

Beispiel: My friends go to school as well. – Meine Freunde gehen auch zur Schule.

So – auch

Kurze Sätze für deutsch „(Person) auch" werden mit "so" gebildet. Ein im Vorsatz vorhandenes Hilfsverb wird wieder aufgegriffen.

Ist im Vorsatz kein Hilfsverb vorhanden, so verwendet man eine entsprechende Form von "to do". Die englische Konstruktion lautet also: *"so" + Hilfsverb + Person*.

Die Reihenfolge Hilfsverb (Prädikat) – Person (Subjekt) entspricht nicht der normalen Satzstellung Subjekt – Prädikat. Man nennt diese Umdrehung *"Inversion"*.

Beispiel: Peter **can** swim. – Peter kann schwimmen.

So **can I. – Ich auch.**

Peter **is** at home. – Peter ist zu Hause.

So **is** his father. – Sein Vater auch.

Peter **likes** ice-cream. – Peter mag Eis.

So **do I. – Ich auch.**

Peter **went** out. – Peter ging aus.

So **did I. – Ich auch.**

Neither/nor – auch nicht

Kurze Sätze für deutsch „(Person) auch nicht" werden mit "neither" oder "nor" gebildet. Das im Vorsatz vorhandene Hilfsverb wird wieder aufgegriffen. Die englische Konstruktion lautet also: *"neither/nor" + Hilfsverb + Person.* (Es liegt eine *Inversion* vor; siehe: so = auch im Kurzsatz.)

Beispiel: I **cannot** swim. – Ich kann nicht schwimmen.

Neither/Nor **can** Peter. – Peter auch nicht.

I **will** not come. – Ich werde nicht kommen.

Neither/Nor **will** Peter. – Peter auch nicht.

I **don't** like hamburgers. – Ich mag keine Hamburger.

Neither/Nor **does** Peter. – Peter auch nicht.

Not ... either – auch nicht

wird mit normaler Wortstellung gebraucht. Hier ist also keine Inversion erforderlich.

Beispiel: Paul does not go home either. – Paul geht auch nicht nach Hause.

Beachte: Bei "not...either" muss im Gegensatz zu "neither/nor" das Vollverb (z. B. go) erwähnt werden.

Das deutsche „wie":
"like", "as" oder "how"?

Like – wie

steht bei einem *bildlichen Vergleich*.

Beispiel: a woman like her – eine Frau wie sie
It's something like a machine. – Es ist so etwas wie eine Maschine.
He behaves like an idiot. – Er benimmt sich wie ein Idiot.

Like – wie

steht bei Vergleichen, wenn nur ein *Nomen/Pronomen* folgt.

Beispiel: Drink like a king! – Trinke wie ein König!

As – wie

steht nach *Adjektiven, Adverbien* und *"the same"*.

Beispiel: sweet as sugar – süß wie Zucker
the same as before – dasselbe wie zuvor

As – wie

steht im *Vergleichssatz* vor dem Nomen oder Pronomen, wenn ein Verb folgt.

Beispiel: Lay the table as they **do** in good restaurants. – Decke den Tisch, wie man es in guten Restaurants tut.

As – als

steht bei *Gleichstellung*.

Beispiel: He works as a teacher. – Er arbeitet als Lehrer (er ist Lehrer).
aber: He speaks like my teacher. – Er spricht wie mein Lehrer (er ist es aber nicht).

As ... as – so ... wie

Zwischen "as ... as" steht ein *Adverb* oder ein *Adjektiv*.

Beispiel: as soon as possible – so bald wie möglich
as tall as Mary – so groß wie Mary

How – wie, auf welche Weise, in welchem Maße

wird als *Fragewort* gebraucht.

Beispiel: How did you manage? – Wie hast du das geschafft?

How old is Mary? – Wie alt ist Mary?

Beachte: „Wie?" wird in einigen Fragen mit "what" übersetzt!

Beispiel: Wie nennt man das?   – What do you call this?

Wie heißt du?   – What is your name?

Wie spät ist es?   – What is the time?

Wie wär's mit ..?   – What about ...?

Wie sieht dein Auto aus?   – What does your car look like?

Final Test: The Conjunction

Abschlusstest: die Konjunktion

I. Put in "if" or "when".
Setze "if" oder "when" ein!

1. The dog always runs to the door...the bell rings.
2. I'll go on holiday next summer...I have time.
3. ...their parents are out, the children get up to all sorts of nonsense.
4. The driver stopped immediately...he saw the child.
5. ...I pass my exam, my father will buy me a car.
6. You'd know the story...you'd read today's paper.
7. What would you do...you found £ 1000?
8. Mother always turns on the radio...she does the washing-up.
9. You'll miss the train...you don't hurry.
10. You can see the Tower...you are standing on the Monument.

II. Put in "during", "while" or "whereas".
Setze "during", "while" oder "whereas" ein.

1. ...our stay in England the weather was fine.
2. ...dinner we talked about our plans for the next day.
3. ...we were having dinner we watched TV.
4. ...we were in Italy we visited some friends.
5. ...the last year we had a lot of work.
6. My brother spent his holiday in Spain...I went to Italy.
7. ...we were on the beach we played some games.
8. I had to work overtime,...my colleagues were on holiday.
9. ...the last week we wrote three class tests.
10. ...she was preparing dinner, the telephone rang.
11. ...the lesson Peter didn't listen.

12. ... the teacher was explaining the text, some of the students were not listening.
13. There may be occasional showers ... the day.
14. ... the examination I didn't feel nervous.
15. Several important letters came ... we were in England.

III. Put in "because", "since", "as" or "for".
   Setze "because", "since", "as" oder "for" ein!

1. He couldn't come to the party, ... he was ill.
2. ... his mother was in hospital, he had to look after himself.
3. ... nobody had told him, he didn't know.
4. He got some extra homework ... he had forgotten his exercise book.
5. ... Sally is not a good student, she couldn't take part in the competition.
6. ... my little brother is ill, I have to stay at home.
7. ... he had lost his purse, I lent him some money.
8. He can't buy the book, ... he hasn't got any pocket money left.
9. Simon got the job ... he has very good reports.
10. I'm very hungry, ... I haven't had my dinner yet.
11. Sam lost his job ... he hadn't done his work properly.
12. ... she doesn't understand German, we had to translate everything.
13. ... I didn't sleep very well last night. I'm very tired today.
14. ... we had missed the last train, we had to take a taxi.
15. ... English pubs close very early, we came home quite early.
16. I'm sorry, I can't come, ... I have to see the doctor.
17. We didn't go to the seaside, ... it was raining.
18. ... Sheila is very lazy, she'll never be successful.
19. On Sunday we stayed in all day ... the weather was terrible.
20. Harry was elected chairman ... he is such a good speaker.

IV. Form short sentences (German „... auch [nicht]") with the persons in brackets.
   Bilde kurze Sätze (deutsch „... auch [nicht]") mit den Personen in Klammern!

1. My father can speak Italian. (I)
2. Sally is a very good student. (her brother)
3. My mother cooks well. (I)
4. The Millers will come to the meeting. (the Meyers)
5. Edith doesn't go out very often. (her sisters)
6. Judith cant' stand stupid persons. (I)
7. He likes science-fiction stories. (I)
8. My sister hasn't got a driving-licence. (my brother)
9. Simon hadn't got his homework. (I)

10. I don't watch TV very often. (he)

11. Billy must go home now. (Peter)

12. I don't like him. (I)

13. Petra can speak English. (Susanne)

14. I can write English letters. (my friend)

15. Michael enjoys sailing. (Carmen)

V. *Put in "like", "as" or "how".*
   Setze "like", "as" oder "how" ein!

   1. Mary dances . . . a queen.

   2. . . . did you find the correct answer?

   3. Sally is a member of the school choir, but she sings . . . a professional singer.

   4. Sam sometimes behaves . . . a baby.

   5. . . . did the thief get into the house?

   6. My car is . . . fast . . . yours.

   7. My sister works . . . a secretary at Simon and Co.

   8. Mr Harris speaks German . . . a German but he's English.

   9. Men . . . Einstein are rare.

10. He did it . . . his uncle had done it.

11. . . . do you do?

12. The old warehouses are used . . . flats now.

13. She looks . . . her sister.

14. When he came back from the playing-ground, he was so dirty, he looked . . . a chimney sweeper.

15. You should try to see yourself . . . others see you.

16. The exercise isn't . . . easy . . . you think.

17. The little child followed me . . . a dog.

18. My father is a clerk, but he can repair things . . . a carpenter.

19. Now we have the same problem . . . we had before.

20. Little Billy sometimes speaks . . . an adult.

Indefinite Quantifiers

Unbestimmte Zahlwörter/ unbestimmte Mengen- bezeichnungen

Unbestimmte Zahlwörter wie "much", "many", "some", "any" etc. werden oft noch als **Indefinitpronomen (unbestimmte Fürwörter)** bezeichnet.
Unbestimmte Zahlwörter stellen eine häufige Fehlerquelle dar, da einige Zahlwörter im Deutschen bedeutungsgleich sind, im Englischen jedoch unterschiedlich verwendet werden.

"Some" und "any"

"Some" und "any" bezeichnen beide eine *unbestimmte Menge oder Anzahl* in der Bedeutung „etwas"/„einige". Sie unterscheiden sich in ihrer Anwendung.

Some: +	Any: - ?
▶ "Some" steht im bejahten Satz. **Beispiel:** There are some books on the table.	▶ "Any" steht im verneinten Satz. **Beispiel:** There aren't any. books on the table.
	▶ "Any" steht im Fragesatz. **Beispiel:** Are there any books on the table?
▶ "Some" steht in Fragesätzen, wenn eine bejahte Antwort erwartet wird (z. B. beim Anbieten) **Beispiel:** Would you like some winne? Unter anderem steht es nach: where, when, how **Beispiel:** Where can I get some books?	▶ "Any" steht in bejahten Sätzen in der Bedeutung „jeder beliebige". **Beispiel:** You can come any time.

Grund-regel

225

Some	Any
▶ "Some" steht im verneinten Satz, wenn der Sprecher auf etwas wirklich Vorhandenes oder Geschehenes hinweist. **Beispiel:** I don't need some books. (I've already got some)	▶ "Any" steht in den Nebensätzen der If-Sätze. **Beispiel:** If I had any idea, I would tell you.

Die gleichen Regeln gelten für die Zusammensetzungen (compounds) mit "some" und "any", wie z. B.

something/anything	– etwas/irgendetwas
somebody/anybody	– jemand/irgendjemand
someone/anyone	– jemand/irgendjemand
somewhere/anywhere	– irgendwo

Exercises

Übungen

I. *Put in "some" or "any".*
    Setze "some" oder "any" ein!

1. Are there ... potatoes in the basket?
2. He hasn't got ... paper.
3. I got ... good books for my birthday.
4. I had to wait for ... minutes.
5. You need ... extra money for your holiday.
6. I've seen ... children in the park.
7. Isn't there ... yoghurt in the fridge?
8. Did you have ... difficulties?
9. Isn't there ... bacon left?
10. I'm sorry. We haven't got ... French wine at the moment.
11. I need ... paper.
12. Did you see ... body near the house?
13. Have you noticed ... differences?
14. Did you buy ... thing special?
15. You can't get ... fresh strawberries at the moment.
16. I'd like ... sweets. Have you got ... ?
17. ... glasses are broken.
18. Have you seen Tom ... where?
19. He hasn't got ... money.
20. ... people were standing around.

Unbestimmte Zahlwörter
Much, many, little, few

II. *Put in "some" or "any". Look out for the exceptions.*
Setze "some" oder "any" ein! Achte auf die Ausnahmen!

1. ...of the pens will do.
2. Would you like...coffee?
3. Did you have...thing particular in mind?
4. You can pay with...credit card.
5. If I had...money, I'd lend you...
6. You wouldn't take...money, would you?
7. ...people never know what they want.
8. I've never seen...thing as stupid as that!
9. May I have...more cake?
10. If...thing goes wrong you can phone me.
11. Won't you take...milk in your coffee?
12. There are...good restaurants in town.
13. Is there...thing else you'd like to know?
14. ...one who has ever been to England must have seen a picture of the Queen.
15. I've never had...thing to do with that.
16. Where can I get...books on Scotland?
17. One of M. Monroe's best films was "...Like It Hot".
18. ...fool knows that 2 + 2 is 4.
19. Has...one called the police yet?
20. Can't I be alone...where?

"Much" und "many"/"little" und "few"

"Much" (viel) und "many" (viele) werden hauptsächlich in *Fragen* und *verneinten Sätzen* verwendet.

Beispiel: She hasn't got much time. – Sie hat nicht viel Zeit.

Have you got many friends? – Hast du viele Freunde?

In bejahten Aussagesätzen stehen "much" und "many" gewöhnlich nur als Subjekt oder in Verbindung mit "as", "so", "how", "too".

Beispiel: Much of what you believe is not true. – Viel von dem, was du glaubst, ist nicht wahr.

Take as much as you want. – Nimm soviel du willst.

Ansonsten werden "much" und "many" in bejahten Aussagesätzen durch folgende Begriffe ersetzt: a lot, lots, plenty, a great quantity, a large quantity, a great/good deal (nur für "much"), a large number (nur für "many") + of.

Beispiel: She has got plenty of time. – Sie hat viel Zeit.

Grund-regel

227

"Much" (viel) und "little" (wenig)

stehen nur vor *nicht zählbaren Begriffen,* d. h. Wörtern im Singular.

Beispiel: We haven't got much sugar left. – Wir haben nicht viel Zucker übrig.
We have little sugar left. – Wir haben wenig Zucker übrig.

"Much" und "little" können auch ohne Bezug auf ein Nomen stehen.

Beispiel: We didn't do much today. – Wir haben heute nicht viel getan.

Die *Steigerungsformen,* für die die gleiche Regel gilt, lauten:

much (viel)   – more (mehr)   – the most (der/die/das meiste)
little (wenig) – less (weniger) – the least (der/die/das wenigste).

"Many" (viele) und "few" (wenige)

stehen nur vor *zählbaren Begriffen,* d. h. vor Wörtern im Plural.

Beispiel: We haven't got many eggs left. – Wir haben nicht viele Eier übrig.
We have few eggs left. – Wir haben wenige Eier übrig.

"Many" und "few" können ohne Bezug auf ein Nomen nur in der Bedeutung von „viele/wenige Leute" stehen.

Beispiel: How many were at the party? – Wie viele (Leute) waren auf der Party?

Die *Steigerungsformen,* für die die gleiche Regel gilt, lauten:

many (viele) – more (mehr)   – the most (am meisten)
few (wenige) – fewer (weniger) – the fewest (am wenigsten)

Exercises

Übungen

I. *Put in "much" or "many".*
   Setze "much" oder "many" ein!

   1. We have written too ... sentences today.
   2. I've eaten too ... cakes.
   3. He reads so ... books.
   4. They have got so ... children.
   5. There wasn't ... dirt in the hall.
   6. The hostess didn't make ... tea.
   7. ... bottles were broken.
   8. We didn't have ... fun.
   9. How ... cigarettes can you buy on the ferry?
   10. How ... is the pullover?
   11. ... of us were very tired.
   12. How ... wine did you drink?
   13. Where did you find so ... stones?

14. There is too . . . smoke in the room.
15. We didn't have . . . rain in England.
16. . . . students don't like homework.
17. The company built so . . . houses.
18. Don't make so . . . noise.
19. He had too . . . drinks.
20. My brother hasn't got . . . time.

II. *Put in "little" or "few" in front of the nouns.*
   Setze "little" oder "few" vor die Nomen!

1. . . . flowers	8. . . . accidents	15. . . . pictures
2. . . . noise	9. . . . letters	16. . . . work
3. . . . music	10. . . . pens	17. . . . trees
4. . . . records	11. . . . cups	18. . . . sleep
5. . . . money	12. . . . salt	19. . . . enthusiasm
6. . . . boys	13. . . . water	20. . . . rivers
7. . . . women	14. . . . sweets	21. . . . books

III. *Form positive statements.*
   Bilde bejahte Aussagesätze!

1. I haven't got much time.
2. He hasn't got much money.
3. The students haven't read many books.
4. I can't eat many hamburgers.
5. There aren't many trees in the park.
6. There isn't much noise upstairs.
7. There aren't many jobs available.
8. We didn't have much wind.
9. I haven't eaten many apples.
10. He hasn't drunk much alcohol.

IV. *Translate the following expressions.*
   Übersetze die folgenden Ausdrücke!

1. weniger Fehler	9. weniger Lampen	17. viel Ärger
2. mehr Geld	10. die wenigsten Schüler	18. weniger Schaden
3. am wenigsten Zeit	11. viele Freunde	19. mehr Schokolade
4. weniger Natur	12. mehr Urlaub	20. die meisten Bücher
5. wenig Wasser	13. die meisten Straßen	21. mehr Lehrer
6. mehr Geschäfte	14. mehr Fenster	22. weniger Hilfe
7. die wenigsten Zimmer	15. weniger Übungen	23. die meiste Zeit
8. mehr Tee	16. die meisten Tiere	24. weniger Häuser

"Each", "every", "any", "all" und "whole"

"Each", "every", "all", "any" und "whole" bereiten aufgrund ihrer ähnlichen Bedeutungen oft Schwierigkeiten:

Übersicht

each	– jeder (Einzelne)
every	– jeder (allgemein verstanden)
any	– jeder (x-Beliebige)
all	– alle (ohne Ausnahme)
whole	– ganz

Each – jeder (Einzelne)

Grundregel

betont eine Person oder ein Ding aus einer *begrenzten Anzahl*. "Each" kann vor einem Nomen stehen (a) oder allein stehend verwendet werden (b).

Beispiel: (a) You must ask each student in your class. – Du musst jeden (einzelnen) Schüler deiner Klasse fragen.

He gave a present to each boy. – Er gab jedem einzelnen Jungen ein Geschenk.

(b) He gave a present to each (one *). – Er gab jedem (Einzelnen) ein Geschenk.

In Verbindung mit Grundzahlen kann nachgestelltes "each" in der Bedeutung „je" verwendet werden.

Beispiel: The oranges are 30 p each. – Die Orangen kosten je (Stück) 30 Pence.

Every – jeder (allgemein verstanden)

und seine Zusammensetzungen (everybody, -one – jeder; everything – alles etc.) werden benutzt, wenn „jeder" (Person oder Ding) *ganz allgemein* gemeint ist (alle ohne Ausnahme).

Beispiel: Every child likes sweets. – Jedes Kind (ohne Ausnahme) mag Süßigkeiten.

Everybody was busy. – Jeder (ohne Ausnahme) war beschäftigt.

We met every day last week. – Wir trafen uns jeden Tag (ohne Ausnahme) letzte Woche.

"Every" steht gewöhnlich vor Nomen im Singular (siehe Beispiele).

Beachte: ▶ Bei Verbindung von "every" mit Grundzahlen tritt das Nomen in den Plural.

Beispiel: every two days – **alle** zwei Tage

▶ Bei Verbindung von „every" mit Ordnungszahlen steht das Nomen jedoch im Singular.

Beispiel: every second day – **jeden** zweiten Tag

---

* *"Each one" betont die Vereinzelung besonders stark.*

Unbestimmte Zahlwörter
Each, every, any, all, whole

Einige Ausdrücke mit "every":

every other day	– jeden zweiten Tag
every now and then	– von Zeit zu Zeit
every now and again	– von Zeit zu Zeit

Ausdrücke

Any – jeder (x-Beliebige)

und seine Zusammensetzungen (anybody, anyone – jeder; anything – alles etc.) bedeuten im *bejahten* Aussagesatz „jeder x-Beliebige", „jeder" im Sinne von „ganz gleich welcher".

Beispiel: Any policeman can tell you the way to the police station. – Jeder (x-beliebige) Polizist kann dir den Weg zur Polizeistation zeigen.
Anybody can become a member. – Jeder (ganz gleich wer) kann Mitglied werden.

All – alle (ohne Ausnahme)

hat *vor Nomen im Plural* allgemeine Bedeutung.

Beispiel: All students have to learn. – Alle Schüler müssen lernen.

"All the (my/his/ . . .)" + *Nomen (im Plural)* hat die Bedeutung „alle einer bestimmten Gruppe".

Beispiel: All the students in this class have to learn. – Alle Schüler dieser Klasse müssen lernen.

"All" + *Adjektiv* hat die Bedeutung „ganz/völlig".

Beispiel: My jeans were all dirty. – Meine Jeans waren ganz schmutzig.

"All" + *Nomen im Singular* bedeutet „ganz".

Beispiel: I worked all day. – Ich arbeitete den ganzen Tag.

"All" allein stehend bedeutet im Singular „alles", im Plural „alle".

Beispiel: All I know is . . . – Alles, was ich weiß, ist . . .
All agreed. – Alle stimmten zu.

Einige Ausdrücke mit "all":

all of a sudden	– ganz plötzlich
at all	– überhaupt
nothing at all	– überhaupt nichts
if at all	– wenn überhaupt
all but	– alle außer
first of all	– zu allererst

Ausdrücke

Whole – ganz

(substantivisch: the whole of) bezeichnet ein unteilbares Ganzes. Es betont die Gesamtheit stärker als "all".

Beispiel: We stayed in the whole day. – Wir blieben den ganzen Tag zu Hause.
Tell me the whole truth! – Sag mir die ganze Wahrheit!

Einige Ausdrücke mit "whole":

Ausdrücke

on the whole	– im Ganzen
as a whole	– als Ganzes
the whole of (England)	– ganz (England)

Übungen

Exercises
Übungen

I. *Put in "each", "every", "any", "all (the)", or "whole".*
Setze "each", "every", "any", "all (the)" oder "whole" ein!

1. ... person makes mistakes.
2. ... child likes playing.
3. The apples are 8 p ...
4. The same can happen to you ... day.
5. ... member of the club came at a different time.
6. ... doors close automatically.
7. We travelled round the ... country.
8. ... member of the party must help.
9. ... people in the theatre clapped.
10. ... of us likes you.
11. ... men must die.
12. You can use ... TV for this video game.
13. ... assault on staff will be prosecuted.
14. ... of these articles are worth reading.
15. ... these years he hasn't written a single letter.
16. The ... club were happy because ... members had won a prize.
17. ... visitors get a free meal.
18. Grandma gave ... of her grandchildren a book.
19. ... individual picture sold for £ 200.
20. We have five different pies, ... kind is delicious.
21. ... parents are invited.
22. We sell the pullovers for £ 10 ...
23. ... people left the building.

24. Serving afternoon tea is the same procedure . . . day.
25. He stayed in bed . . . day.
26. At . . . meeting we discussed the . . . question over and over again.
27. . . . members of the family looked at . . . other.
28. . . . members of the family looked at . . . others.
29. He told . . . one the whole story.
30. . . . the answers are correct.

"No", "not", "none", "nobody" ("no one") und "nothing"

no	– kein
not	– nicht
none	– keiner

Übersicht

No – kein

wird *attributiv vor Nomen* gebraucht.
Beispiel: no money– kein Geld
no help   – keine Hilfe
No (nicht, um nichts) kann in adverbialer Funktion vor Komparativen (2. Steigerungsform) gebraucht werden.
Beispiel: There were no fewer than 20 people at the party. – Es waren nicht weniger als 20 Leute auf der Party.

Grund-regel

Not – nicht

steht als *Verneinungspartikel* meist hinter dem *Hilfsverb*.
Beispiel: I cannot come. – Ich kann nicht kommen.
I do not like him. – Ich mag ihn nicht.
"Not" kann aber nicht nur das Verb, sondern auch ein *anderes Wort* verneinen.
Beispiel: Not everybody came. – Nicht jeder kam.
Who wants to start? – Not me. – Wer möchte beginnen? – Ich nicht!
Not a sound could be heard. – Nicht ein Laut war zu hören.

None – keiner

wird *substantivisch* in Bezug auf ein vorangegangenes oder folgendes *Nomen* gebraucht.
Beispiel: Is there any coffee left? – Ist noch Kaffee übrig?
No, none at all. – Nein, überhaupt keiner.
None of my friends helped me. – Keiner meiner Freunde hat mir geholfen.

"None" kann *in adverbialer Funktion* vor "too" im Sinne von „nicht besonders"
und vor "the" + Komparativ (2. Steigerungsform) im Sinne von „keineswegs"
verwendet werden.

Beispiel: The wine was none too good. – Der Wein war nicht besonders gut.
The food was none the better. – Das Essen war keineswegs besser.

Nobody (no one) – keiner, niemand

wird *substantivisch* ohne Bezugsnomen für *Personen* verwendet.

Beispiel: Nobody (no one) could answer the question. – Keiner (niemand)
konnte die Frage beantworten.

Nothing – nichts

wird *substantivisch* ohne Bezugsnomen für *Dinge* verwendet.

Beispiel: Nothing could be done. – Nichts konnte getan werden.

Exercises

Übungen

I. *Put in "no", "not", "none", "nobody" ("no one"), or "nothing".*
Setze "no", "not", "none", "nobody" ("no one") oder "nothing" ein!

1. He did . . . come.
2. . . . of the boys complained.
3. These results are . . . too bad.
4. There were . . . pictures in the room.
5. . . . answered the phone.
6. You are . . . the better than your friend.
7. I'm sorry. I can . . . tell you the way.
8. . . . likes him.
9. . . . remains to be done.
10. Who wants to help me? – . . . me!
11. He practised all day, but he can play . . . the better.
12. . . . of my friends helped me.
13. He has . . . friends.
14. He does . . . have any friends.
15. . . . was done because . . . was there.
16. . . . a single car was sold.
17. . . . could help him because we wanted . . . help.
18. He had . . . money with him.
19. It was . . . easy to find him.
20. He failed in the test although he was . . . too stupid.

21. ... even my brother visited me when I was ill.
22. Bob tried everything but his car was ... the faster.
23. He knew ... of the whole matter.
24. ... has ever seen him in person.
25. I can tell you ... It's all secret.
26. We knew ... of our neighbours when we moved here.
27. We have ... idea where our sister is.
28. ... is worse than losing all your papers.
29. There is ... that can make me change my mind.
30. ... of his answers were wrong.

"Both", "either" und "neither"

Both – (alle) beide

betont die *Zusammengehörigkeit* zweier Personen oder Dinge. Es wird nur verwendet, wenn bekannt ist, dass es sich um eine *Zweiergruppe* handelt (sonst: "two").

Beispiel: Both men were caught by the police.
    oder: Both (of) the men were caught by the police.
        Beide Männer wurden von der Polizei geschnappt.

"Both" kann substantivisch allein stehend mit Bezug auf Pluralnomen gebraucht werden.

Beispiel: Both came. – Beide kamen.

Either – der eine (oder andere) von zweien, jener eine

drückt aus, dass *jeder der Zweiergruppe für sich* betrachtet wird. "Either" kann adjektivisch (vor Singularnomen) gebraucht werden.

Beispiel: You can use either entrance. – Du kannst jeden (der beiden) Eingänge benutzen.

"Either" kann auch substantivisch (allein stehend mit Bezug auf Pluralnomen) gebraucht werden.

Beispiel: Either will be all right. – Das eine wie das andere wird in Ordnung sein.

Neither – keiner (von beiden)

ist die *Verneinung von "either"* und kann ebenfalls adjektivisch (vor Nomen im Singular) oder substantivisch (allein stehend mit Bezug auf Nomen im Plural) gebraucht werden.

Beispiel: Neither answer is correct. – Keine der beiden Antworten ist richtig.
        Neither was successful. – Keiner von beiden war erfolgreich.

Grund-regel

Exercises

Übungen

I. Put in "both" or "either".
   Setze "both" oder "either" ein!

1. ...the parents agreed.

2. You can go along...street.

3. ...buses go to the station.

4. The 10 and the 12 go to the station. You can take...bus.

5. ...of the children are very good students.

6. ...of us were invited.

7. ...these books are mine.

8. London is situated on...side of the Thames.

9. ...teams are good.

10. ...of the teams may win.

11. Two people were injured...had serious injuries.

12. ...the witnesses were questioned by the police.

13. I lost...my gloves.

14. There are fields on...side of the road.

15. ...her eyes are injured.

16. He speaks...languages, English and French.

17. There were candles at...end of the table.

18. She has two children...are taller than she is.

19. Do you like the two poems? – I don't like...(of them).

20. ...thieves were arrested.

21. Two people applied for the job...of the two had good chances.

22. Tom had two sons,...wanted to help him.

23. ...roads lead to London.

24. ...way would take him home.

25. He had to sell...his cars.

Final Test: Indefinite Quantifiers

Abschlusstest: unbestimmte Zahlwörter

I. *Translate the following sentences.*
   Übersetze die folgenden Sätze!

1. Ich gehe jeden Tag spazieren.
2. Dieses Jahr sind viele Kirschen am Baum.
3. Fast jeder Schüler hasst Hausaufgaben.
4. Wir haben zwei Nachbarn. Beide sind sehr nett.
5. Herr S. scheint viel Geld zu haben.
6. Alle Arbeiter dieser Firma werden mehr Lohn bekommen.
7. Möchtest du etwas zu trinken?
8. Einige Sätze sind recht schwierig.
9. Wenn ich etwas Zeit hätte, würde ich dir helfen.
10. Nichts wird meine Meinung ändern.
11. Ich muss noch so viele Briefe schreiben, dass ich wahrscheinlich noch viele Stunden beschäftigt sein werde.
12. Niemand ist ohne Fehler.
13. Nur wenige Bilder auf der Ausstellung gefielen mir.
14. Viele Leute wissen nicht, wie viel Energie gespart werden könnte, wenn einige Regeln beachtet würden.
15. Wie viele Meilen sind es bis London?
16. Es gab nur wenig Hoffnung die Jungen wiederzufinden.
17. Wie viele Gäste werden kommen?
18. Ich werde dich in einigen Minuten zurückrufen.
19. Einige Leute meinen, Französisch sei leichter als Englisch.
20. Alle Schüler freuen sich auf die Ferien.
21. Erzähl mir etwas über deine Amerikareise.
22. Der Lehrer gab jedem von uns eine Kopie.
23. Du musst diese Tabletten jeden Abend nehmen.
24. Weil das Wetter so schlecht war, waren keine Leute am Strand.
25. Keiner der Besucher durfte die Privatgemächer sehen.
26. Keiner der beiden Vorschläge war gut.
27. Du kannst die Platte in jedem Plattengeschäft kaufen.
28. Alles muss ein Ende haben.
29. Das hilft mir überhaupt nicht.
30. Nur wenige Frauen sind im Parlament.

Word Order

Die Wortstellung

Synthetische Sprachen, wie z. B. das Lateinische, verdeutlichen die Beziehungen der Satzteile zueinander durch Flexionsendungen. Durch den Wegfall fast aller Flexionsendungen im Englischen sind Subjekt und Objekt im Englischen der Form nach gleich (außer bei Pronomen). Um dennoch Subjekt und Objekt eindeutig kennzeichnen zu können ist eine feste Wortstellung erforderlich. Sprachen, die die Beziehungen der Satzteile zueinander durch feste Wortstellung verdeutlichen, nennt man **analytische Sprachen.**

Word Order in Statements

Die Wortstellung in Aussagesätzen

Die normale Wortstellung ist:

Grund-regel

Subjekt (S)	Prädikat (P)	Objekt (O)
(Subject)	(Predicate)	(Object)

Beispiel:

Sally	buys	a record.
I	can speak	English.
The Millers	have	a house.
She	has written	a letter.
He	doesn't like	football.

Besonder-heiten

Beachte: Anders als im Deutschen besteht diese feste Wortstellung auch:

▶ wenn eine adverbiale Bestimmung am Satzanfang steht.

Beispiel: Now they entered the house.

S   P   O

Nun betraten sie das Haus.

P   S   O

▶ wenn ein Nebensatz dem Hauptsatz vorausgeht.

Beispiel: When I came in, <u>my friend</u> <u>was reading</u> <u>a book.</u>
$\quad\quad\quad\quad\quad\quad\quad$ S $\quad\quad\quad$ P $\quad\quad\quad$ O

Als ich hereinkam, <u>las</u> <u>mein Freund</u> <u>ein Buch.</u>
$\quad\quad\quad\quad\quad\quad$ P $\quad\quad\quad$ S $\quad\quad\quad$ O

▶ bei zusammengesetzten Zeiten.

Beispiel: <u>I</u> <u>have written</u> <u>a postcard.</u>
$\quad\quad\quad\quad$ S $\quad\quad$ P $\quad\quad\quad$ O

<u>Ich</u> <u>habe</u> <u>eine Postkarte</u> <u>geschrieben.</u>
$\quad\quad$ S $\quad$ P₁ $\quad\quad$ O $\quad\quad\quad$ P₂

▶ im Nachsatz der direkten Rede.

Beispiel: "I'll come", <u>he</u> <u>said</u> <u>to me.</u>
$\quad\quad\quad\quad\quad\quad\quad$ S $\quad$ P $\quad$ O

„Ich werde kommen", <u>sagte</u> <u>er</u> <u>zu mir.</u>
$\quad\quad\quad\quad\quad\quad\quad\quad$ P $\quad\quad$ S $\quad$ O

Word Order in Sentences with Two Objects
Die Wortstellung in Sätzen mit zwei Objekten

Ein Satz kann ein *direktes Objekt (O$_d$)* und ein *indirektes Objekt (O$_i$)* haben. Ein indirektes Objekt liegt vor, wenn eine Person (selten ein Ding) als an der Handlung nur indirekt beteiligt gekennzeichnet wird.

Grund-regel

Beispiel: <u>I</u> <u>gave</u> <u>Paul</u> <u>the book.</u>
$\quad\quad\quad$ S $\quad$ P $\quad$ O$_i$ $\quad$ O$_d$

<u>Ich</u> <u>gab</u> <u>Paul</u> <u>das Buch.</u>
$\quad$ S $\quad$ P $\quad$ O$_i$ $\quad$ O$_d$

Gewöhnlich steht *indirektes Objekt vor direktem Objekt* (siehe Beispiel). Soll das indirekte Objekt jedoch stark betont werden, so steht direktes Objekt vor indirektem Objekt.

Beispiel: <u>I</u> <u>gave</u> <u>the book</u> <u>to Paul.</u>
$\quad\quad\quad$ S $\quad$ P $\quad$ O$_d$ $\quad\quad$ O$_i$

<u>Ich</u> <u>gab</u> <u>das Buch</u> <u>Paul.</u>
$\quad$ S $\quad$ P $\quad$ O$_d$ $\quad\quad$ O$_i$

Beachte: ▶ Stellt man das indirekte Objekt hinter das direkte Objekt, so muss man bei zahlreichen Verben *"to"* einfügen.

Dazu gehören: to announce, to bring, to deliver, to describe, to dictate, to explain, to give, to grant, to hand, to introduce, to lend, to mention, to offer, to owe, to pay, to point out, to promise, to read (vorlesen), to report, to say, to sell, to send, to suggest, to teach, to tell, to wish, to write.

Beispiel: I brought the book to him.

           S   P O_d O_i

           Ich brachte ihm das Buch.

▶ Stellt man das indirekte Objekt hinter das direkte Objekt, so muss man bei manchen Verben *"for"* einfügen.

Dazu gehören: to buy, to cook, to find (suchen), to get (besorgen), to leave (übrig lassen), to make, to order, to pour, to spare (erübrigen).

Beispiel: I bought a book for him.

           S   P O_d O_i

           Ich kaufte ein Buch für ihn. (Ich kaufte ihm ein Buch.)

▶ *Nicht zulässig* sind Umstellungen mit "to" / "for" bei den Verben

to ask s. o. s. th.	– jdn. (nach) etwas fragen
to envy s. o. s. th.	– jdn. um etwas beneiden
to forgive s. o. s. th.	– jdm. etwas verzeihen
to save s. o. s. th.	– jdm. etwas ersparen

(s. o. – someone; s. th. – something; jdn./m. – jemanden/m

Beispiel: I envy you your new car.

           S   P O_i O_d

           Ich beneide dich um dein neues Auto.

Exceptions to the S–P–O–Rule (Inversion)
Ausnahmen zur S–P–O–Regel (Inversion)

In einigen Fällen wird die feste Wortstellung S-P-O durchbrochen und das Prädikat tritt vor das Subjekt (diese Umstellung wird **Inversion** genannt):

▶ In Ausrufen ohne Objekt nach *satzeinleitendem "here" oder "there"* tritt das Prädikat vor das Subjekt (meist bei "to come", "to go", "to be"), jedoch nur, wenn das Verb im Present Tense Simple oder Past Tense Simple steht.

Die Wortstellung
In Aussagesätzen

Beispiel: Here <u>comes</u> <u>the bus!</u> – Hier kommt der Bus!

              P   S

There <u>goes</u> <u>the train!</u> – Dort fährt der Zug!

       P   S

▶ In Ausrufen ohne Objekt nach *satzeinleitenden Ortsadverbien,* die fest zum Verb gehören, kann das Prädikat vor das Subjekt treten, wenn die Ortsadverbien stark betont werden sollen.

Beispiel: In <u>came</u> <u>the boss.</u> – Herein kam der Chef!

         P   S

Out <u>went</u> <u>the lights.</u> – (Da) gingen (tatsächlich) die Lichter aus.

       P   S

▶ Wenn *Zeitadverbien* oder *prädikativ gebrauchte Adjektive* an den Satzanfang in gefühlsbetonter Rede treten, erfolgt auch Inversion.

Beispiel: First <u>came</u> <u>the news.</u> – Zuerst kamen die Nachrichten.

         P   S

Great <u>was</u> <u>the joy.</u> – Groß war die Freude.

        P   S

▶ Wenn Adverbien oder Konjunktionen *mit verneinendem oder einschränkendem Sinn* an den Satzanfang treten, tritt das Hilfsverb (HV) vor das Subjekt. Dazu gehören: hardly, in vain, little, neither ... nor, never, no sooner ... than, nor, not only ... but also, rarely, scarcely, seldom.

Beispiel: No sooner <u>had</u> <u>he</u> <u>started</u> <u>his speech</u> than the lights

              P₁ (HV) S P₂ (VV)   O   went out.

Kaum hatte er mit seiner Rede begonnen, als die Lichter ausgingen.

▶ In *Wunschsätzen* tritt das Hilfsverb vor das Subjekt.

Beispiel: <u>May</u> <u>he</u> <u>rest</u> in peace. – Er ruhe in Frieden.

        P₁ (HV) S P₂ (VV)

▶ In *Bedingungssätzen ohne Konjunktion* tritt das Hilfsverb (HV) vor das Subjekt.

Beispiel: <u>Had</u> <u>I</u> <u>met</u> <u>him</u> earlier, all would have been better.

        P₁ (HV) S P₂ (VV) O

Hätte ich ihn früher getroffen, wäre alles besser gewesen.

▶ In *Zwischen- oder Nachsätzen bei direkter Rede* kann das Subjekt (wenn es ein Nomen ist!) hinter dem Prädikat stehen.

Beispiel: "Tell me the truth", <u>said</u> <u>Maud.</u>
$$\text{P}\quad\ \text{S}$$

„Sag mir die Wahrheit!" sagte Maud.

Word Order in Questions

Die Wortstellung in Fragen

Die normale Wortstellung Subjekt – Prädikat – Objekt findet sich nur in Fragen, in denen das *Fragewort Subjekt* (immer bei who – wer) oder mit dem Subjekt verbunden ist.

Beispiel: <u>Who</u> <u>is calling</u> <u>me?</u>
$$\text{S}\qquad\ \text{P}\qquad\ \text{O}$$

What <u>car</u> <u>is standing</u> in the garage?
$$\text{S}\qquad\text{P}$$

Grund-regel

In allen anderen Fragen tritt das Hilfsverb (HV) vor das Subjekt (Inversion!).

Beispiel: <u>Has</u> <u>he</u> <u>written</u> <u>a letter?</u>
$$\text{P}_1\,\text{(HV)}\quad\text{S}\quad\text{P}_2\,\text{(VV)}\qquad\text{O}$$

What <u>can</u> <u>I</u> <u>do?</u>
$$\text{P}_1\,\text{(HV)}\quad\ \text{S}\quad\text{P}_2\,\text{(VV)}$$

Where <u>did</u> <u>you</u> <u>get</u> <u>this pullover?</u>
$$\text{P}_1\,\text{(HV)}\quad\text{S}\quad\text{P}_2\,\text{(VV)}\qquad\text{O}$$

Beachte: Die zum Fragewort gehörende Präposition steht gewöhnlich am Ende einer Frage.

Beispiel: What is it for? – Wofür ist es?

Exercises
Übungen

I. *Form statements.*
   Bilde Aussagesätze!

1. my father / a new car/ bought / some years ago
2. watch / I / TV / sometimes / in the evening
3. lent / Micheal / me / £ 10
4. his father / didn't / him / see
5. sent / my aunt / last week / a parcel
6. drank / lemonade / at the party / the children
7. you / wish / for the future / all the best / I
8. cooked / she / a meal / for her husband
9. told / he / the story / has / to everybody
10. I / written / have / him / a letter / today
11. has / shown / just / the guide / to the visitors / the rooms
12. brought / us / the postman / a letter
13. coffee / the secretary / will / for the boss / make
14. I / have / such beautiful flowers / seen / never
15. Mary / for her father / a drink / got
16. you / forgive / should / his bad behaviour
17. repaired / for me / my bike / my father / last week
18. will / some trouble / save / her / that
19. is / a pullover / for me / knitting / just / my mother
20. have / his name / him / asked / I
21. explained / the teacher / the sentences / the students
22. bought / my father / me / the record
23. he / not / understand / could / me
24. envy / I / her / her nice dress

II. *Form questions*
   Bilde Fragen!

1. the children / are / in the garden / playing
2. broke / the vase / who
3. whose mother / you / did / yesterday / meet
4. Peter / how long / has / English / now / been learning
5. you / did / come / why / so late
6. where / going / all the people / are / to
7. you / did / him / ask / the money / to give / back
8. what boy / the window / broke
9. where / you / bought / have / this good book
10. you / who / this present / gave

11. he / what time / come / will
12. haven't / you / why / asked / him
13. took / these photos / who
14. did / you / whose books / find / in the classroom
15. which / do / car / prefer / you
16. did / meet / yesterday / who / your brother
17. since when / you / not / have / him / seen
18. how / you / do / do
19. you / call / do / what / this animal
20. your mother / is / how
21. ever / been / you / have / to Paris
22. you / like / do / Sam's little brother
23. your secretary / can / speak / fluently / English
24. your homework / have / finished / you

Final Test: Word Order

Abschlusstest: die Wortstellung

I. Translate the following sentences.
Übersetze die folgenden Sätze!

1. Möge Gott dir vergeben!
2. Kannst du mir £ 20 leihen?
3. Nach Regen kommt Sonnenschein.
4. So ist das Leben.
5. Ich kann nicht Fahrrad fahren. – Ich auch nicht.
6. Ich habe ihm gestern ein Paket geschickt.
7. Er hat sich den Arm gebrochen.
8. Als er aus dem Haus kam, sah er eine fremde Person.
9. Er ging um 7 Uhr aus dem Haus.
10. Welches Kind meinst du?
11. Sollte es morgen regnen, werde ich zu Hause bleiben.
12. Hat sie einen Fehler gemacht?
13. Wen hast du gestern in der Stadt getroffen?
14. Wo wirst du deine Ferien verbringen?
15. Peter liest seinem Großvater eine Geschichte vor.
16. Würdest du deinem Vater bitte den Brief zeigen!
17. Wie viele Leute wohnen in diesem Haus?
18. Spricht dein Freund Italienisch?
19. Soll ich dir den Brief schicken?
20. Dort kommt der Zug!

British and American English in Contrast

Britisches und amerikanisches Englisch im Vergleich

Britisches (BE) und amerikanisches (AE) Englisch weisen Unterschiede in folgenden Bereichen auf:

▶ **Aussprache**　　▶ **Schreibung**　　▶ **Grammatik**　　▶ **Wortschatz**

Pronunciation

Aussprache

BE	AE
→ [ɑ:] z. B. dance [dɑ:ns]	→ häufig: [æ] z. B. dance [dæns]
→ nach n, d, t, th, s wird [j] vor [u:] gesprochen z. B. student [ˈstju:dənt]	→ nach n, d, t, th, s wird kein [j] vor [u:] gesprochen z. B. student [ˈstu:dənt]
→ "r" bleibt vor Konsonanten und am Wortende stumm z. B. art [ɑ:t]	→ "r" wird vor Konsonanten und am Wortende gesprochen z. B. art [ɑrt]
→ "t" zwischen Vokalen wird [t] gesprochen z. B. water [ˈwɔ:tə]	→ "t" zwischen Vokalen wird [d] gesprochen z. B. water [ˈwɔ:də]
→ die Endsilbe "-ile" wird [ail] gesprochen z. B. missile [ˈmisail]	→ die Endsilbe "-ile" wird [əl] gesprochen z. B. missile [ˈmisəl]

Spelling

Schreibweisen

BE	AE
unbetonte Endsilbe "-our" z. B. neighbour	"-or" z. B. neighbor
betonte Endung "-ence" z. B. offence	"-ense" z. B. offense
Endung "-re" z. B. centre	"-er" z. B. center
Beim Anhängen von "-ing", "-ed", "-er", "-est" an die unbetonten Silben "-el", "-al", "-ol", "-il" wird das "l" verdoppelt. z. B. quarrelling	Beim Anhängen von "-ing", "-ed", "-er", "-est" an die unbetonten Silben "-el", "-al", "-ol", "-il" wird das "l" nicht verdoppelt. z. B. quarreling
"-ise/-ize" z. B. to organise/to organize	"-ize" z. B. to organize
"-logue" z. B. catalogue	"-log" z. B. catalog
"-gramme" z. B. programme	"-gram" z. B. program

Grammar

Grammatik

BE	AE
Have you got ...?	Do you have ..?
to get – got – got to prove – proved – proved	to get – got – gotten to prove – proved – proven
Present Perfect z. B. I have already written a letter.	umgangssprachlich: Past Tense z. B. I already wrote a letter.
Adverb z. B. He writes awfully.	häufig: Adjektiv z. B. He writes awful.

Vocabulary

Wortschatz

BE	AE	Deutsch
Essen:		
aubergine	egg-plant	Aubergine
biscuit	cookie	Keks
chips	French fries	Pommes frites
cooker	stove	Herd
crisps	chips	(Kartoffel)chips
jug	pitcher	Krug
mince	hamburger meat	Hackfleisch
maize (corn)	corn	Mais
sweets	candy	Süßigkeiten
tin	can	Dose
Verkehr:		
aeroplane	airplane	Flugzeug
boot	trunk	Kofferraum
car	car/auto(mobile)	Auto
car park	parking lot	Parkplatz
diversion	detour	Umleitung
dual carriageway	divided highway	Schnellstraße
filling station	gas station	Tankstelle
goods train	freight train	Güterzug
lorry	truck	LKW
motorway	highway, freeway	Autobahn
number plate	license plate	Nummernschild
petrol	gas(oline)	Benzin
pavement	sidewalk	Bürgersteig
railway	railroad	Eisenbahn
return ticket	round trip ticket	Rückfahrkarte
single ticket	one way ticket	einfache Fahrkarte
traffic lights	stop lights	Verkehrsampel
underground	subway	Untergrundbahn
windscreen	windshield	Windschutzscheibe

Haupt-unterschiede

247

BE	AE	Deutsch
Natur:		
autumn	fall	Herbst
embankment	levee	Uferbefestigung
insect	insect/bug	Insekt
Kleidung:		
braces	suspender	Hosenträger
dressing-gown	bathrobe	Morgenmantel
handbag	handbag/purse	Handtasche
trousers	pants/trousers	Hosen
andere Bereiche:		
at home	home	zu Hause
bookshop	bookstore	Buchhandlung
chemist's	drugstore	Drogerie
company	corporation	Gesellschaft (Firma)
dustbin	garbage can	Mülleimer
dustman	garbage man	Müllmann
film	movie	Spielfilm
flat	apartment	Wohnung
ground floor	first floor	Erdgeschoss
launderette	laundromat	Waschsalon
lift	elevator	Aufzug
luggage	baggage	Gepäck
post	mail	Post
post code	zip code	Postleitzahl
postman	mailman	Briefträger
prison	jail/penitentiary	Gefängnis
(public) toilets	restrooms	öffentliche Toiletten
rubber	eraser	Radiergummi
shop assistant	sales-clerk	Verkäufer(in)

Final Test: British and American English

Abschlusstest: britisches und amerikanisches Englisch

Rewrite the letter in BE.
Übertrage den Brief in BE!

Dear Cathy,

I live in a house not far from the town center. Our apartment is on the first floor, so we don't have to take the elevator to take the rubbish to the garbage cans as the other neighbors have to do. My father owns a truck, so my mother and I often spend the evenings together. There are some nice theaters in the neighborhood. Gasoline is not very cheap here. So the best way of traveling is to take the subway or the railroad. In fall I prefer reading books, but the bookstores are getting more and more expensive and the sales-clerks are often very unfriendly, but it's no use quarreling with them. I have to stop now in order to mail this letter in time.

Yours,
Mary

Appendix

Anhang

Appendix 1: Irregular Verbs
Anhang 1: unregelmäßige Verben

B

be	was/were	been	sein
beat	beat	beaten	schlagen
become	became	become	werden
begin	began	begun	beginnen
bet	bet	bet	wetten
bite	bit	bitten	beißen
blow	blew	blown	wehen, blasen
break	broke	broken	brechen
bring	brought	brought	bringen

build	built	built	bauen
burn	burnt	burnt	(ver-/an)brennen
buy	bought	bought	kaufen

C

catch	caught	caught	fangen
choose	chose	chosen	(aus-)wählen
come	came	come	kommen
cost	cost	cost	kosten
cut	cut	cut	schneiden

D

deal	dealt	dealt	umgehen mit, handeln
draw	drew	drawn	ziehen, zeichnen
dream	dreamt	dreamt	träumen
drink	drank	drunk	trinken
drive	drove	driven	fahren
do	did	done	tun

E

eat	ate	eaten	essen

F

fall	fell	fallen	fallen
feed	fed	fed	füttern
feel	felt	felt	(sich) fühlen
fight	fought	fought	kämpfen
find	found	found	finden
fly	flew	flown	fliegen
forget	forgot	forgotten	vergessen
forgive	forgave	forgiven	vergeben
freeze	froze	frozen	frieren

G

get	got	got	bekommen
give	gave	given	geben
go	went	gone	gehen
grow	grew	grown	wachsen, anbauen

H

hang	hung	hung	hängen
have	had	had	haben

hear	heard	heard	hören
hide	hid	hidden	(sich) verstecken
hit	hit	hit	schlagen, treffen
hold	held	held	halten
hurt	hurt	hurt	verletzen

K

keep	kept	kept	(be-/er-)halten
knit	knitted/knit	knitted/knit	stricken
know	knew	known	wissen, kennen

L

lay	laid	laid	legen
lead	led	led	führen
learn	learnt/learned	learnt/learned	lernen, erfahren
leave	left	left	verlassen
lend	lent	lent	leihen
let	let	let	lassen, vermieten
lie	lay	lain	liegen
light	lit/lighted	lit/lighted	(an-)zünden
lose	lost	lost	verlieren

M

make	made	made	machen
mean	meant	meant	bedeuten, meinen
meet	met	met	treffen

O

overtake	overtook	overtaken	überholen

P

pay	paid	paid	bezahlen
prove	proved	proved/proven	beweisen
put	put	put	setzen, stellen

R

read	read	read	lesen
ride	rode	ridden	reiten
ring	rang	rung	läuten, anrufen
run	ran	run	rennen, laufen

S

say	said	said	sagen
see	saw	seen	sehen
sell	sold	sold	verkaufen
send	sent	sent	schicken, senden
set	set	set	setzen, stellen
shake	shook	shaken	schütteln
shine	shone	shone	scheinen, leuchten
shoot	shot	shot	(er-)schießen
shut	shut	shut	schließen
sing	sang	sung	singen
sink	sank	sunk	sinken
sit	sat	sat	sitzen
sleep	slept	slept	schlafen
smell	smelt/smelled	smelt/smelled	riechen
speak	spoke	spoken	sprechen
spell	spelt/spelled	spelt/spelled	buchstabieren
spend	spent	spent	verbringen, ausgeben
split	split	split	teilen, spalten
spoil	spoilt/spoiled	spoilt/spoiled	verderben, verwöhnen
spread	spread	spread	ausbreiten
stand	stood	stood	stehen
steal	stole	stolen	stehlen
swear	swore	sworn	fluchen, schwören

T

take	took	taken	nehmen
teach	taught	taught	lehren
tear	tore	torn	(zer-)reißen
tell	told	told	erzählen, sagen
think	thought	thought	denken, meinen
throw	threw	thrown	werfen

U

understand	understood	understood	verstehen

W

wake	woke	woken	aufwachen
wear	wore	worn	tragen (Kleidung)
weep	wept	wept	weinen
win	won	won	gewinnen
write	wrote	written	schreiben

Appendix 2: Grammatical Terms
Anhang 2: grammatikalische Ausdrücke

Englisch	Fremdwort	Deutsch
A		
accusative	Akkusativ	4. Fall/Wenfall
active voice	Aktiv	Tatform
adjective	Adjektiv	Eigenschaftswort
adverb	Adverb	Umstandswort
of degree	Gradadverb	des Grades
of frequency	Häufigkeitsadverb	der Häufigkeit
of manner	Adverb der Art und Weise	der Art und Weise
of place	Ortsadverb	des Ortes
of time	Zeitadverb	der Zeit
article	Artikel	Geschlechtswort
definite article	bestimmter Artikel	bestimmtes Geschlechtswort
indefinite article	unbestimmter Artikel	unbestimmtes Geschlechtswort
auxiliary verb	Hilfsverb	Hilfszeitwort
B		
backshift	Tempusverschiebung	Zeitverschiebung
C		
case	Kasus	Fall
collective noun	Kollektivnomen	Sammelname
command	Imperativsatz	Befehlsatz
comparative	Komparativ	Steigerungsstufe
comparison	Komparation	Steigerung/Vergleich
conditional	Konditional	---
conditional clause	Konditionalsatz	Bedingungssatz
conjugation	Konjugation	Beugung eines Tätigkeitswortes
conjunction	Konjunktion	Bindewort
co-ordinating conjunction	nebenordnende Konjunktion	nebenordnendes Bindewort
subordinating conjunction	unterordnende Konjunktion	unterordnendes Bindewort
consonant	Konsonant	Mitlaut

Englisch	Fremdwort	Deutsch
contact clause	Relativsatz ohne Relativpronomen	bezüglicher Nebensatz ohne bezügliches Fürwort
continuous form	---	Verlaufsform

D

dative	Dativ	3. Fall/Wemfall
declension	Deklination	Beugung eines Hauptwortes
direct object	direktes Objekt (Akkusativobjekt)	direkte Satzergänzung (Satzergänzung im 4. Fall)
direct speech	direkte Rede	wörtliche Rede

F

finite verb	finites Verb	gebeugtes Tätigkeitswort
future I	Futur I	Zukunft
future II	Futur II	vollendete Zukunft

G

genitive	Genitiv	2. Fall/Wesfall
gerund	Gerundium	Tätigkeitswort als Hauptwort

I

imperative	Imperativ	Befehlsform
indirect object	indirektes Objekt (Dativobjekt)	indirekte Satzergänzung (Satzergänzung im 3. Fall)
infinitive	Infinitiv	Grundform des Tätigkeitswortes
inversion	Inversion	vertauschte Wortstellung
irregular verb	unregelmäßiges Verb	unregelmäßiges Tätigkeitswort

M

main clause	---	Hauptsatz
main verb	Vollverb	Volltätigkeitswort
modal auxiliary	modales Hilfsverb	unvollständiges Hilfszeitwort

Englisch	Fremdwort	Deutsch
N		
negative sentence	negativer Satz	verneinter Satz
nominative	Nominativ	1. Fall/Werfall
non-finite form	infinite Form	nicht veränderbare Form des Tätigkeitswortes
noun	Nomen/Substantiv	Hauptwort/Namenwort
O		
object	Objekt	Satzergänzung
P		
participle	Partizip	Mittelwort
present participle	Partizip Präsens/	der Gegenwart
past participle	Partizip I	der Vergangenheit
	Partizip Perfekt/	
	Partizip II	
passive voice	Passiv	Leideform
past perfect	Plusquamperfekt	Vorvergangenheit
past tense	Imperfekt/Präteritum	Vergangenheit
plural	Plural	Mehrzahl
positive	Positiv	Grundstufe des Eigenschaftswortes
positive sentence	positiver Satz	bejahter Satz
predicate	Prädikat	Satzaussage
preposition	Präposition	Verhältniswort
present tense	Präsens	Gegenwart
present perfect	Perfekt	vollendete Gegenwart
primary auxiliary	vollständiges Hilfsverb	vollständiges Hilfszeitwort
pronoun	Pronomen	Fürwort
demonstrative pronoun	Demonstrativpronomen	hinweisendes Fürwort
indefinite pronoun	Indefinitpronomen	unbestimmtes Fürwort
interrogative pronoun	Interrogativpronomen	Fragewort
personal pronoun	Personalpronomen	persönliches Fürwort
possessive pronoun	Possessivpronomen	besitzanzeigendes Fürwort
reflexive pronoun	Reflexivpronomen	rückbezügliches Fürwort
relative pronoun	Relativpronomen	bezügliches Fürwort

Englisch	Fremdwort	Deutsch
Q		
quantifier	Indefinitpronomen	Mengenbezeichnung (unbestimmtes Fürwort)
question	---	Frage
question tag	---	Frageanhängsel
question word	Interrogativpronomen	Fragewort
R		
regular verb	regelmäßiges Verb	regelmäßiges Tätigkeitswort
relative clause	Relativsatz	bezüglicher Nebensatz
defining r.cl.	notwendiger Relativsatz	notwendiger bezüglicher Nebensatz
non-defining r.cl.	nicht notwendiger Relativsatz	nicht notwendiger bezüglicher Nebensatz
reported speech	indirekte Rede	abhängige Rede
S		
short answer	---	Kurzantwort
singular	Singular	Einzahl
statement	---	Aussagesatz
subject	Subjekt	Satzgegenstand
subordinate clause	---	Nebensatz
superlative	Superlativ	Höchststufe des Eigenschaftswortes
T		
tense	Tempus	Zeit
V		
verb	Verb	Tätigkeitswort
vowel	Vokal	Selbstlaut
W		
word formation	---	Wortbildung
word order	---	Wortstellung

Appendix 3: Key to Exercises and Tests

Anhang 3: Schlüssel zu Übungen und Tests

Seite 19f.

I. 1. -; 2. -s; 3. -; 4. -; 5. -; 6. -; 7. -; 8. -s; 9. -; 10. -s; 11. -s; 12. -; 13. -s; 14. -s; 15. -; 16. -; 17. -s; 18. -s; 19. -s; 20. -; 21. -; 22. -s; 23. -s; 24. -.

II. 1. -; 2. e; 3. e; 4. e; 5. -; 6. -; 7. -; 8. e; 9. e; 10. -.

III. 1. ie; 2. y; 3. y; 4. y; 5. ie; 6. y; 7. ie; 8. ie; 9. ie; 10. ie.

IV. 1. Do you live; 2. I don't live; 3. live; 4. works; 5. doesn't like; 6. likes; 7. doesn't want; 8. go; 9. goes/attends; 10. come; 11. wear; 12. takes, 13. has/cycles; 14. watch/play; 15. don't go/get up.

Seite 22f.

I. 1. leaving; 2. riding; 3. referring; 4. sitting; 5. hiding; 6. reading; 7. cooking; 8. typing; 9. meeting; 10. having; 11. bringing; 12. getting; 13. repairing; 14. coming.

II. 1. are discussing; 2. is playing; 3. are opening; 4. are making; 5. are writing; 6. is leaving; 7. are cleaning; 8. is telephoning; 9. is shining; 10. is playing; 11. am watching; 12. is cutting; 13. is correcting; 14. is going; 15. is baking; 16. are sleeping; 17. are having; 18. is washing; 19. is climbing; 20. are having.

III. 1. Next Saturday we are having a football game. 2. At the moment I am practising for our class test. 3. Mr Steiger is just repairing his car. 4. We are just having dinner. 5. Listen! The neighbour's dog is barking again. 6. He is just reading an interesting book. 7. My father is working in the garden at the moment. 8. Susan is just visiting her friend. 9. The secretary is just telephoning. 10. Come on, let's go swimming. The sun is shining. 11. Mr Meyer is just writing a letter, and Mrs Meyer is knitting. 12. Look! The fire brigade is coming. 13. Mrs Cooper is just lying on the balcony and is sunbathing. 14. The workers are just building a new house. 15. He is just taking photos of the sights. 16. The students are just having a reading competition. 17. At the moment we are taking part in a French course. 18. She is just sitting in her room and is reading. 19. Mother is just shouting at her son, because he isn't writing properly. 20. He is just taking the dog for a walk.

Seite 25f.

I. 1. watches/prefers; 2. is working/starts; 3. are going; 4. answer/am having; 5. eat/are having; 6. see/go; 7. meet/go; 8. is playing/hear; 9. sleeps/talks; 10. speak/am; 11. go/are staying; 12. goes/goes; 13. isn't/is working; 14. don't like; 15. sings/is having; 16. is raining/ go; 17. hates/thinks/are; 18. go/are waiting; 19. go/is visiting; 20. loves/eats.

II. 1. Listen! Mrs Simon is playing the piano again, although she knows that her neighbour is ill and (is) lying in bed. 2. Sometimes the old lady doesn't leave her flat the whole day, but today she is spending all day in the garden. 3. He occasionally visits his brother in Hampstead, but apart from that he doesn't travel very often. 4. Lady Mary has her tea at

257

5 o'clock daily. But butler Charles is ill. Therefore Sue is serving the tea today. **5.** Bill is just learning his French words, although he usually plays outside at this time, but tomorrow he is writing a class test. **6.** Look! Here in this photo Susan and Mary are just lying on the beach. **7.** At the moment my brothers are working in the park, but it's only a holiday job. They attend college, but are having summer holidays at the moment. **8.** Mrs Cooper loves Italian food, but at the moment she is eating only vegetables and fruit because she wants to lose weight. **9.** "What are you doing here in the hospital?" – "I'm here with Sam. He is just having an X-ray." **10.** I am just reporting about the car race in Indianapolis. Car No. 5 is just overtaking car No. 3. It's a surprise because car No. 3 usually wins.

Seite 28 f.   **I.**   1. occurred; **2.** came; **3.** planned; **4.** gave; **5.** saw; **6.** destroyed; **7.** changed; **8.** applied; **9.** painted; **10.** worked; **11.** enjoyed; **12.** heard; **13.** listened to; **14.** arrived; **15.** drank; **16.** put; **17.** wrote; **18.** drove; **19.** read; **20.** understood.

       II.   1. didn't go; **2.** went; **3.** got up/went/opened; **4.** invented; **5.** did you buy; **6.** Did you see; **7.** did you like; **8.** opened/began; **9.** wrote/was; **10.** rang/got; **11.** passed/started; **12.** was; **13.** had/was not allowed to leave; **14.** sold/moved; **15.** was/could already play (he was already able to play).

       III.   He was born at Bridges Creek in 1732. In the 1750s he became commander-in-chief- of Virginia. In 1759 he married a wealthy young widow. In 1759 the people elected him to the Virginia Parliament. From 1774 to 1775 he was a delegate to the 1st and 2nd Continental Congress, which chose him commander-in-chief of the Continental Army in the Revolutionary War. In 1781 he defeated the British Army in the battle of Yorktown. In 1789 he became the first President of the United States. He kept America neutral during the French Revolution. The Americans elected him for a second term of office in 1793. In 1799 he died at Mount Vernon, Virginia.

Seite 31 ff.   **I.**   1. Bob was dancing; **2.** Peter was drinking; **3.** Susan and Mary were using; **4.** Some children were having; **5.** The dog was lying; **6.** Paula was wearing; **7.** The children were playing; **8.** Some hamburgers were lying; **9.** Three children were dancing; **10.** Empty bottles were lying; **11.** Bob was smoking; **12.** Four girls were playing; **13.** The cat was trying; **14.** The neighbours were coming; **15.** The telephone was ringing.

       II.   1. While father was typing...; I was tidying...; **2.** While the stewardesses were serving..., Mr Scott was sleeping...; **3.** While Mrs Martin was trying..., the children were making...; **4.** While the boys were playing..., their mothers were enjoying...; **5.** While the band was playing..., all the spectators were waiting. **6.** While the actors were practising..., the workers were decorating...; **7.** While my aunt was talking..., I was doing...; **8.** While the children were sleeping, their parents were watching TV. **9.** While Lord and Lady S. were having tea, their servants were preparing...; **10.** While the patient was telling..., the doctor was looking...; **11.** While the reporter was interviewing..., she was polishing...; **12.** While the students were writing..., the teacher was watching...; **13.** While Mrs B. was doing..., Mr B. was collecting...; **14.** While the children were having..., Mrs. C. was visiting...; **15.** While the new neighbours were moving in, we were working...

III. **1.** We were sleeping...; **2.** ... the old lady was waiting... **3.** The B. were having...; **4.** I was writing...; **5.** The band was playing...; **6.** We were driving...; **7.** Mrs C. was doing...; **8.** Mr S. was playing...; **9.** ...her friend was waiting...; **10.** ... he was still breathing. **11.** ... he was trying...; **12.** We were sitting...; **13.** ... my parents were already sleeping. **14.** The teacher was explaining...; **15.** We were standing...

Seite 34 f. **I.** **1.** were lying/were having; **2.** was walking/met; **3.** was getting off/were trying; **4.** wanted/were not/was/were you doing; **5.** recognized/was wearing; **6.** was trying/came/hit; **7.** ate/helped; **8.** came/could not come/was having; **9.** started/were trying; **10.** climbed/switched on/went; **11.** heard/burst; **12.** was examining/was waiting; **13.** broke/went; **14.** were you doing/took place; **15.** was checking/was waiting; **16.** were watching/started/switched off/was; **17.** announced/appeared; **18.** was working/didn't like; **19.** was/were playing/was sitting/(was) studying; **20.** visited/went.

II. **1.** The Inspector entered the bar with the stranger and asked, "What were you doing between 9 and 10 o'clock yesterday?" **2.** The stranger answered, "When the murder took place, I was sitting in the bar and (was) playing cards with Mr Doodle." **3.** "Did anybody see you?" Inspector Monday wanted to know. **4.** "While we were playing cards, a young man who was standing at the bar all the time, was watching us." **5.** Slowly, the Inspector got was getting (becoming) nervous. **6.** Finally he thought for a moment and then asked the stranger, "What was the man doing at the moment when you entered the bar?" **7.** "When I saw him for the first time, he was standing in the corner and was talking to the waiter in a low voice. **8.** Monday seemed to be very surprised when he heard this. **9.** While he was talking to the stranger, he heard that Mr Doodle was talking to the waiter. **10.** Monday didn't understand what they were talking about. **11.** While he was still trying to understand the two of them, Inspector Datson came in. **12.** When he saw what was going on (happening) in the bar, he rushed to Inspector Monday. **13.** He gave him a piece of paper which the stranger recognized at once. **14.** While Monday was staring at the piece of paper, the stranger thought for a moment how he could escape from the bar. **15.** When he suddenly ran to the door, he was arrested by the two policemen who were waiting outside.

I. 1. has smoked; 2. has never gone; 3. hasn't been; 4. has never written; 5. has already written; 6. has never gone; 7. has taken; 8. has done; 9. hasn't helped; 10. has always been/has always caused.

II. 1. Have you ever worked; 2. Have you ever organized; 3. Have you already passed; 4. Since when have you been; 5. Have you already learned; 6. Have you applied; 7. Have you ever had; 8. Have you already asked; 9. Have you ever been; 10. Have you ever had.

III. 1. How long have you known him? 2. He has just closed the window. 3. We have already solved five exercises. 4. They have already walked 10 miles. 5. He hasn't spoken to anybody all evening. 6. I have never been to Australia. 7. Since he became a dog owner he has gone for a walk twice a day. 8. Fred has never read Shakespeare. 9. I haven't seen him for a long time. 10. He has just left the office. 11. Have you ever walked to Greenwich? 12. He has had this illness for 2 years. 13. For 4 weeks she hasn't done anything for school. 14. She has always been a good student. 15. I haven't spoken to the director yet. 16. She hasn't spoken to him for 2 years. 17. Have you already listened to the new record by David Bowie? 18. Our neighbour has always been very friendly so far. 19. I haven't been on holiday for 2 years. 20. Since he joined this company he has earned much more.

I. 1. S. has been doing; 2. P. and P. have been playing; 3. Mother has been working; 4. I have been; 5. The young children have been playing; 6. The neighbours have been lying; 7. S. has been knitting; 8. D. has been trying; 9. Grandfather has been sitting ... and reading; 10. The cat has been chasing ... and playing.

II. 1. I have been learning; 2. We have been living; 3. He has already solved; 4. It has been raining; 5. you haven't been waiting; 6. He hasn't eaten; 7. has been working; 8. He has known him; 9. Have you ever seen; 10. have you been sitting; 11. They haven't finished; 12. My uncle has already found; 13. Mr C. has been driving ... He has already driven; 14. You have told ... I have never believed; 15. M. has been drinking ... He has already drunk; 16. Mrs S. has been talking ... She hasn't talked; 17. S. has just cleaned; 18. you haven't been listening; 19. What have you been doing? 20. The M. have been taking ... They have already taken.

III. 1. Susan has been on a diet for 3 weeks and has already lost 5 pounds. 2. Mr S. has already been having customers all morning. He has already sold two cars. 3. Paul has been playing chess for 2 hours. He has never played against Tom. 4. I have been living in the USA for 2 years now and haven't missed my home country yet. 5. Mrs C. has been telephoning with her friend for half an hour. She has already spent more than £ 5 for the phone call. 6. What have you been doing all afternoon? Have you been waiting for me? 7. H. has been saving for a motorbike for months. He has already saved £ 100. 8. I have already been looking for my glasses since 10 o'clock, but I haven't found them yet. **9.** I have never been to America, but I've already read a lot about his country. **10.** He has been working in this firm for 5 years and there have never been any problems so far. **11.** M. has already been sitting at her desk for 2 hours and still hasn't answered all the questions yet. **12.** He has been playing golf in the club for 2 years and has already won some prizes. **13.** Have you already had breakfast or have you been sleeping till now? **14.** "Has the postman already been here?" – "Yes, I've already put the post on your desk." **15.** He has been living here for 2 months, but he hasn't found a new job yet.

Seite 44 f. **I.** **1.** hasn't seen/arrived; **2.** looked at/hasn't decided; **3.** have never liked/didn't watch; **4.** enjoyed/had/hasn't even looked at; **5.** arrived/ couldn't speak (weren't able to speak); **6.** found out/had to learn; **7.** have made; **8.** was/have continuously been trying/landed; **9.** has considered; **10.** came/has been living; **11.** got/has already taught; **12.** have visited/have never wanted; **13.** saw/were; **14.** have visited; **15.** came/were; **16.** (have) never liked/went up/have also stopped; **17.** have always hated/have never played; **18.** has been working/has not visited; **19.** were/came/has been staying/has been making/arrived; **20.** Did you really enjoy...? I have never seen.

II. **1.** S. hasn't been here for a long time; but he has already eaten three steaks. **2.** When J. came to Germany for the first time, he couldn't (wasn't able to) speak a word of German. **3.** We have been living in our new house for 3 weeks and haven't got to know our neighbours yet. **4.** Since Mr S. moved to Hamburg, we haven't heard from him. **5.** Erwin has never been to the Wild West. **6.** When he came to New Mexiko last year, he was surprised that there were still Indians there. **7.** He has been living in New Mexico for 8 months now and has already learned many Indian words. **8.** When I visited him some weeks ago, he was just trying to talk to an old chief. **9.** Some days later the chief told me in English; **10.** "In the 8 months since he came here Erwin has learned more words than I have ever known." **11.** Although he has already seen hundreds of Indians, he hasn't met a cowboy yet. **12.** When he came to the West he thought that only cowboys lived there. **13.** He soon found out that there were more Indians than real cowboys in New Mexico. **14.** Since the beginning of this century the number of Indians in the USA has quadrupled. **15.** When Columbus discovered America, 1 million Indians lived in today's USA. **16.** In the following 4 centuries their number got smaller and smaller. **17.** In the second half of the 19th century it reached its lowest level. **18.** Since then the number of Indians has been growing steadily. **19.** In contrast to this the real cowboys have nearly died out today. **20.** In the last decades more and more white Americans have shown an interest in Indian culture.

I. 1. had tidied up/played; 2. had visited/had; 3. had had/opened; 4. had mixed/started; 5. had made/called; 6. had passed/went; 7. had made/sang; 8. had taken/bought; 9. had been/found; 10. had learned/got.

II. 1. had been walking; 2. had already laid; 3. had you been working; 4. had lived in; 5. had you been learning; 6. had been; 7. had studied; 8. had broken; 9. had had; 10. had already applied; 11. had heard; 12. had taken; 13. had finished/had forgotten; 14. had got; 15. had had; 16. had missed; 17. had still not arrived; 18. had discovered; 19. had given; 20. had been.

I. 1. came/had been waiting; 2. didn't you come/has been; 3. wanted/had to stay; 4. did you do/had to stay; 5. came/were jumping; 6. haven't heard; 7. arrived/found/had been committed; 8. had not been standing/wanted; 9. said/had been watching/had heard; 10. had run/had seen; 11. had been wearing, 12. mentioned/knew/was; 13. wrote/told; 14. did/was told; 15. smiled/said/have already solved; 16. have had/was/came; 17. was/had finished; 18. returned; 19. had arrested/had been trying; 20. was promoted/has been.

II. 1. When Columbus discovered America, he thought that he had found a shorter way to India. 2. Since then we have found out that Columbus was wrong. 3. After the first settlers had come to America, they soon began to build villages and towns everywhere. 4. From the end of the 17th century till the end of the 19th century a continuous westward movement took place. 5. By 1890 the last great open areas had been settled. 6. Since then the situation for the immigrants has changed completely. 7. While/(whereas) they found work in the industrial centres in the first decades of this century, the immigrants have become a problem during recent years. 8. Before World War II the immigrants mainly came from Europe, but since the 1950s the number of immigrants from the Third World has been increasing steadily; 9. In addition, the number of illegal immigrants has increased recently. 10. In 1987 the government began to give many illegal immigrants the chance to become American citizens. 11. Never before had so many people had the possibility of becoming citizens of the United States at one time. 12. When we were in the USA the last time, we learned that many Mexicans had been waiting for the new law for many years. 13. In England the number of immigrants also strongly increased in the 1970s and early 1980s. 14. In 1986 the British government tried to stop the flood of immigrants by a new law. 15. Since then fewer immigrants have come to Great Britain. 16. When he came in, he noticed that the other guests had already eaten all the sandwiches. 17. Although he had been looking forward to a steak all afternoon, he couldn't (wasn't able to) eat anything now. 18. The host told him, "We had been waiting for you for 2 hours, but when you weren't here by 8 o'clock we started dinner." **19.** "We were just talking about/of you when you came in." **20.** The guest replied, "Unfortunately, I couldn't come earlier, because I still had to work at the office."

Seite 54 ff. **I.** **1.** We will arrive on the evening of the 4th of June. **2.** We will spend 3 days there. **3.** We will not visit the Empire State Building, but we will see the Statue of Liberty. **4.** We will not stay at the Hilton, but we will stay at a cheaper hotel. **5.** We will fly to Chicago. **6.** We will visit an uncle of mine. **7.** We will only stay 2 days. **8.** We will not have time for that. **9.** We will go to L. A. by Greyhound bus. **10.** Yes, after that we will return to England.

II. **1.** We will arrive; **2.** We will take; **3.** We will arrive; **4.** We will not go; **5.** We will only have; **6.** We will go; **7.** We will visit Portobello Road Market the next morning; **8.** Perhaps we will buy; **9.** We will have; **10.** In the afternoon we will go; **11.** On Sunday morning we will go ... and (will) listen; **12.** We will not stay ... because we will meet; **13.** In the evening we will go; **14.** On Monday morning we will take; **15.** There we will see; **16.** In the afternoon we will go; **17.** We will visit ... and (will) admire; **18.** Later we will have; **19.** We will not have ... because we will return; **20.** At 8 o'clock we will have.

III. **1.** We will be watching; **2.** Mother will be preparing; **3.** The cat will be lying; **4.** Later we will be playing; **5.** Our parents will be talking; **6.** Paul will be helping; **7.** The baby will already be sleeping; **8.** we will be having; **9.** Grandma will be sitting; **10.** We hope the sun will be shining.

IV. **1.** will be sitting/will be clapping; **2.** will be crying; **3.** will be trying; **4.** will be working; **5.** will be checking; **6.** will be sitting/(will be) hoping; **7.** will be preparing; **8.** will be waiting; **9.** will be controlling; **10.** will already be scribbling.

Seite 58 f. **I.** **1.** are going to serve; **2.** is going to make; **3.** is going to welcome; **4.** is going to give; **5.** is going to start; **6.** is going to perform; **7.** are going to dance; **8.** is going to be; **9.** are going to show; **10.** are going to answer.

II. **1.** It's going to rain; **2.** leaves; **3.** will be (are); **4.** will happen; **5.** will be lying; **6.** is going to lose; **7.** will tell; **8.** will go; **9.** isn't going to get (won't get); **10.** is having; **11.** will be seeing; **12.** is going to be; **13.** leaves; **14.** Will you visit; **15.** will probably be; **16.** will never marry; **17.** will fall (is going to fall); **18.** will never travel (is never going to travel); **19.** will be writing; **20.** will be/will get.

Seite 62 **I.** **1.** will have asked; **2.** will have given; **3.** will have taken; **4.** will have checked; **5.** will have done; **6.** will have done; **7.** will have checked; **8.** will have packed; **9.** will have bought; **10.** will have informed; **11.** will have watered; **12.** will have pulled; **13.** will have turned off; **14.** will have put; **15.** will have taken.

II. 1. he will have been sleeping; 2. they will have been building; 3. The dancers will have been practising; 4. we will have been living; 5. they will have been playing; 6. Jack will have been staying; 7. I will have been going; 8. Simon will have been playing; 9. father will have been repairing; 10. we will have been travelling.

Seite 65 **I.** 1. you wouldn't fall; 2. Would you mind; 3. I would like; 4. I would learn; 5. they would go out; 6. he would not listen; 7. would you like; 8. he would get; 9. she would be able; 10. would you do; 11. Would you open; 2. would help; 13. would make; 14. I would buy; 15. it wouldn't open.

II. 1. I would like to reserve/book a double room with a shower. 2. Would you like another tea? 3. Would you please take the letters to the post office as soon as possible? 4. In earlier years my father would go to his club every Sunday. 5. The gangsters told him to open the safe, but he wouldn't. 6. If I were you, I would phone him at once. 7. Would you mind me (my) coming an hour later? 8. Waiter, we would like to pay. 9. Would you please come to my place (call in) tomorrow evening. 10. He said he would fly to New York the following week.

Seite 69 **I.** 1. would have gone; 2. would you have done; 3. would have done; 4. would have stayed; 5. would have caught; 6. would have gone; 7. would never have asked; 8. would have done; 9. would have stopped; 10. would have met; 11. would have been glad; 12. would have been; 13. would have been; 14. would have finished; 15. would have been able to; 16. would not have been allowed; 17. would have been drowned; 18. would have liked; 19. would have bought; 20. would have painted.

Seite 75 f. **I.** 1. came/found out/had already cleaned; 2. couldn't believe/saw/ entered; 3. was playing cards/was working; 4. would not eat; 5. will have been; 6. hasn't come/left; 7. told/would look/ were travelling; 8. does the sun always rise; 9. have been sitting/has arrived; 10. Why do workers nowadays never come/have promised; 11. would like/wouldn't allow; 12. accepted/had been working; 13. Have you ever visited; 14. was/would like; 15. had seen/recognized/came; 16. has not been sleeping/gets up; 17. was examining/was preparing; 18. would never have remembered/hadn't helped; 19. are/am/is going to rain; 20. didn't you tell/had never seen/came.

II. 1. I would like to visit him, but he hasn't phoned me for 2 weeks. 2. Two years ago when he came back to Germany for the first time in 10 years, he didn't know any more that we drive on the right side of the road. 3. When we were in the factory the last time, everyone was working very hard. 4. If I hadn't been to England so often, I would have liked to go to London once more. 5. When we were at the theatre last Friday, we met an old friend who we hadn't seen for

2 years. **6.** Next year in October we will have been married for 20 years.
7. We have been living in this flat for 7 years now. Today it's not as
nice as it was when we moved in. **8.** During the last 2 years Virginia
has constantly been ill. **9.** After Sepp had been living in the USA for
5 years, he was glad to be allowed to return to Bavaria at last. **10.** If Mr
O'Neill had saved his money regularly, he would be a millionaire today.
11. After Ian had been robbed in his holidays last year, he said he
would never come to Europe again. **12.** During his last stay thieves had
stolen his golden wristwatch, which his grandfather had given (to) him
years before. **13.** Aaron didn't want to go home again, because he was
afraid of his father. **14.** Unfortunately, I cannot (won't be able to) visit
you tomorrow, because I will be playing tennis from 10 to 12 o'clock.
15. When the filmstar came in, everybody stared at her as if they had
never seen an actress before. **16.** Olliver is just learning English,
although he hates grammar. **17.** Mr M. plays football with his son every
Saturday, but he isn't playing this Saturday, because he hurt himself
last week. **18.** He has never been abroad in his life, but at Christmas he
is going to fly (is flying/will fly) to Rio. **19.** When the fire brigade
arrived the whole house was on fire, although everybody had tried to
extinguish the fire. **20.** As a child I would have liked to go to the
seaside, but my parents went to the mountains every year.

Seite 81 f. **I.** **1.** A motorbike was bought by S. last week. **2.** The old lady was helped
by the boyscouts. **3.** The letters will be typed by Mrs S. tomorrow.
4. The bike is being repaired by the boys. **5.** The prize will be won by
the best student. **6.** German is spoken in A. **7.** A hundred radios and
TVs had been stolen by the thieves before the police caught them
(before the thieves were caught by the police). **8.** The drinks will be
sent to us by the grocer tonight. We will be sent the drinks by the
grocer tonight. **9.** Books aren't sold any longer (by them). **10.** The
children have been told a good story by the nurse. A good story has
been told to the children by the nurse. **11.** The lazy workers were fired
by the firm. **12.** The postman was bitten by our dog some days ago.
13. The tyre was invented by Dunlop. **14.** After the engine had been
mended, they... **15.** The suitcases have already been carried to the taxi
by the porters. **16.** Free soup was given to the poor by the church. The
poor were given free soup by the church. **17.** I have been given the
necklace as a present by my sister. The necklace has been given to me
as a present by my sister. **18.** Good efforts were being made by the
students. **19.** The newspaper wasn't published any longer (by them).
20. Buckingham Palace is used as a city residence by the Royal Family.

II. **1.** The police discovered the burglary. **2.** People in many countries speak
English. **3.** They will elect Mr Carter. **4.** They use the Tower of London
as a museum nowadays. **5.** They will pull down the house next year.
6. Noone had opened this old trunk before. **7.** ... her husband had
already done the washing-up. **8.** The cook was preparing the meal.

9. The weather forecast has announced bad weather. 10. The Duke sold the R. R. 11. The electrician has put the aerial on the roof. 12. I will translate the book. 13. Clever thieves have stolen the jewellery. 14. An earthquake destroyed the town completely. 15. Mrs C. has already watered the plants.

III. Next year the new shopping-centre will be opened. 2. Last week the prize was given to us. We were given the prize last week. 3. 2 years ago the disco was closed, but it will be reopened soon by the new owner. 4. The lonely village had never been entered by a stranger before. 5. Before he came to London, a house had been rented for him by his firm.

Seite 84 f.   I.   1. The roof must be mended (by us). 2. The windows should be cleaned at least twice a month (by them). 3. This question cannot be answered. 4. Their homework ought to be done properly (by them). 5. The dentist should be consulted regularly by children. 6. The problems couldn't be solved by the members of the committee. 7. This room mustn't be entered by the children. 8. The presents may be opened by the students after dinner. 9. The letters should be written by the secretary. 10. The best will be chosen by us.

II. 1. the methods to be used; 2. time to be lost; 3. problems to be solved; 4. letters to be written; 5. relatives to be visited.

III. 1. She really is to be pitied. 2. Many repairs are to be done. 3. The letters must be posted today. 4. Little remains to be said. 5. This tin mustn't be put near an open fire. 6. This book leaves many questions to be answered. 7. He is to be sent for at once. 8. This should be done by tomorrow. 9. The keys couldn't be found anywhere. 10. This question should have been asked earlier.

Seite 85 f.   I.   1. Most of the houses were destroyed by a thunderstorm. 2. The explanations weren't understood. 3. The bills have to be paid by us. 4. We were offered tea and biscuits by our hostess. Tea and biscuits were offered to us by our hostess. 5. The poem had to be learned by heart by us. 6. The cat is fed by Uncle R. every morning. 7. Meat is liked by lions. 8. "War and Peace" was written by Tolstoy. 9. The Egyptian grave was discovered by some scientists last year. 10. She was told the secret by Sam. The secret was told to her by Sam. 11. The castle was built in the 17th century. 12. The Museum of London can be visited every day except Mondays. 13. Mr S. was given notice by the boss some weeks ago. 14. The dog hadn't been looked after properly (by them) before it got ill. 15. The recipe hadn't been tried by the housewife before. 16. This old vase mustn't be touched (by you). 17. I haven't been shown the document. The document hasn't been shown to me. 18. Will her letter be answered by you? 19. We were shown the way by the friendly gentleman. The way was shown to us by the friendly gentleman. 20. An interesting radio play is just being broadcast by the radio station.

II. 1. We (you) made the discovery yesterday. 2. A careless driver killed two people. 3. Nobody has slept in this bed. 4. People were (Somebody was) laughing at them. 5. My boss gave me the opportunity. 6. Electricity drives the machine. 7. His son was helping him. 8. The same author wrote the books. 9. The police had warned the population. 10. The mountain rescue team had rescued him.

III. 1. Such things should be abolished. 2. It's reported that he is seriously injured. 3. The mistake couldn't be found. 4. Such hats are mostly worn by natives. 5. The missed purse was found by a little boy. 6. Some years ago the population was evacuated, a reservoir was built and the village was flooded. 7. He is said to be intelligent. 8. The heating must be (has to be) repaired before winter. 9. The cellar should be tidied up. 10. He was given a prize.

Seite 91 ff. **I.** **Statements** 1. (that) she has; 2. (that) we will all have to come in on Saturday. 3. The speaker says (that) it's going to rain. 4. (that) if the weather is fine, we can have a picnics. 5. (that) the Millers moved house last week. **Questions** 1. who broke this window; 2. Grandma asks when he will arrive. 3. The new neighbour asks where I/you do my/your weekly shopping. 4. if I/you have ever been. 5. where I was between 6 p. m. and 8 p. m. last Monday. **Commands** 1. Father tells me not to go; 2. to copy; 3. not to turn her/his radio; 4. The guide tells the visitors to be careful. 5. The label tells us not to iron this blouse.

II. **Statements** 1. (that) many houses had been destroyed by the thunderstorm, so that the inhabitants had been taken to a school building in the next village. 2. (that) he would join the school orchestra as soon as possible. 3. (that) we would have a meeting for the parents the following Monday. The headmaster wanted to know how many of the parents would come. 4. My brother said (that) they had been living in that town for many years and he thought they would stay there for the next few years. 5. Grandma told me (that) when she had been young, they had used to walk to school. 6. The teacher said (that) we would have to hand in the papers the next day, because he was going to correct them over the weekend. 7. My father remarked (that) somebody seemed to be in the living-room, he had just heard a strange noise. 8. S. said to her brother (that) they would celebrate their parents' anniversary the following week and (that) she was planning to buy something really nice for them. 9. The photographer said (that) when he had taken those photos he hadn't known that they would become . . . 10. My Indian classmate told me (that) in India parents often chose the future husband for their daughter and that they sometimes hadn't even met . . . **Questions** 1. when she was going to work; 2. if I could tell him; 3. if he would be able to finish those papers; 4. who could tell him where they had stopped the lesson before; 5. The new boy wanted to know for how long I had been a member . . . 6. where and when S. had been born and what his most famous plays were; 7. how I had done my maths homework before Dad had bought me; **8.** if she could look after her cat while she was; **9.** why young people always spoke; **10.** The doctor wanted to know if Mr B. had called while he had been out. **Commands 1.** not to use; **2.** to find out what had happened the night before; **3.** not to be; **4.** The announcer in the underground station told the passengers to mind the gap. **5.** The teacher told Bob to stop talking; **6.** not to feed; **7.** The doctor told me to take; **8.** to see him again the following Tuesday; **9.** not to play with the video while they were away; **10.** to finish the essay till the following week.

III. **1.** (that) since I had been elected, the school magazine had very much improved and that he had even enjoyed the article about himself; **2.** (that) their holidays had been terrible that year and that they had only got one hotel room instead of the two they had booked; **3.** that water boils; **4.** (that) his parents are; **5.** (that) I mustn't drink coffee or smoke; **6.** when my pop career had started and what my plans for the future were; **7.** that years before the Thames had been so polluted that no fish had been able to live in it; **8.** why I had been out of work for 6 months and if I was not willing to work in a different job than the one I had had before; **9.** (that) that had been a near miss and that he had suddenly seen a plane right in front off him and (that) there had been nothing he had been able to do; **10.** if I could help him and (he) said (that) he had been trying to solve that problem for 20 minutes then; **11.** to fasten our seatbelts and to stop smoking; **12.** (that) anybody who found the necklace and took it to the lost property office would get; **13.** where he had lived before and which school he had gone to; **14.** (that) 100 years before people had thought women should look; **15.** (that) she had been driving along a lonely country road when suddenly a shining circulating object had landed right in front of her and (that) she was sure it had been a UFO; **16.** how I had felt when my team had won the match the day before; **17.** if they won the next election, they would change everything; **18.** (that) he had called me at 5 o'clock but I hadn't answered the phone, so he hadn't been able to tell me; **19.** (that) there would be little rain ... the day it would get; **20.** if I could lend him £ 15 because he had forgotten his purse but (that) he would like to buy that CD.

Seite 94 f. **I.** **1.** when the teacher had asked him, he had been so nervous that he hadn't been able to answer although he had known; **2.** to put those 20 sentences ... and to learn; **3.** (that) due to bad weather conditions the flight to B. will be delayed; **4.** if I would like; **5.** if he wanted her to phone; **6.** (that) my mother phoned half an hour ago and that she wanted to know if I was in. **7.** if he had ever been to E. before or if that was his; **8.** (that) that castle belonged to the Duke and (that) it had been open; **9.** if she has received the postcard she wrote her from Spain; **10.** (that) when they went to F., they would all have to look after their luggage themselves.

II. 1. ... asked me, "Do you prefer to wait for the alteration of shall we send it to you?" 2. ... told me, "Somebody has been (was) at the door." 3. ... told us, "You have the wrong ticket and can't take this bus." 4. "When will Mrs K. arrive and shall I pick her up?" 5. "Be at the stadium at 8 o'clock!" 6. ... waitress, "Will you accept cheques?" 7. "When is dinner ready?" 8. ... told him, "I have never been abroad before but I would like ..." 9. ... said, "The concert was the most ..." 10. ... said, "You can move ..."

Seite 106 f. **I.** 1. S. will have to wear; 2. S. will have to stay; 3. S. won't be able to have; 4. S. will be able to play; 5. S. will not be allowed to leave; 6. S. will have to attend; 7. S. won't have to do; 8. S. will have; 9. S. will have to make; 10. S. won't be able to speak.

II. 1. Children could swim; 2. Many children had to work because the family needed; 3. Mothers had to do; 4. Women weren't allowed to take; 5. Students had to walk; 6. Fathers couldn't spend ... – They had to go; 7. The air was cleaner; 8. People had to spend; 9. Water had to be carried; 10. Girls weren't allowed to wear.

III. 1. I have been able to read; 2. I have been allowed to go; 3. I have had; 4. I have never needed; 5. I have never had to repeat; 6. I have been given; 7. I have always been able to do; 8. I have been allowed to drive; 9. I have never had to help; 10. I have been able to work.

IV. 1. You needn't help me if you haven't got time. 2. You should learn 20 words every day. 3. Could you please ask your brother if I can come tomorrow. 4. We had to stay longer, because we had to tidy up the classroom. 5. In 1960 a worker used to earn only £ 1.20 per hour. 6. Where shall I put the books? 7. Could you do me a favour? 8. You really shouldn't drink so much. 9. Since when has Mr P. been able to speak English so well? 10. Unfortunately, I won't be able to come (cannot come) tomorrow, because I'll have to (I have to) take my mother to the doctor. 11. The engine simply wouldn't start. 12. I would like to help you if I could. 13. Couldn't we go to the cinema? 14. We might visit aunt Paula at the weekend. 15. Would you like a single or a double room? 16. You mustn't (are not allowed to) open the parcel before your birthday. 17. If you can type these letters for me today, you'll be allowed to (you may) come an hour later tomorrow morning. 18. When will you finally be able to do your homework alone? 19. Since he had the accident he hasn't been able to walk. 20. Would you please phone the doctor and ask when I can come.

Seite 109 ff. **I.** 1. B. cannot speak; 2. The children don't like; 3. I won't be able to come; 4. He didn't phone; 5. He hasn't always been; 6. I couldn't read; 7. He hadn't known; 8. Sue isn't watching; 9. The neighbour's boy doesn't go; 10. You may not open; 11. He didn't come; 12. The children aren't; 13. The Millers didn't spend; 14. They don't always go; 15. I don't learn; 16. Mrs Burl wasn't; 17. I haven't heard; 18. The accident didn't happen; 19. You don't have; 20. Mr Cut doesn't work.

II. 1. Where were you born? 2. When were you born? 3. Where do you live? 4. How long have you been living in F.? 5. Where did you live before? 6. What is your job? 7. Where do you work? 8. Where did you go to school? 9. Where do your parents live? 10. How long have you been working in this firm? 11. Do you like your job? 12. How many children have you got? 13. Where do your children go to school? 14. Does your wife work? 15. Where did you learn German? 16. What do you do in your free time; 17. When do you start work in the morning? 18. When do you get home . . .? 19. Do you like German food? 20. What is your favourite German meal?

III. 1. a) When did they open . . .? b) Where did they open . . .? c) What did they open . . .? 2. a) Who lives in London? b) Where do the C. live? 3. a) When does P. play football? b) Who plays football . . .? c) What does P. do/play . . .? d) Where does P. play football? 4. a) Who goes to work by underground? b) How does Mr C. go to work? 5. a) Who has been working hard . . .? b) How long has he been working hard . . .? c) How has he been working for this test? 6. a) Where did C. C. start his career? b) Who started his career in London? 7. a) Where did the students have to look up . . .? b) Who had to look up . . .? c) What did the students have to look up . . .? 8. a) What happened at 4 o'clock . . .? b) Where did the accident happen? c) When did the accident happen? 9. a) Why didn't you go out? 10. a) How often do you go to the cinema? b) Where do you go to once a week?

IV. 1. When do you usually go to bed? 2. How long haven't you spoken to him? 3. When did the famous actor die? 4. What did he get? 5. When did they build the department store? 6. When does she usually prepare dinner? 7. What did the butler do? 8. When did he stop smoking? 9. What does the secretary speak? 10. Who moved last month? 11. What does Grandpa drink every evening? 12. What did scientists discover years ago? 13. When will he arrive? 14. Why did you stay at home? 15. Where did she learn typing? 16. Who(m) did the police arrest? 17. Who is just painting the house?

V. 1. My parents don't go out very often. 2. Do you see the building over there? 3. Do you still go to work by bike? 4. I don't live in Munich. 5. Why didn't you come yesterday evening? 6. I didn't have time. 7. Do you like pizza? 8. Did you watch the film yesterday? 9. I don't know Mr M. 10. Where does your father work? 11. Why don't you phone Mary? 12. Last week she didn't visit her sick aunt. 13. She doesn't work properly. 14. When did you go to bed yesterday? 15. Why didn't you ask me last week?

Seite 113 f.

1. didn't he? 2. don't you? 3. isn't he? 4. is she? 5. won't you? 6. wasn't she? 7. don't you? 8. don't they? 9. did she? 10. haven't you; 11. has she? 12. do they? 13. doesn't he? 14. won't he? 15. was she? 16. do you? 17. would she? 18. must they? 19. could they? 20. mightn't it? 21. isn't he? 22. does she? 23. can't you? 24. can you? 25. didn't they? 26. isn't it? 27. doesn't he? 28. wasn't it? 29. will you? 30. doesn't he?

Seite 115

1. I can; 2. she is; 3. I have; 4. she didn't; 5. they aren't; 6. I have; 7. I won't; 8. she wasn't; 9. I needn't; 10. I didn't; 11. I would; 12. he has; 13. he may not; 14. she hadn't; 15. he did; 16. she wasn't; 17. I won't; 18. I'm not; 19. she hasn't; 20. he did; 21. he may; 22. she doesn't; 23. I haven't; 24. I wasn't; 25. you shan't; 26. I haven't; 27. I can; 28. I have; 29. I don't; 30. he did.

Seite 116 f.

I. 1. could (was able to); 2. will be able to; 3. will have to; 4. wasn't allowed to; 5. has never been; 6. I didn't have to; 7. couldn't (wasn't able to); 8. has never been able to; 9. haven't got (don't have); 10. had to; 11. will be able to; 12. will not be allowed to; 13. was; 14. didn't you; 15. had had to; 16. are not allowed to; 17. will not have to; 18. are not allowed to; 19. had to/was; 20. will not be able to.

II. 1. Could you lend me your pencil, please? 2. May I introduce Mr M. to you? 3. May the children (Are the children allowed to) play in the garden? 4. He will not be able to enter the house, because he has forgotten his keys. 5. Can't your glasses lie on the dining-table? 6. She doesn't have to (She needn't) work on Monday. 7. Can't we go to the theatre? 8. Since when have you been able to speak F.? 9. P. doesn't like classical music, does he? 10. Do you know G. O.? – Yes, I do. 11. He didn't forget to lock the car yesterday. 12. In former times food used to cost much less. 13. M. hopes to be able to speak so much English in 2 years that she will be able to (can) speak with the foreign tourists in her souvenir shop. 14. They have had to take their son to the dentist every day for 2 weeks. 15. When entering a mosque, shoes must be (have to be) taken off. 16. Does your neighbour really clean her windows every day? 17. Did your friend move to Spain last year? 18. This pullover mustn't be washed. 19. The Baker children have never been allowed to have a party. 20. Could I have left my hat in the car?

Seite 120 ff.

I. 1. to see; 2. to help; 3. to annoy; 4. answer; 5. to spell; 6. let/drive; 7. to phone; 8. to repair; 9. to get; 10. to land; 11. be repaired; 12. to be; 13. to study; 14. to arrive; 15. to let.

II. 1. to answer; 2. be left; 3. to stay; 4. to become; 5. to come; 6. to hear; 7. to listen; 8. to lock/get; 9. to elect; 10. to be painted; 11. to be discussed; 12. to be able to spend; 13. not to be found; 14. to get; 15. to blame.

III. 1. where to go to; 2. student to deserve the prize; 3. paper to leave the note on; 4. somebody to look after our children; 5. land to live on; 6. second to reach; 7. person to be hurt; 8. somebody to talk to; 9. pullover to go with; 10. whether to accept the invitation: 11. Englishman to sail; 12. how to take; 13. person to arrive and the last person to leave; 14. boy to act; 15. how to translate.

IV. 1. The caretaker wants all students to leave the school at 1 o'clock. 2. Mr C. is the second to fall off the horse today. 3. It's not easy to learn English grammar. 4. John is the only boy to have enrolled for the sewing course. **5.** Mr K. is much too old to take part in the dancing competition. **6.** The homework should be done properly. **7.** The new boss wants me to stay longer in the office on Friday. **8.** Yesterday our neighbour saw a man enter the garden. **9.** Could you please come next weekend to help me with the preparations for the party? **10.** It's time for him to look for a new job. **11.** I can show you how to repair a tyre. **12.** The police looked everywhere, but the pistol wasn't to be found. **13.** Before we can move in a lot of work remains to be done. **14.** John must be having his dinner right now. **15.** There is no time to be lost.

Seite 127 f.   **I.**   **1.** H. promised to give up smoking. **2.** The guide said we had the opportunity of visiting ...; **3.** He is very proud of having passed his exam. **4.** He complains about not earning enough money. **5.** "You have the choice between learning your new words and not getting a good mark." **6.** He dreams of being ...; **7.** It's no use relying on S. **8.** She's busy preparing dinner. **9.** He is not used to working long. **10.** I'm looking forward to meeting ...; **11.** I'll have to pay the workers for painting ...; **12.** It's not worth reading ...; **13.** We had difficulties in finding ... **14.** I'm fond of playing tennis ...; **15.** It's no use phoning him. **16.** I won't be able to avoid meeting her. **17.** I missed seeing the film. **18.** He succeeded in getting ...; **19.** After having dinner ...; **20.** He is very good at dancing.

II.   **1.** He was always afraid of flying. **2.** I risk losing my job if I help you. **3.** The children are not used to staying up so late. **4.** He was very disappointed about you(r) not having come to his birthday. **5.** They came to England in the hope of being able to lead a better life there. **6.** He didn't want to admit having made a mistake. **7.** What is the reason for you(r) coming too late again? **8.** I can't stand waiting long. **9.** The customer insists on talking to the manager. **10.** The vicar went on making his speech. **11.** It's no use visiting him in hospital. **12.** Do you mind me (my) opening the window? **13.** He went on holiday instead of finishing his work. **14.** I didn't have any opportunity of asking questions. **15.** You can prevent the plants from dying if you water them regularly. **16.** You should consider working together with S. **17.** He was against spending more money on holidays. **18.** Instead of finally telling me the truth, he made up more lies. **19.** He has always been fond of travelling. **20.** Judith was very angry about not having met you.

Seite 128   **1.** to have; **2.** go/walk; **3.** to write; **4.** seeing; **5.** to be run; **6.** to understand; **7.** laughing; **8.** cutting; **9.** to go; **10.** to go; **11.** to swim; **12.** leaving; **13.** to get; **14.** winning (having won); **15.** repairing; **16.** to say; **17.** trying to make; **18.** to finish/looking up; **19.** to tell/playing; **20.** practising/to play (playing); **21.** leave; **22.** to come; **23.** Looking at/being; **24.** robbing (having robbed).

Seite 131f.   **I.**   1. 'll go; 2. 'll give; 3. 'll jump; 4. 'll catch; 5. sends/'ll go; 6. have; 7. 'll telephone; 8. shines/'ll have; 9. 'll take; 10. finds/'ll move; 11. 'll buy/have; 12. 'll run; 13. 'll be; 14. send/'ll get; 15. write/'ll be; 16. 'll call for/doesn't feel; 17. go on/'ll lose; 18. comes/'ll be; 19. 'll fly; 20. lends/'ll be able to.

         II.   1. If I have today off, I'll go out. 2. If she should come, I'll tell you. 3. If you meet Mrs B., will you please tell her to phone me. 4. If C. 's repairing her bike at the moment, she'll be ready by 5 o'clock. 5. If the parcel doesn't come soon, I'll phone the firm. 6. If you water flowers during the day, they grow better. 7. If S. hasn't booked the journey yet, he should hurry. 8. If I find the city map, I can show you the street. 9. If C. has decided to stay in L., he should look for a flat. 10. If R. comes to G., he will phone you directly.

Seite 134   **I.**   1. would lend; 2. would call; 3. were; 4. lived; 5. would be; 6. wore/would laugh; 7. left/would be stolen; 8. would phone/knew; 9. was/would become; 10. believed/would become; 11. knew/could tell you (would be able to tell you); 12. were (was)/would get; 13. would your father say/didn't pass; 14. had/wouldn't have; 15. would be/saw; 16. had/could play (would be able to play); 17. could (would be able to) apply/passed; 18. had/could go out (would be able to go out); 19. won/would buy; 20. read/would be.

         II.   1. If I had enough money, I would already have bought the recorder. 2. He would catch the train if he hurried. 3. If the weather was better, we could go swimming. 4. If Carmen was a little bit more polite, she wouldn't get into trouble so often. 5. If there were fewer students in a class, the students could learn more. 6. If you got the £ 1000, you should really open a savings account. 7. I wouldn't have a free minute if I went to the tennis court as often as you do. 8. If my party were in the government, everything would be better. 9. If I were well I could go walking with you. 10. If we had to buy a new car, we would choose a faster car.

Seite 136f.   **I.**   1. would have been; 2. would have met; 3. would have caught; 4. had known; 5. had left; 6. had found/could have saved (would have been able to save); 7. hadn't worn/would have been; 8. had known/would have picked; 9. had been/would not have locked; 10. had done/wouldn't have happened; 11. had phoned/would have been able to reserve (could have reserved); 12. had gone/would have stayed; 13. had gone/wouldn't have been; 14. would have left/hadn't told; 15. had spent/wouldn't have become; 16. hadn't drunk/wouldn't have lost; 17. had asked/would have got; 18. had been raised/wouldn't have gone; 19. had applied/would have got; 20. had had/would have bought.

         II.   1. We would have liked to help you moving house if we hadn't been on holiday. 2. If Carl hadn't had his sister with him; it would have become a boring evening. 3. If you hadn't driven so fast, you would have seen the traffic-lights. **4.** I also wouldn't have believed it if I hadn't seen the photo. **5.** My mother would like to go to the theatre if she hadn't been so ill. **6.** I would have lent you the book if I hadn't needed it myself. **7.** If Sheila hadn't been so spoiled by her parents, she wouldn't be so selfish. **8.** I could have repaired (would have been able to repair) the car myself if I had had the right tools. **9.** If Leo hadn't always been so lazy, he could have passed (would have been able to pass) the exam. **10.** It would have been better if you had asked the doctor.

Seite 137 f. **I.**   **1.** 'll go; **2.** would know; **3.** would be; **4.** 'll go; **5.** would stay; **6.** 'll go; **7.** like; **8.** 'll have to go; **9.** wouldn't have broken; **10.** 'll be; **11.** were/wouldn't visit; **12.** could have taken (would have been able to take); oder: could take (would be able to take); **13.** would have been able to get (could have got); **14.** hadn't gone; **15.** doesn't run; **16.** was (were); **17.** had obeyed; **18.** hadn't robbed; **19.** marries/'ll be; **20.** hadn't worked.

      II.   **1.** If he weren't (wasn't) such a fool, he would never have done this. **2.** If I speak, I don't like to be interrupted. **3.** He wouldn't have been dismissed if he had admitted the mistake at once. **4.** If S. isn't feeling well at the moment, she should go to the doctor. **5.** If P. sells the car, he must ('ll have to) go by bus again. **6.** If R. comes in time, we can ('ll be able to) go to the zoo. **7.** If we had found the papers earlier, it would have saved us a lot of work. **8.** The two girls would have been drowned if a boat had not been nearby.

Seite 140   **1.** Leave your brother alone! **2.** I will allow the children to go (let the children go) into the garden. **3.** Mother had the washing machine repaired. **4.** The boss let me go home. **5.** Leave the building at once, please. **6.** I will have the letter written. **7.** Let us buy a present for him together. **8.** The neighbour let the children (allowed the children to) play in the garden. **9.** My mother let me watch the late night film. **10.** Stop this nonsense. **11.** Give me one hour. **12.** Let us go to a youth hostel. **13.** Mr S. kept me waiting for half an hour. **14.** The doctor didn't let the patient (didn't allow the patient to) get up. **15.** Leave the book there. **16.** He had his lawn cut. **17.** The police made him empty his bags. **18.** He had his hair cut. **19.** I have my pullovers drycleaned. **20.** My parents have the house wallpapered. **21.** The coach made the sportsmen train one extra hour. **22.** Sue didn't leave her little brother alone. **23.** He left his suitcase at the airport. **24.** The pilot had the plane checked. **25.** The headmaster makes the students tidy up the yard.

Seite 143 f. **I.**   **1.** shops; **2.** children; **3.** hovercraft; **4.** bookshelves; **5.** families; **6.** days; **7.** wives; **8.** photos; **9.** tomatoes; **10.** cars; **11.** buses; **12.** friends; **13.** companies; **14.** boats; **15.** bushes; **16.** boys;

17. gentlemen; **18.** Americans; **19.** Japanese; **20.** feet; **21.** cigarettes; **22.** glasses; **23.** pens; **24.** clocks; **25.** pieces; **26.** tickets; **27.** houses; **28.** ferries; **29.** windows; **30.** noses; **31.** toys; **32.** bodies; **33.** chiefs; **34.** apples; **35.** streets; **36.** managers; **37.** teachers; **38.** bases; **39.** letters; **40.** parrots; **41.** donkeys; **42.** brothers; **43.** keys; **44.** purses; **45.** radios; **46.** pictures; **47.** trees; **48.** boxes; **49.** flowers; **50.** bags.

II. 1. chairmen; **2.** handbags; **3.** record-shops; **4.** bathing-costumes; **5.** sons–in-law; **6.** air traffic controllers; **7.** teach-ins; **8.** mouse-traps; **9.** menservants; **10.** women-haters; **11.** horsemen; **12.** passers-by; **13.** sit-ins; **14.** schoolboys; **15.** armchairs; **16.** bookcases; **17.** men students; **18.** forget-me-nots; **19.** roundabouts; **20.** broadcasting stations; **21.** bus-drivers; **22.** ticket-collectors; **23.** have-nots; **24.** snowmen; **25.** fellows; **26.** schoolmasters; **27.** onlookers; **28.** bedrooms; **29.** good-for-nothings; **30.** dining-tables.

Seite 146f. **I.** 1. are; **2.** are; **3.** is; **4.** supports; **5.** is; **6.** is; **7.** are; **8.** are; **9.** lead; **10.** are; **11.** isn't; **12.** are lying; **13.** is; **14.** have; **15.** have; **16.** aren't; **17.** is turning; **18.** is found; **19.** are just having; **20.** consists; **21.** are; **22.** are; **23.** are; **24.** are; **25.** are.

II. 1. The staff are on holiday. 2. The audience is requested to be quiet. 3. The class are just writing a test. 4. The homework is very difficult. 5. This information wasn't written in the newspaper. 6. Great progress has been made. 7. Your jeans are torn. 8. The people were very excited. 9. Mumps is an unpleasant disease. 10. The binoculars belong to my grandfather. 11. The jury withdraw for their consultations: 12. The choir is just singing my favourite song. 13. The shorts are already in the suitcase. 14. The group consists of 10 members. 15. The firm needs new office rooms.

Seite 150f. **I.** 1. my cat's; **2.** mother's; **3.** the ladies'; **4.** Fred's; **5.** the women's; **6.** my sister's; **7.** father's; **8.** the girls'; **9.** James'; **10.** a five minutes'; **11.** grandfather's; **12.** today's; **13.** the greengrocer's; **14.** America's; **15.** the chemist's; **16.** your aunt's; **17.** the Smiths'; **18.** our neighbours'; **19.** the dog's; **20.** the secretaries'; **21.** my little brother's; **22.** the boss'; **23.** my brother's; **24.** Anne's; **25.** my friends'; **26.** tomorrow's; **27.** Mr Carter's; **28.** the morning's; **29.** my parents'; **30.** the students'.

II. 1. the wall of the garden; **2.** cup of tea; **3.** page of the book; **4.** 3 minutes' discussion; **5.** the bird's cage; **6.** my employer's office; **7.** the frame of the picture; **8.** loss of the briefcase; **9.** Shakespeare's work; **10.** Madame Tussaud's; **11.** University of London; **12.** last month's business; **13.** Mr Red's secretary; **14.** headline of the article; **15.** at the Porters'; **16.** length of the letter; **17.** the teachers' room; **18.** the old man's coat; **19.** the Beatles' records; **20.** the manager's salary; **21.** lock of the door; **22.** the waiter's purse; **23.** size of the book; **24.** the guests' order; **25.** the men's suitcases; **26.** colour of the painting; **27.** my sister's CD-player; **28.** my friend's party; **29.** Paul's birthday; **30.** growth of the flowers.

1. Yesterday's news was shocking. **2.** One of Mr Grant's colleagues has fallen ill. **3.** The crowd were standing around when I came and all were waiting at the baker's to get the sportsman's autograph. **4.** After a 2 hours' meeting all the members of the club were rather tired. **5.** The crew of the plane are just striking. Therefore we'll have to go by one of my boss' private planes. **6.** The second of Karl's ideas seems to be the best. **7.** Davis' pyjamas have disappeared again. He'll have to take some of Tom's. **8.** The beggar's belongings consisted of a suitcase and a pair of old uniform trousers. **9.** The group are still working at their project, but the financial situation of the firm will soon put an end to the project. **10.** Great damage was caused by the explosion of the gas-stove.

I. **1.** a; **2.** an; **3.** an; **4.** a; **5.** an; **6.** a; **7.** a; **8.** an; **9.** a; **10.** a; **11.** an; **12.** a; **13.** a; **14.** a; **15.** a; **16.** an; **17.** an; **18.** a; **19.** an; **20.** a; **21.** an; **22.** an; **23.** a; **24.** an; **25.** a; **26.** an; **27.** a; **28.** a; **29.** a; **30.** a.

II. **1.** a; **2.** an; **3.** a/a; **4.** a; **5.** an; **6.** a; **7.** a; **8.** a/a; **9.** a; **10.** –; **11.** an; **12.** a; **13.** a; **14.** a; **15.** a; **16.** a/a; **17.** an; **18.** a; **19.** a; **20.** a/an.

III. **1.** –; **2.** the; **3.** the; **4.** –; **5.** –; **6.** the/–; **7.** –/–; **8.** the/the; **9.** the/the; **10.** –/–; **11.** the/–; **12.** –; **13.** the/–; **14.** –; **15.** the/the/the; **16.** the/–/the; **17.** the; **18.** –; **19.** –/–; **20.** the.

IV. **1.** such a; **2.** half a bottle; **3.** absurd a story; **4.** quite a nice; **5.** Both the parents; **6.** as a good lawyer; **7.** £ 5.50 a bottle; **8.** What a good; **9.** half the sum; **10.** such a hurry.

I. **1.** –; **2.** the; **3.** a; **4.** –/a; **5.** –; **6.** –; **7.** –; **8.** –/the; **9.** –/the/the; **10.** the/a; **11.** –; **12.** –; **13.** –/a; **14.** a; **15.** a.

II. **1.** Nature is sometimes cruel. **2.** The work I am doing at the moment is boring. **3.** After his A-levels my son will go to university. **4.** The caretaker fixed a loudspeaker on the roof of the school. **5.** When S. saw the dog, he took (to) flight. **6.** As a rule our secretary is very reliable. **7.** He is such a difficult boy. **8.** As a good friend I can give you the following advice. **9.** Yesterday was rather a cold day. **10.** Peter is rather a strong boy. He always has a good appetite. **11.** He worked five hours without a break. **12.** It is really a pity that you can't come. **13.** Most students don't like grammar. **14.** My uncle works as a psychiatrist in the prison. **15.** One of the patients is "Big Sam", who has been in prison for five years.

I. **1.** cleaner – cleanest; **2.** hotter – hottest; **3.** more radical – most radical; **4.** thirstier – thirstiest; **5.** nicer – nicest; **6.** softer – softest; **7.** happier – happiest; **8.** more democratic – most democratic; **9.** thicker – thickest; **10.** fatter – fattest; **11.** greater – greatest; **12.** narrower – narrowest; **13.** smaller – smallest; **14.** younger – youngest; **15.** quicker – quickest; **16.** more polite – most polite; **17.** larger – largest; **18.** more difficult – most difficult; **19.** cooler –

coolest; **20.** simpler – simplest; **21.** more efficient – most efficient; **22.** more nervous – most nervous; **23.** cheaper – cheapest; **24.** dirtier – dirtiest; **25.** more characteristic – most characteristic; **26.** sunnier – sunniest; **27.** prettier – prettiest; **28.** luckier – luckiest; **29.** uglier – ugliest; **30.** more competent – most competent.

II. **1.** easier than; **2.** as expensive as; **3.** the sooner the better; **4.** the smallest; **5.** as nice as; **6.** not as old as; **7.** less big than; **8.** more and more expensive; **9.** the best; **10.** lazier than; **11.** as cheap as; **12.** longer than; **13.** better and better; **14.** the most difficult; **15.** less nice than; **16.** the most interesting; **17.** newer than; **18.** as thick as; **19.** less polite than; **20.** the more children the livelier; **21.** as tired as; **22.** the richest; **23.** not as long as; **24.** thirstier than.

Seite 165

1. The rich can afford servants. **2.** This exercise is more difficult than the last (one). **3.** My father's car is nearly as fast as a sportscar. **4.** Mr Pit is the oldest inhabitant of this town. **5.** Food is getting more and more expensive. **6.** Sometimes the young don't understand the old. **7.** My elder brother works in a bank. **8.** The police make further investigations. **9.** Where is the nearest bus-stop? **10.** The students become more and more childish. **11.** Fewer people than expected came to the concert. **12.** My friend is 2 years older than me. **13.** The more he has, the more he wants. **14.** He is less stupid than I thought. **15.** My friend ist the most intelligent boy in class. **16.** In the last half of the century there were economic difficulties. **17.** Sam is not as good as Kelly at school. **18.** The more he speaks, the better his English becomes. **19.** Fewer and fewer people go to church. **20.** I'll give you further details later.

Seite 172

I. **1.** directly; **2.** fast; **3.** fully; **4.** fantastically; **5.** correctly; **6.** carefully; **7.** happily; **8.** truly; **9.** extremely; **10.** in a silly way; **11.** cheaply; **12.** probably; **13.** busily; **14.** pretty/prettily; **15.** fair/fairly; **16.** rarely; **17.** recently; **18.** intelligently; **19.** well; **20.** sadly; **21.** far; **22.** powerfully; **23.** sweetly; **24.** loudly; **25.** sensibly; **26.** bravely; **27.** slowly; **28.** hopefully; **29.** basically; **30.** wisely; **31.** angrily; **32.** wholly; **33.** politely; **34.** weekly; **35.** fluently; **36.** regularly.

II. **1.** better – best; **2.** more slowly – most slowly; **3.** longer – longest; **4.** more quietly – most quietly; **5.** more deeply – most deeply; **6.** more nervously – most nervously; **7.** less – least; **8.** more – most; **9.** more extremely – most extremely; **10.** more quickly – most quickly; **11.** worse – worst; **12.** more fluently – most fluently; **13.** more softly – most softly; **14.** more nicely – most nicely; **15.** more prettily – most prettily; **16.** more sweetly – most sweetly; **17.** more gladly – most gladly; **18.** more loudly – most loudly; **19.** sooner – soonest; **20.** earlier – earliest; **21.** higher – highest; **22.** more angrily – most angrily; **23.** faster – fastest; **24.** worse – worst.

III. 1. . . . to the bus-stop at 7 o'clock. **2.** My sister Maud was studying very hard in her room all day yesterday. **3.** He has never been to London in his life. **4.** Let's go to the cinema this evening. **5.** Sue sang very well at the competition in Oxford 2 days ago. **6.** The visitors had to wait in front of the door a little while. **7.** Come again soon! **8.** He had never seen a musical on stage before. **9.** He has been in the park twice today. **10.** She walked once before supper. **11.** Unfortunately, he had to stay in hospital for 3 days. **12.** Our friend usually helps me in the garden at the weekend. **13.** The cat was lying quietly on the sofa. **14.** I seldom go shopping in Paris.

Seite 174 1. seriously; **2.** serious; **3.** seriously; **4.** usually/loudly; **5.** usual; **6.** loud/terrible; **7.** happily; **8.** Happy; **9.** happily; **10.** high; **11.** high; **12.** highly elegant; **13.** surprising; **14.** surprisingly/really; **15.** surprisingly polite; **16.** well; **17.** good; **18.** good; **19.** completely; **20.** complete; **21.** completely; **22.** regularly; **23.** regularly; **24.** easy; **25.** easily; **26.** easily; **27.** careless; **28.** especially/carelessly; **29.** really; **30.** real; **31.** nervous; **32.** great; **33.** sad; **34.** carefully; **35.** weak; **36.** good (well); **37.** angrily.

Seite 175 1. Sally looks very nice in her extremely long coat. **2.** At first his explanations sounded strange, but then they turned out to be true. **3.** If the cake remains in the oven any longer, it won't taste so good any more. **4.** From the plane the mountains didn't look so high. **5.** The cat was lying in front of the fireplace. Its fur felt soft and warm. **6.** He worked very hard, but had hardly any success. **7.** Have you already tasted the good jam? **8.** Kevin is very ill. Yesterday he felt worse than ever before. **9.** When he suddenly heard a noise, he excitedly looked behind him. **10.** Why must Sam always behave so stupidly? After all, he is fairly intelligent. **11.** She felt so tired that she could hardly keep her eyes open. **12.** Every rule will be explained as simply as possible. **13.** The patient impatiently waited for the doctor. **14.** Fortunately, he wasn't seriously injured. **15.** As he doesn't take his studies very seriously; he probably won't do very well in the exam. **16.** The beef looks delicious and smells very good. **17.** As usual my grandfather was sitting on the comfortably warm porch. **18.** When he heard a strange noice in the cellar, he carefully felt his pistol. **19.** Mary doesn't see very well, but nevertheless she is a good student. **20.** Sam sounded very happy when he heard the good news.

Seite 177 f. **I.** 1. She; **2.** them; **3.** It; **4.** them; **5.** It; **6.** it; **7.** it; **8.** It; **9.** them; **10.** She/it; **11.** it; **12.** He; **13.** them; **14.** They; **15.** them; **16.** it; **17.** He/it; **18.** it/him; **19.** they; **20.** We/it; **21.** it; **22.** It; **23.** it; **24.** them; **25.** They; **26.** She; **27.** He/it.

II. 1. I think you are nicer than all of them (them all). **2.** Who is knocking? – It's me. **3.** Can you introduce him to me? **4.** I saw you only yesterday. **5.** I have never seen them here. **6.** He is as old as me. **7.** Who is coming to the cinema? – Me! **8.** Can you give them the letters, please? **9.** You must always do your duty. **10.** They say this winter is going to be very cold.

Seite 180 f. **I.** **1.** His; **2.** Her; **3.** his; **4.** his; **5.** his; **6.** Her; **7.** His; **8.** hers; **9.** their; **10.** mine (ours); **11.** hers; **12.** hers; **13.** hers; **14.** his; **15.** his; **16.** our; **17.** Their; **18.** my; **19.** Their; **20.** His; **21.** their; **22.** my; **23.** Her; **24.** their; **25.** his; **26.** their; **27.** his; **28.** her; **29.** Their; **30.** my.

II. **1.** Have you seen my bag? **2.** The cover of my book is missing. **3.** He is a colleague of his. **4.** Peter has always had a room of his own. **5.** They attended their three months' French course. **6.** That is not your suitcase. It's mine. **7.** I can't get the idea out of my mind. **8.** I have already met his sister. **9.** Your house is very nice. **10.** Have you got a room of your own?

Seite 183 f. **I.** **1.** which; **2.** what; **3.** which; **4.** which; **5.** what; **6.** what; **7.** which; **8.** which; **9.** what; **10.** which; **11.** what; **12.** which; **13.** which; **14.** which; **15.** which; **16.** what; **17.** which; **18.** which; **19.** what; **20.** what.

II. **1.** what; **2.** what (who/m); **3.** who(m); **4.** what; **5.** what (who); **6.** whose; **7.** what; **8.** whose; **9.** what; **10.** which; **11.** what; **12.** who; **13.** what (who/m); **14.** what; **15.** who(m); **16.** who; **17.** which; **18.** who (which); **19.** whose; **20.** who.

III. **1.** Who would you like to spend your holiday with? **2.** What kind of magazine is your father looking at? **3.** What is your favourite pop group? **4.** Who were you introduced to? **5.** Who did your brother sell his car to? **6.** Who called me ...? **7.** Who do you have to send the photos to at once? **8.** What is in the wardrobe? **9.** Who are the boys laughing at? **10.** Which one is yours? **11.** Who have you seen before? **12.** Who knows Mr Baker? **13.** What films do you like best? **14.** What is published by a brewery? **15.** Who would your mother like to talk to?

Seite 186 ff. **I.** **1.** myself; **2.** herself; **3.** himself; **4.** yourself (yourselves); **5.** ourselves; **6.** himself; **7.** himself; **8.** himself; **9.** himself; **10.** themselves; **11.** himself; **12.** herself; **13.** yourself; **14.** yourself; **15.** myself; **16.** myself; **17.** themselves; **18.** yourself (yourselves); **19.** herself; **20.** yourself (yourselves).

II. **1.** you; **2.** ourselves; **3.** ourselves; **4.** him; **5.** her; **6.** herself; **7.** herself; **8.** himself; **9.** itself; **10.** themselves; **11.** him; **12.** us; **13.** yourself (yourselves); **14.** herself; **15.** herself.

III. **1.** –; **2.** you; **3.** itself; **4.** herself; **5.** itself; **6.** yourself (yourselves); **7.** –; **8.** –; **9.** herself; **10.** himself; **11.** herself; **12.** you; **13.** –; **14.** himself; **15.** himself; **16.** themselves; **17.** –; **18.** –; **19.** –; **20.** herself; **21.** himself; **22.** herself; **23.** –; **24.** herself; **25.** yourself (yourselves).

IV. **1.** each other; **2.** each other (ourselves); **3.** herself; **4.** each other; **5.** yourself (yourselves); **6.** each other; **7.** myself; **8.** myself; **9.** each other/each other; **10.** ourselves.

I. 1. this/that; 2. these/those; 3. this/those; 4. these/those; 5. this/that; 6. this/that; 7. this/that; 8. this/that; 9. this/that; 10. this/those; 11. this/that; 12. this/that; 13. this/those; 14. this/that; 15. this/those.

II. 1. those; 2. that; 3. these/those; 4. that/this; 5. this/that; 6. this/that; 7. this/that; 8. that; 9. those; 10. those.

III. 1. Our house is much smaller than that of our neighbour. 2. Are those your suitcases over there? 3. These are my friends, Pit and Herbert. 4. Which of the girls is Sue? – This one here. 5. I think these chairs are much more comfortable than those ones. 6. Which suit do you think is nicer? This one or that one? 7. I cannot walk that far. 8. Isn't that the famous singer over there? 9. You can take either this or that way. 10. I have never seen that lady over there.

I. 1. who; 2. which; 3. who; 4. which; 5. who; 6. which; 7. who(m); 8. which; 9. which; 10. which; 11. which; 12. which; 13. which; 14. which; 15. which; 16. who; 17. who; 18. which; 19. which; 20. who.

II. 1. whose; 2. which; 3. who; 4. which; 5. who(m); 6. which; 7. which; 8. who; 9. whose (of which); 10. who; 11. whose; 12. who; 13. whose; 14. who; 15. which; 16. which; 17. who; 18. which; 19. which; 20. whose.

III. 1. which; 2. –; 3. which; 4. –; 5. –; 6. –; 7. –; 8. –; 9. –; 10. which; 11. which; 12. which; 13. who; 14. whose; 15. which; 16. who; 17. –; 18. which; 19. which; 20. –.

1. He always leaves the door open behind him. 2. The Great Fire of London, which broke out in a bakery in Pudding Lane in 1666, destroyed large parts of London. 3. The Museum of London, which shows the history of the town, is closed on Mondays. 4. Whose coat are you wearing? – Isn't it mine? 5. Is this my bag here? – No, that one over there is yours. 6. He cut himself in his finger yesterday. 7. Those roses over there are really beautiful. Do you think your aunt would give me some? 8. Who have you lent your new bike to? 9. Could you please write down your phone number for me? 10. Who are you writing to? 11. I can't remember having seen your sister before. 12. My friend, whose mother is a cook, cannot cook at all. 13. Who lives in that big house over there? 14. The man the police are looking for has escaped from that prison. 15. He has got three daughters, who all work for the same firm. 16. He hasn't given her the book back yet. 17. They talked to each other like good friends although they didn't know each other. 18. May I sit down or is this seat taken? 19. Which coat shall I take, the thick blue one or the thin black one? 20. I need the book as a present for him, not for myself. 21. The glass you are drinking out of is still dirty. 22. The parcel she sent me was damaged. 23. I don't like these people. 24. Peter offered his help at once, which was very surprising. 25. What colour is your hair? 26. He lives with his sister in that little house over there.

27. Simon went to buy Christmas presents all by himself. **28.** He came with his hat in his hand. **29.** I haven't met him personally. **30.** Who are you thinking of?

Seite 206 ff. **I.** **"At", "in", or "on"?** **1.** in; **2.** in; **3.** At; **4.** in; **5.** at … at; **6.** In; **7.** On; **8.** in; **9.** on; **10.** on; **11.** on; **12.** in; **13.** on; **14.** at; **15.** at; **16.** in; **17.** on; **18.** on; **19.** at; **20.** on. **"Above", "over", "across" or "via"?** **1.** over; **2.** above; **3.** over; **4.** above; **5.** via; **6.** over; **7.** over; **8.** above; **9.** across; **10.** via; **11.** across; **12.** above; **13.** across; **14.** over; **15.** across. **"Under" or "below"?** **1.** below; **2.** under; **3.** below; **4.** under; **5.** below; **6.** below; **7.** under; **8.** under; **9.** under; **10.** below. **"Between" or "among"?** **1.** between, **2.** between; **3.** among; **4.** between; **5.** among; **6.** among; **7.** among; **8.** between; **9.** among; **10.** among. **"To" or "towards"?** **1.** to; **2.** towards; **3.** towards; **4.** to; **5.** to; **6.** towards; **7.** to; **8.** to; **9.** to; **10.** towards. **"To" or "as far as"?** **1.** to; **2.** to; **3.** to/as far as; **4.** to; **5.** as far as; **6.** to; **7.** to; **8.** as far as; **9.** to; **10.** to. **"After", "behind", "beyond" or "past"?** **1.** behind (past); **2.** behind; **3.** behind; **4.** behind; **5.** behind; **6.** behind (beyond); **7.** behind; **8.** after; **9.** after; **10.** after; **11.** behind; **12.** after; **13.** beyond; **14.** after; **15.** behind. **"In front of" or "before"?** **1.** in front of; **2.** in front of; **3.** before; **4.** in front of/before; **5.** before; **6.** in front of; **7.** before; **8.** before; **9.** in front of; **10.** before. **"Ago" or "before"?** **1.** before; **2.** ago; **3.** ago; **4.** before; **5.** ago; **6.** before; **7.** before; **8.** ago; **9.** before; **10.** ago. **"Since" or "for"?** **1.** since; **2.** since; **3.** since; **4.** since; **5.** for; **6.** since; **7.** for; **8.** for; **9.** since; **10.** since; **11.** since; **12.** for; **13.** since; **14.** since; **15.** for. **"By" or "with"?** **1.** by; **2.** with; **3.** by; **4.** by; **5.** by; **6.** with; **7.** by; **8.** with; **9.** by; **10.** with.

Seite 214 **I.** **1.** off; **2.** for; **3.** about; **4.** to; **5.** by; **6.** for; **7.** out; **8.** by; **9.** for; **10.** off; **11.** about (of); **12.** of (from); **13.** to; **14.** with; **15.** on; **16.** in; **17.** down; **18.** for (with); **19.** by; **20.** up; **21.** in/in; **22.** to; **23.** for; **24.** across; **25.** with; **26.** into; **27.** for; **28.** for; **29.** like; **30.** after; **31.** into; **32.** up; **33.** up; **34.** (up)on as; **35.** out; **36.** on; **37.** about.

Seite 215 f. **I.** **1.** at/at; **2.** about (for); **3.** between; **4.** about; **5.** for; **6.** among; **7.** to/via; **8.** ago; **9.** by/by; **10.** at; **11.** to/since; **12.** in; **13.** on; **14.** before/in (to); **15.** to; **16.** from; **17.** for; **18.** with; **19.** with; **20.** of; **21.** with; **22.** behind; **23.** in; **24.** out; **25.** out.

II. **1.** We have been living at 25 Church Street since 1995. **2.** He insisted on opening the safe. **3.** Children under 16 may not go in a pub. **4.** I have already been waiting for Tom for an hour. **5.** He died from (of) heart failure 2 days ago. **6.** I have already heard so much about her that I'm looking forward to meeting her. **7.** Please be on time tomorrow. **8.** We have a small garden behind our house. **9.** He lost his wallet in the tube yesterday. **10.** She applied for the job of secretary at (the firm) Cup Ltd. 1 week ago. **11.** On the right side you can see our house in the picture. **12.** I'm usually at home at 6 o'clock in the evening. **13.** You can reach

281

me in the office between 1 and 2 o'clock. **14.** He wrote a letter to his aunt and sent it by airmail. **15.** He was found on a rock below the top of the mountain. **16.** My mother has been working in this supermarket for 3 years. **17.** He lived among the Indians for 5 years. **18.** He understood the warning between the lines. **19.** Three suitable candidates were among the applicants. **20.** We arrived at the hotel in time for dinner. **21.** When he went over the bridge, he saw a plane above him. **22.** The accident happened on the evening of the 13th of October. **23.** He liked living among the Indians in the jungle. **24.** Look over your essay again. There is a mistake in line 2. **25.** They have already been talking about his problems for half an hour now.

Seite 222 ff.

I. **1.** when; **2.** if; **3.** when; **4.** when; **5.** if; **6.** if; **7.** if; **8.** when; **9.** if; **10.** when.

II. **1.** during; **2.** during, **3.** while; **4.** while; **5.** during; **6.** whereas; **7.** while; **8.** whereas; **9.** during; **10.** while; **11.** during; **12.** while; **13.** during; **14.** during; **15.** while.

III. **1.** because; **2.** since/as; **3.** since/as; **4.** because; **5.** since/as; **6.** since/as; **7.** since/as; **8.** because; **9.** because; **10.** because/for; **11.** because; **12.** since/as; **13.** since/as; **14.** since/as; **15.** since/as; **16.** because; **17.** because; **18.** since/as; **19.** because; **20.** because.

IV. **1.** So can I. **2.** So is her brother. **3.** So do I. **4.** So will the Meyers. **5.** Neither/Nor do her sisters. **6.** Neither/Nor can I. **7.** So do I. **8.** Neither/Nor has my brother. **9.** Neither/Nor had I. **10.** Neither/Nor does he. **11.** So must Peter. **12.** Neither/Nor do I. **13.** So can Susanne. **14.** So can my friend. **15.** So does Carmen.

V. **1.** like; **2.** how; **3.** like; **4.** like; **5.** how; **6.** as ... as; **7.** as; **8.** like; **9.** like; **10.** as; **11.** how; **12.** as; **13.** like; **14.** like; **15.** as; **16.** as ... as; **17.** like; **18.** like; **19.** as; **20.** like.

Seite 226 f.

I. **1.** any; **2.** any; **3.** some; **4.** some; **5.** some; **6.** some; **7.** any; **8.** any; **9.** any; **10.** any; **11.** some; **12.** any; **13.** any; **14.** any; **15.** any; **16.** some/any; **17.** some; **18.** any; **19.** any; **20.** some.

II. **1.** any; **2.** some; **3.** any; **4.** any; **5.** any/some; **6.** any; **7.** some; **8.** any; **9.** some; **10.** any; **11.** some; **12.** some; **13.** any; **14.** any; **15.** any; **16.** some; **17.** Some; **18.** any; **19.** any; **20.** any.

Seite 228 f.

I. **1.** many; **2.** many; **3.** many; **4.** many; **5.** much; **6.** much; **7.** many; **8.** much; **9.** many; **10.** much; **11.** many; **12.** much; **13.** many; **14.** much; **15.** much; **16.** many; **17.** many; **18.** much; **19.** many; **20.** much.

II. **1.** few; **2.** little; **3.** little; **4.** few; **5.** little; **6.** few; **7.** few; **8.** few; **9.** few; **10.** few; **11.** few; **12.** little; **13.** little; **14.** few; **15.** few; **16.** little; **17.** few; **18.** little; **19.** little; **20.** few; **21.** few.

III. **1.** I have got a lot of time. **2.** He has got a lot of money. **3.** The students have read a lot of books. **4.** I can eat a lot of hamburgers.

5. There are a lot of trees in the park. **6.** There is a lot of noise upstairs. **7.** There are a lot of jobs available. **8.** We had a lot of wind. **9.** I have eaten a lot of apples. **10.** He has drunk a lot of alcohol.

IV. **1.** fewer mistakes; **2.** more money; **3.** the least time; **4.** less nature; **5.** little water; **6.** more shops; **7.** the fewest rooms; **8.** more tea; **9.** fewer lamps; **10.** the fewest students; **11.** many friends; **12.** more holidays; **13.** most streets; **14.** more windows; **15.** fewer exercises; **16.** most animals; **17.** much trouble; **18.** less damage; **19.** more chocolate; **20.** most books; **21.** more teachers; **22.** less help; **23.** most time; **24.** fewer houses.

Seite 232 f. **I.** **1.** every; **2.** every; **3.** each; **4.** any; **5.** each; **6.** all; **7.** whole; **8.** each; **9.** all the; **10.** each; **11.** all; **12.** any; **13.** any; **14.** all; **15.** all; **16.** whole/all; **17.** all; **18.** each; **19.** each; **20.** each; **21.** all; **22.** each; **23.** all; **24.** every; **25.** all (the whole); **26.** every/whole; **27.** all the/each; **28.** all/all the; **29.** every; **30.** all.

Seite 234 f. **1.** not; **2.** none; **3.** not; **4.** no; **5.** nobody; **6.** none; **7.** not; **8.** nobody; **9.** nothing; **10.** not; **11.** none; **12.** none; **13.** no; **14.** not; **15.** nothing/nobody; **16.** not; **17.** nobody/no; **18.** no; **19.** not; **20.** not; **21.** not; **22.** none; **23.** nothing; **24.** nobody; **25.** nothing; **26.** none; **27.** no; **28.** nothing; **29.** nothing; **30.** none.

Seite 236 **I.** **1.** both; **2.** either; **3.** both; **4.** either; **5.** both; **6.** both; **7.** both; **8.** either; **9.** both; **10.** either; **11.** both; **12.** both; **13.** both; **14.** either; **15.** both; **16.** both; **17.** either; **18.** both; **19.** either; **20.** both; **21.** either; **22.** both; **23.** both; **24.** either; **25.** both.

Seite 237 **1.** I go for a walk every day. **2.** This year there are many cherries on the tree. **3.** Nearly every student hates homework. **4.** We have two neighbours. Both are very nice. **5.** Mr S. seems to have plenty of (a lot of) money. **6.** All the workers in this firm will get higher wages. **7.** Would you like something to drink? **8.** Some sentences are rather difficult. **9.** If I had any time, I would help you. **10.** Nothing will change my mind. **11.** I still have to write so many letters that I will probably be busy for many more hours. **12.** Nobody is without fault. **13.** I liked only a few of the pictures at the exhibition. **14.** Many people don't know how much energy could be saved by following some rules. **15.** How many miles is it to London? **16.** There was only little hope of finding the boys. **17.** How many guests will come? **18.** I will call you back in a few minutes. **19.** Some people think French is easier than English. **20.** All students look forward to the holidays. **21.** Tell me something about your trip to America. **22.** The teacher gave each of us a copy. **23.** You must take these tablets every evening. **24.** Since the weather was so bad, no people were on the beach. **25.** None of the visitors was allowed to see the private rooms. **26.** Neither of the two suggestions

was good. **27.** You can buy the record in any record shop.
28. Everything must come to an end. **29.** That doesn't help me at all.
30. Only few women are in Parliament.

Seite 243 f. **I.** **1.** My father bought a new car some years ago. **2.** I sometimes watch TV in the evening. **3.** Michael lent me £ 10. **4.** His father didn't see him. **5.** My aunt sent a parcel last week. **6.** The children drank lemonade at the party. **7.** I wish you all the best for the future. **8.** She cooked a meal for her husband. **9.** He has told the story to everybody. **10.** I have written him a letter today. **11.** The guide has just shown the rooms to the visitors. **12.** The postman brought us a letter. **13.** The secretary will make coffee for the boss. **14.** I have never seen such beautiful flowers. **15.** Mary got a drink for her father. **16.** You should forgive his bad behaviour. **17.** My father repaired my bike for me last week. **18.** That will save her some trouble. **19.** My mother is just knitting a pullover for me. **20.** I have asked him his name. **21.** The teacher explained the students the sentences. **22.** My father bought me the record. **23.** He could not understand me. **24.** I envy her her nice dress.

II. **1.** Are the Children playing in the garden? **2.** Who broke the vase? **3.** Whose mother did you meet yesterday? **4.** How long has Peter been learning English now? **5.** Why did you come so late? **6.** Where are all the people going to? **7.** Did you ask him to give the money back? **8.** What boy broke the window? **9.** Where have you bought this good book? **10.** Who gave you this present? **11.** What time will he come? **12.** Why haven't you asked him? **13.** Who took these photos? **14.** Whose books did you find in the classroom? **15.** Which car do you prefer? **16.** Who did your brother meet yesterday? **17.** Since when have you not seen him? **18.** How do you do? **19.** What do you call this animal? **20.** How is your mother? **21.** Have you ever been to Paris? **22.** Do you like Sam's little brother? **23.** Can your secretary speak English fluently? **24.** Have you finished your homework?

Seite 244 **1.** May God forgive you! **2.** Can you lend me £ 20? **3.** After rain comes sunshine. **4.** Such is life. **5.** I cannot ride a bike. – Nor (Neither) can I. **6.** I sent him a parcel yesterday. **7.** He has broken his arm. **8.** When he came out of the house he saw a strange person. **9.** He left the house at 7 o'clock. **10.** What child do you mean? **11.** Should it rain tomorrow, I'll stay at home. **12.** Has she made a mistake? **13.** Who(m) did you meet in town yesterday? **14.** Where will you spend your holidays? **15.** Peter is reading a story to his grandfather. **16.** Would you please show your father the letter! **17.** How many people live in this house? **18.** Does your friend speak Italian? **19.** Shall I send you the letter? **20.** There comes the train!

Seite 249 centre – flat – ground floor – lift – dustbins – neighbours – lorry – theatres – neighbourhood – petrol – travelling – underground – railway – autumn – bookshops – shop assistants – quarrelling – post.

284

Index

Register

Das Register verzeichnet die wichtigsten Fundstellen behandelter Themen (Normalschrift) und Vokabeln *(Kursivschrift)*.